AF616824

State Planning : A Handbook

About the Author

Bedprakas Syam Roy, an MA in Economics (1968) from the Calcutta University did his Ph.D. from the North Bengal University (1987). Earlier, he had joined in the West Bengal Civil Service (1970 batch) and specialised in developmental administration. After his selection in the IAS (1989 batch), he worked in District Administration, Area Development, Health and Family Welfare and then spent a considerable time in the State Planning Department as Special Secretary. He was also the Nodal Officer for the State Plan for Human Development in West Bengal. After retirement, he served as a Member of the Third State Finance Commission, West Bengal.

State Planning: A Handbook

Dr. Bedprakas Syam Roy

CONCEPT PUBLISHING COMPANY PVT. LTD.
NEW DELHI-110059

ISBN-13: 978-81-8069-928-3

First Published 2013

Published and Printed by

Concept Publishing Company Pvt. Ltd.
A/15-16, Commerical Block, Mohan Garden
New Delhi - 110059 (India)
T : 25351460, 25351794, F : 091-11-25357109
E : publishing@conceptpub.com, W : www.conceptpub.com
Editorial Office : H-13, Bali Nagar, New Delhi-110015, India

Cataloging in Publication Data--*Courtesy:* D.K. Agencies (P) Ltd. <docinfo@dkagencies.com>

Shyamroy, Bedprakash.
State planning : a handbook / Bedprakas Syam Roy.
p. cm.
Includes index.
ISBN 9788180699283

1. Central planning—India—Handbooks, manuals, etc. 2. India—Economic policy—1991- I. Title.

DDC 338.954 23

To

The Planning Units of the
State Governments

Preface

The Planning for the State is an annual event for the Government in any State. It is also a part of constitutional obligation of the Government of the State as well. Normally, in matters related to planning, guidelines of the Planning Commission are followed for its adoption and implementation by the concerned State government. Such guidelines range from National Five Year Plan to Annual Plan. It also includes comments and suggested way-forward on Half-yearly, Annual and Mid-term appraisal of the Five Year Plan performances. Such inputs are useful ingredients to formulate objectives and realistic State Plan. Additionally, several national and State level surveys and reports also provide wider background and valuable inputs to design realistic Plan for the State.

This Handbook on State Planning intends to cover the broad areas in which the State Plan needs to address. It focuses from the perspective of human development and also from the angle of last mile journey of outreach. It also covers how the plan projections are to be presented in terms of Annexure designed by the Planning Commission, its related significance and interlinkage, and finally how to fill in the same with simplest possible narration.

Planning is a serious and knowledge based job and requires periodical update. It also necessitates continuity and development of institutional knowledge and memory. The reality of transfer and retirement very often hits the professional resources and stands in the way of transmission of knowledge. Further, the knowledge back-up support for the planning units of several Line Departments in the States are not well structured making even the routine plan presentation suffer from dependence syndrome on individuals.

The Handbook on State Planning intends to address this void area in simple operational language to enable it to qualify as a reference book on State Plan for planning units of the Line Departments, for the officials of the State Planning Board and also for the Planning Department of the State Government. It has, however, not dwelt elaborately on District Plan as it has been addressed in a separate publication (*The Niceties of District Planning—An Operational Framework*).

In preparing this Handbook, I have made use of my knowledge and experiences acquired in course of my posting in the Planning Department of the Government of West Bengal. At the first instance, therefore, I thank the Government of West Bengal for putting me in the Planning Department for a number of years with opportunity to interact with Line Departments in the State, Finance Department of the State, State Planning Board and the Planning Commission. To all of them, I owe my personal gratitude. For the focus on human development, I am indebted to UNDP, Delhi office for assisting me to broaden my understanding on Strengthening State Plan for human development through several seminars and workshops. I am also grateful to interactions with District Planning Committees to understand the nexus between the State Plan and the District Plan and to development professionals for their various observations on State Plan related issues.

Finally, I owe a great debt to the Planning Commission and to the various Ministries of the Government of India for making liberal use of relevant materials to complete the Manual. As a matter of record, the schemes of various Ministries have been taken from their departmental websites and adopted here with minimum editing to maintain the purity of its original form. The incorporation of such schemes would serve also as a compendium and facilitate as reference materials during State planning exercise.

My daughter, Maniparna, has been my constant source of inspiration to complete the publication in time. Chandan, my son-in-law, helped me a lot for formatting statistical presentation.

I am grateful to Shri Ashok Kumar Mittal, Proprietor, Concept Publishing Company Pvt. Ltd., New Delhi to agree to publish the book at the quickest possible time.

21.1.2012 **Dr. Bedprakas Syam Roy**

JC-2, Flat-4, Sector-3, Salt Lake, bpsyamroy@yahoo.co.in
Kolkata, 700098

Contents

PART-A

1

Introduction

The National Five Year Plan sets the approach, objectives, and the goal for the economic and social agenda of the country. It sets the macro-economic targets for the country as well. This is very important in a federal system like ours where the state organs enjoy considerable planning sovereignty in respect of items mentioned in the State List and Concurrent List in the Seventh Schedule of the Constitution. The National Five Year Plan creates the planning environment and the broader framework in which the activities during the plan period need to be directed. At the introductory level, some conceptual issues will be discussed to have common understanding on aspects related to State Planning.

State List and Concurrent List

The Constitution of India provides under Article 246 the Seventh Schedule of the Constitution which delineates the functional jurisdiction in between the Union Government and the State governments in three Lists—the Union List (List-I), the State List (List-II) and the Concurrent List (List-III). The Union List contains items which the Union Government will alone exercise. The State List empowers absolute legislative and executive jurisdiction to the Government in the State on items included therein. Such jurisdiction includes planning rights as well. The same right exists to the Government in the State on items in the Concurrent List as well with the rider that in the event the Union Government exercises any authority on any of such items, the decision of the Union Government would prevail. This right is equally applicable for planning function on such items.

Plan and Non-Plan Scheme

The conceptual clarity on classification of Plan and Non-Plan activities is very important from planning point of view. Any new scheme taken up in any Annual Plan or under a Five Year Plan belongs to the category of plan scheme. The salient feature of a Plan scheme is that it has an outcome content connected with the basic objective and goal of an Annual Plan or under a Five Year Plan. The nature of such outcome may be different depending on whether such scheme belongs to Primary sector, Secondary sector or Tertiary sector. Non-Plan items, on the other hand, falls in the category of maintenance of those schemes which were completed earlier. It is a kind of committed liability of plan schemes completed earlier but whose maintenance now falls under Non-Plan. However, upgradation of a previously completed scheme falls under Plan scheme. Additionally, organisational expenses including contingencies related expenditures fall under Non-Plan. For the same reason, Non-Plan items do not qualify to be included under Plan. This classification for the State Plan is maintained under the watchful eyes of the Accountant General in the State. This classification *ipso facto* is also applicable for all programme partners of the State Plan. Planning Commission issues guidelines on the eve of every Five Year Plan. The Planning Commission has issued guidelines this time also and has been discussed separately.

Planning, Plan and Plan of Actions

Clarity on concepts is a prerequisite for good planning. However, uniformity of understanding is an ideal condition and it does not always exist in real world, more particularly in planning scenario in the departments of the State Government. In such planning scenario two concepts namely, (i) Planning; and (ii) Plan are often liberally used to convey the same kind of meaning and in the process make the entire planning environment confused. These need to be comprehensively resolved at the first instance. As a matter of fact these concepts are mutually exclusive and are not substitutable one for the other. It is imperative, therefore, that these concepts are briefly discussed for role clarification to facilitate proper planning:

(I) Planning

Planning is a process in which vision is settled and objectives are outlined with due regard to human development deficit. It is in the same process that felt needs of the stakeholders are assessed by direct interaction or otherwise and stocktaking of resources—physical, financial and human—are made. In this process prioritisation is decided after examining all possible alternatives and then final decision is made on schemes, its location and its financial provisioning. The issues of inclusiveness, bridging the divide, targeting the BPL, SC, ST, Children, Women and the Aged are all addressed in the domain of planning.

(II) Plan

Plan is the document in which the final decisions on planning are captured. The document could be simple; it can also be detailed depending on requirement to present the Plan, e.g., the presentation of Annual Plan of a State to the Planning Commission has to be made in 13 annexures. However, there are some common characters for presentation of any Plan like the name of the planning authority, the nature of plan—Annual or Revised, the planning year, sector-wise presentation of schemes along with proposed outlay, etc. It may also include physical targets, separate provisioning for SC/ST/Women/NGOs, etc.

(III) Plan of Action

Plan of Action comes into the picture after a programme/scheme is finally approved under a Plan. This is a next order function of the concerned government functionary. This is a component of a function relating to execution of schemes already approved in the Plan. In other words, Plan of Action is a subsequent layer of activity and not a part of those directly connected with the process of planning, a first layer of activity which has already been over. Plan of Action has only connectivity with implementation of schemes taken up in the Plan. This is true for all approved schemes in a Plan irrespective of whether it is a national programme, State programme or for any scheme of the local bodies. There is no scope for *de novo* planning at this stage of way forward. The focused responsibility at this stage is only to work out sequence of action points for proper execution of schemes, popularly known as 'Plan of Action'.

The Plan of Action has assumed importance with the assignment of planning and implementation responsibility of NAREGA, BRGF, RKVY, etc., to the tiers of Panchayats. Such schemes have tied up big resources which in a way determine the spending image of the related local body.

For these schemes, separate planning and Plan of Action have come as conditionalities for eligibility of fund under such schemes. These new dimensions have complicated the area of planning.

Planning is a time bound job of the State Government, for a tier of Panchayats or Municipalities for its Annual Plan. There is normally no scope for parallel planning for each of the assigned schemes separately at different points of time. Such guidelines of BRGF, RKVY, etc., need to address the timeliness of Planning of the local body and integrate it with the original plan of the local body. Once included under the Plan, the Plan of Action would be separate and different for each of the Programme/Schemes which may be shared with the assignee and execute it thereafter.

Devolution *vs.* Assigned Schemes

Devolution denotes transferring functional jurisdiction on given items from the Government of the State to the local bodies—Panchayats and/or the Municipalities. Devolution has three essential qualifying components, namely, autonomy in respect of selection of scheme, its financial provisioning and also of its implementation. The concept is relevant in the context of empowering planning and implementation responsibility to the local bodies. The concerned local body would be acting like a sovereign body in respect of schemes devolved on to them and it need not refer to the government functionary for its approval or fund. The Constitution of India requires institutional devolution to put in place by the Legislature of a State, under Article 243G, on items of the Eleventh Schedule to each of the tiers of the Panchayat and also on items of the Twelfth Schedule to the Municipalities as per Article 243W. The functional items so devolved on to the Panchayats or the Municipalities would automatically get excluded from the functional jurisdiction of the State Government.

Assigned schemes are those entrusted to any tier of the Panchayats or to the Municipalities either by the departments of the State Government or by the Ministries of the Central Government under defined terms and conditions. The Assignment of schemes is an executive decision of the Government and it has no linkage either with Devolution or with any constitutional provision. The terms and conditions of Assigned schemes may be rigid; it can be very flexible also. Unlike devolved responsibilities, it is not a kind of institutional empowerment by the Legislature of a State on functional items under the Eleventh Schedule to each tier of the

Panchayat or to the Municipalities on items of the Twelfth Schedule. It is scheme specific and not functional responsibility specific. Assigned schemes are also not permanent in nature but valid for the term of assignment. Such assignment may be revoked by the assignee at any time on ground of exigency of the government. Here the role of the local body is akin to the role of an agency and that it has also to comply with all the conditionalities and directions of its assignee. It has in that sense less sovereign power over the scheme and is liable to be controlled by the assignee or its representatives. Assigned schemes are thus not devolved schemes as it does not meet the devolution criteria. Finally, assignment is a task concept while devolution is a right concept under Articles 243G and 243W.

It is in this context that the role of devolved schemes and the role of assigned schemes on the State Annual Plan assume importance and need comprehensive resolution. Article 243G and Article 243W have empowered respectively the levels of Panchayats and the Municipalities to plan for devolved items; it has not mentioned anything about Planning from assigned schemes. Article 243ZD empowers the District Planning Committee to consolidate to Plans prepared by the Panchayats and the Municipalities and prepare the District Plan. There is no constitutional provision to incorporate plans of the Panchayats or of the Municipalities with the State Plan. This is linked with the broader issue of relationship with State Plan and District Plan and will be discussed separately under the following sub-points.

(i) The Role of Line Departments in the District and its Role in the District Plan

There exists understanding variations on the rolc of the Line Departments of the Government working in the District and their relation in the District Plan. The District Plan, under Article 243ZD, is a consolidation outcome of Plans prepared by the Panchayats and the Municipalities. Legally speaking, there is no scope for the plans of the Line Departments of the State Government to be part of such District Plan. On the basis of devolved functional items out of the 11th Schedule under Article 243G or out of the 12th Schedule under Article 243W, the Panchayats and the Municipalities are to plan on them and then submit it to the DPC. Similarly, as per Rules of Business, under Article 166(3) of the Constitution of India, the Line Departments of the Government are to plan and implement schemes as are covered under List-II and List-III of the Seventh Schedule.

There is no constitutional provision for the Panchayats or the Municipalities to plan for items covered under List-II and List-III of the Seventh Schedule. In the context of the District Plan, the exclusion of planning efforts of Line Departments and resultant district plan components from the purview of the constitutionally mandated District Planning Committee, make the entire District Planning exercise less wholesome. From planning angle, those planning efforts are needed to be captured and made part of the District Plan. This is a critical area of reforms under District Plan and needs to be addressed early.

(ii) The Relationship between the District Plans and the State Plan

There are variations of understanding on the relation between the District Plans and the State Plan. The popular perception is that the State Plan is the summation of district plans. This symbiotic relationship between the State plan and the District plans is based on an ideal premise where it is presumed that the State Government would disaggregate the total plan outlay among its districts on some defined norms and asks the concerned District Planning authority to plan for them. The District Plans, thus emerged, would add up to the State Plan. This ideal premise does not exist nor is it practicable to exist in real life situation. It is just not possible to have a different Planning authority at the district level to plan for subjects meant for State Government Departments just as it is not permissible for any District Planning Committee to plan for non-devolved subjects and State level projects spanning over a number of districts.

Another way of looking at the issue is that at the end of the day, irrespective of the authority of plan formulations, all plans meant for the districts have necessarily to add up to the total of the State Plan outlay. This is, however, a truism and a very simplistic way of looking on the subject. Besides, it does not factor in planning functions as a premise for arriving at such views.

The basic point that remains to be resolved is whether all draft plans prepared at the level of the Constitution mandated District Planning Committees would have any integrating linkage with the State Plan. The answer is linked with the niceties of planning and the State Government's constitutional responsibility on State Plan and its budgeting.

The State Plan embodies in general the planning efforts on items included in State List and Concurrent List under the Seventh Schedule of the Constitution. More specifically, it covers items of the Line Departments in the State Plan as per notification issued under the Rules of Business of

Article 166(3) of the Constitution of India. The District Plan, on the other hand, reflects a consolidated picture of plans prepared by the Panchayats and the Municipalities for devolved items under the Eleventh and the Twelfth Schedule of the Constitution respectively. In other words, the planning responsibilities of the departments of a State Government are different from the planning responsibilities of the tiers of the Panchayat and the Municipalities. The jurisdiction over functional items is thus important and it finally determines the areas on planning. Further, in the era of right based environment scenario, empowerment of defined subjects of planning to any local body has also led to the emergence of planning rights over them in favour of the said local body. In the case of Line Departments of the State Government, the planning rights span over items of the State List and Concurrent List as entrusted to them under Article 166(3) of the Constitution. The planning rights of the three tiers of the Panchayats in the rural areas are confined over items as devolved on to them under the Eleventh Schedule of the Constitution. Similarly, the planning rights of the Municipalities in the urban areas are centred over items as devolved on to them under the Twelfth Schedule of the Constitution. Such planning rights cannot be delegated or usurped by any other planning authority. It is for the same reason that the DPC cannot arrogate to itself the planning rights either of the Panchayats or the Municipalities nor can it subsume the planning rights of the State Planning departments.

Now the jurisdiction of the planning rights of the Panchayats and the Municipalities is limited to devolved items only. It does have neither the mandate nor the competency to plan for items included under State List or Concurrent List. Therefore, the plan schemes of Line Departments located in the rural or urban areas of the districts fall outside the planning jurisdiction of the Panchayats or the Municipalities. There does not exist any planning authority, other than officials of the Line Departments, to plan for them and send them to the DPC for consolidation. However, Article 243ZD does not permit such officials of the Line Departments to send district plan components of Line Departments to the DPC. The Panchayats or the Municipalities cannot also plan for them and lawfully send them to the DPC for consolidation. It is for the same reason that plans of the Panchayats for rural areas and plans of the Municipalities for urban areas when consolidated into the draft District Plan has no scope to capture district plan components of Line Departments. Leaving such plan-components of Line Departments outside the scheme of consolidation renders the draft District Plan ineligible to represent 'wholesome' District plan. Thus, the draft District Plan cannot be looked upon as sub-sets of the State Plan. The planning areas are distinct and different for the State and for each of the tiers of the Panchayats or for the Municipalities.

There is, however, no doubt of existence of inherent linkage between schemes of the State plan with schemes of the decentralised local body plans on any development functional area. Productive interactions in between such schemes in defined development area in a time format broaden planning vision and shared perception and are also instrumental in reordering planning priorities and revisiting its sectoral allocation. Such planning connectivity enriches sectoral planning and activates programme convergence to achieve desired outcome. The nature, scope and character of State Plan and District Plans remains, however, different as per constitutional provision.

As mentioned earlier, the State Plan, in ideal setting, could have been an amalgamation of all items included in the District Plans and also those included in the Plans of the Line Departments of the State Government. However, this ideal setting of amalgamation is not possible for other valid reasons also. Unlike resources meant for the State Plan, the District Plans, in most cases, are not prepared on the basis of firm resources. Further, own resources of the Panchayats and the Municipalities, however big or small as it may be, happen to be very significant components of resources for local level planning. Such resources are not usually taken into consideration for computing resources meant for the State Plan. Additionally, in the absence of real devolution in most States, the items in the District Plans also include projected fund for assigned schemes in favour of the Panchayats or the Municipalities, which incidentally have already been booked by the concerned plan implementing departments in their departmental State Annual Plan. There is real danger of double counting on this crucial area. On top of it all, there is no provision in the Constitution of India requiring the Planning Commission either to approve or to disapprove of District Plans and, therefore, incorporation of such District Plans within State Plan would amount to seek Planning Commission's approval in a round about way which is not permissible under the constitutional mandate. The State Plan, in real terms, is the aggregation of the plans of the Line Departments only. The Planning Commission approves this aggregated State Plan Outlay of Line Departments, presented under Major or Minor heads of development, after due process of assessment of State resources, Working Group discussions in the Planning Commission with the secretaries of the Line Departments only and finally after Deputy Chairman or Chief Minister level of interactions. The State Plan, as approved by the Planning

Commission, is also required to be approved by the State Cabinet before taking it up for budgeting by the State. The State Plan becomes functional from the next financial year after it is so budgeted.

The District Plans in the constitutional scheme of things on the other hand are, required to be sent to the State Government as per Article 243ZD (4) *ibid.* Such District Plan comes back to the concerned District Planning Committee with State Government's comments, if any. There is no scope to accord Cabinet approval or approval by any department of State government on such District Plans. There is also no scope to take up budgeting exercise on District Plans either by the State Government or by the DPC. The responsibility of budgeting its Annual Plan lies with the related unit of the tier of Panchayats as provided under the State Panchayat Act or with the Municipalities under the State Municipal Act. The District Planning Committee is required only to send back the State Government's observations, if any, on the Draft Annual Plan to all units of Panchayats and Municipalities for appropriate action. The respective local bodies, after due consideration of such observations, then approve its plan and take measures to budget for them. The procedural format for plan approval and its budgeting is also different for each tier of the Panchayat or the Municipalities. It is an independent function not connected in any way with the budgeting of the State Plan. In the circumstances, it would not be fair to hold that State Plan is an aggregated version of District Plans of any State. The District Plans are in fact by its own nature functionally different and in no way qualify to be sub-sets of the State Plan.

Perspective Plan

The perspective planning is concerned with medium term or long term planning. Here the long range targets are set in advance for the period, say 10 to 20 years. Since longer range vision and projected growth are important consideration in a perspective plan, it is by itself not an implementation plan; it is a model guidance to fix objectives and targets for shorter duration of plan with overall long term perspective. From this angle, the perspective plan can be conceived of a summation of certain short term plans. As a matter of fact a perspective plan is split up in shorter plans consisting of 5 years or so. The goal of any Perspective Plan is to optimise resource constraints along the growth path and meet the projected vision through incremental outcome by way of moving sectoral adjustments.

Annual Plan

The National Five Year Plan is a kind of perspective plan. It is divided into five annual plans. Accordingly, the year-wise plan of a country is called the annual plan. The State Annual Plan exercise usually commences in the third quarter of the financial year and the Draft Plan is required to be sent thereafter to the Planning Commission. The Draft Plan after Working Group discussions and further interactions in between the Deputy Chairman, Planning Commission and the Chief Minister of the State is approved by the Planning Commission. The approved Annual Plan after its budgeting by the State becomes operational from the beginning of the new financial year.

2

The Background of the State Plan

The background of the State Plan is varied and plural. It is both bottom-up and top-down. It is top-down in the sense that the Approach of the National Five Year Plan sets the overarching goals and such goals are also the shared goals of any State Plan. The National Development Council with due interaction with the Chief Ministers of the States determines the vision, goal and objectives of any National Five Year Plan. The State governments prepare its own Approach of the Five Year Plan based on the overall approach of the National Five Year Plan combined with considerations of State level priorities that needed to be carried along. Similarly, after the Plan Documents of the National Five Year Plan are prepared by the Planning Commission and shared with the State governments, a clear picture on sectoral planning cnvironment is available. It intends to address development deficit and quality carc by programme intervention. Such sectoral analysis and planning initiatives in the national plan are immensely helpful in conceptualising the related sector, the core of its national focus, the status of national development in the area or the extent of its weakness. The required level of intervention at the State level and possible investment requirement are also learnt in the process. The State Five Year Plan document is thus immensely benefited from top-down approach of the National Five Year Plan.

There is another level of planning pressure emerging from across the rural and urban areas of the State that demand due cognizance in the planning process. This is related to ground realities of bottom-up priorities. Based on day-to-day problems of real life, a consensus on local level priorities slowly builds up and gets strength through endorsements of its democratic forces and other stakeholders. The perceived priorities reach the State Planners also from the decentralised planning forums of the

Panchayats and the Municipalities. The State is obliged to accommodate such inputs during the process of State planning. The bottom-up inputs for State planning are then plugged in to ensure that plan is realistic and addresses felt needs of the people as planning is after all a device to accommodate the collective voice of the society. The State Five Year plan is thus a balance of national and State priorities.

The State Annual Plan is not an end itself. It tends to be more or less a reflection of the Five Year Plan of the State. It is a sub-set of the State Five Year Plan and has to embody its priorities. Moreover, since planning is a rolling concept, the unfinished task of a previous Annual Plan is also included in the work items of the next Annual Plan. It has to carry forward the tasks of the State Five Year Plan by annual instalments. In the process, it follows up the core agenda of the National Five Year Plan as well. Additionally, Planning Commission also issues guidelines for the Annual State Plan on a yearly basis with focus on national issues and also on emerging issues of the economy that are needed to take due consideration on them. The overarching human development issues as per shared commitment on the MDGs also feature as important area for the background of State Planning.

The State Government has accountability to its Legislature on issues included in the State List and those covered under Concurrent List. The Ministers of the State Government also give assurances from time to time in the floor of the Assembly and also to various Committees under it on issues bearing State Plan. Such items also act as background for State Plan and are needed to be appropriately taken into account.

The Annual State Plan *per se* is important but not so until it is budgeted. It is a constitutional obligation of the State to plan for a financial year, secure its concurrence from the Planning Commission and then budget for the same. The Annual State Plan becomes functional after it is approved in the State Legislature and its budgetary sanction secured. It is a fact that planning process is budget neutral but that process is also conditioned by the outer limit of availability of fund. The availability of fund is only assured through its budgetary sanction. Thus, the limitation of budgetary fund acts as the final background of the State Planning.

3

Guidelines of the Planning Commission

Planning Commission as the apex planning authority in the country frames guidelines on issues relating to national and State planning, on aspects relating to schemes of financing plan and also on areas how the plan assistance for States have to be addressed. Additionally, it issues instructions on areas of mid-term course corrections of Annual Plan or Five Year Plan. Through different forums of Task-force, etc., it also opens up critical areas of State planning on which policy responses need to be made by the States of India. The monitoring and evaluation studies under the auspices of the Planning Commission usually highlights areas on which the States need to take follow-up actions. In other words, Planning Commission plays over-arching supervisory role for the planning process in the country at different levels of the governance. Its role spans from initiation of planning process to ensuring its final outcome.

For operational guidelines on Planning, it might be useful to discuss the role of Planning Commission under three areas, namely, (a) Guidelines in relation to State Planning; (b) Guidelines in relation to assessment of Financial Resources for the Annual Plan; and (c) Guidelines in relation to the plan assistance for States:

I. Guidelines in relation to State Planning

Planning Commission as the apex planning authority in the country prepares the Approach to the Five Year Plan of the country and places them before the National Development Council for interactions, refinement and adoption. Apart from sharing the final Approach and detailed sectoral planning as worked out by the Planning Commission on the Five Year Plan, it also issues guidelines for the Five Year Plans to the

State governments based on priorities as per the decisions of the NDC by way of focused reminder. Additionally, the Planning Commission also issues guidelines on yearly basis—based on past performances and emerging issues on the planning horizon—for the preparation of the Annual plan of the State government for appropriate follow-up. Needless to mention, the guidelines are recommendatory in nature and under no circumstances it aims to interfere with planning sovereignty of any State government.

In line with that tradition, the Planning Commission interacts with the State governments at the preparatory stage of the Five Year Plan, as it did during the Eleventh Five Year Plan on its worked out projected figures on overall growth targets of the country as well as State-wise disaggregated monitorable targets for the views of the States to develop a broad consensus in the NDC meeting. The monitorable targets so worked out were on the following areas:

1. Infant Mortality Ratio;
2. Maternal Mortality Ratio;
3. Total Fertility Rate;
4. Malnutrition of Children (0-3 years);
5. Anaemia among women (15-49 years);
6. Sex ratio (0-6 years);
7. Dropout rate in elementary education;
8. Literacy rate; and
9. Gender gap in literacy rate.

Additionally, State-wise targets for employment creation and jobs were also given.

The monitorable targets were suggestive in nature inspired by the best spirit of cooperative federalism for initiating a consultation process for reaching a broader consensus on national targets at the decentralised level. The targets were initially worked out on the basis of human development deficit for the country and then disaggregated among the States in India with the desire that such inter-State disparities on human development frontier need to be evened out as early as possible in the greater interest of the country as a whole. The State governments were required to introspect on the suggested targets, assess them in the light of current situation obtaining in the field, own a target for each as considered appropriate and organise mechanism to outperform them in the course of the Five Year Plan.

The various State governments in the country undertook interactive discussions on the suggested monitorable targets within the planning forum of their respective State and then firmed up the State level monitorable targets and communicated the same to the Planning Commission.

The Planning Commission in its circular on the Eleventh Five Year Plan reiterated that while working on targets for average rate of growth, plan priorities, sectoral policies and thrust areas for inclusive growth, the State government need to look into the Approach Paper to the Eleventh Five Year Plan, as approved by National Development Council, and be appropriately guided. Further, sufficient outlay may be earmarked for Special Component Plan, Tribal Sub-Plan and State schemes covered under Bharat Nirman and Flagship Programmes. It also underscored that the States are needed to give appropriate consideration for taking care of the counterpart fund required for Centrally Sponsored Schemes at the time of drawing their Five Year Plan and Annual Plan.

Additionally, the Planning Commission took note of current status of implementation of the Constitutional mandate for local level planning at the village panchayats, intermediate panchayats and district panchayat levels as well as in urban local governments under the Seventythird and the Seventyfourth Amendments respectively and observed that it has not made much progress. Accordingly, the Planning Commission reiterated the imperatives of compliance of such Constitutional mandate with required vigour and spirit by issuing focused guidelines on the District Plans while preparing the Eleventh Five Year Plan. The Guidelines were structured on the basis of the Report of the Expert Group on planning at the grassroot level presented to the Central Government in March 2006.

Similarly, during the preparation of the Approach to the Twelfth Plan, apart from providing an interactive forum to the citizens of this country to share their views, the Planning Commission also requested the State governments to give their considered views on the Draft Approach paper of the Twelfth Plan before placing it at the National Development Council meeting. Such inputs were also the basis of the interactive discussion at the NDC meeting held on October 2011 to firm up national approach to the Twelfth Five Year Plan. The Approach to the Twelfth Plan thus became a validated document of the country, including by the State governments. The Approach Paper to the Twelfth Plan would thus be the overall guiding focus for the State plans as well.

As mentioned earlier, the Planning Commission also issues guidelines to the State governments on the eve of each planning season reminding the priorities of the national plan, the emerging new concerns that need to be attended with appropriate consideration and the kind of special importance that may be further accorded for inclusive growth. One or two examples may be given. On the eve of the Annual Plan, 2010-11 the Planning Commission observed that because of lower rate of growth than projected and the impact of drought on kharif crops, floods in the southern States and increase in Finance Commission's transfers, there would be severe pressure on resources. Such guidelines required the States to give appropriate consideration while working on State Plan. Similarly, for the Annual Plan, 2012-13, the Planning Commission required the State governments to undertake a detailed review of all existing programmes to determine whether those should be continued during the Twelfth Plan or not and whether those need to be suitably altered to achieve the new objectives set for them. Further, it is also required to make a comprehensive review of State's own resources in the context of slowing down in growth in an uncertain global economic situation and the imperatives of the State to fund certain ongoing schemes from its own resources. Planning Commission also issued guidelines on classification of expenditure in the context of the Twelfth Plan, which is being separately discussed.

Apart from issuing such guidelines on State Planning in a more or less routine fashion, the Planning Commission also shares its views on quality of planning and implementations after its Midterm Review of the Five Year Plan. In its Annual and Half-Yearly Plan Review held with the State Government officials at the State Headquarters, high valued professional comments and observations are made that also fall in the category of informal guidelines for its follow-up and adoption in course of the next Annual Plan.

It would be appropriate here to mention the role of informal guidelines by the Working Groups in the Planning Commission as well. The Working Groups in the Planning Commission usually examines in details the vision, its approach, its suggested programmes and commensurate investment on the Draft Annual Plan proposals of the State governments, interacts with the secretaries of the State Government and then record its observations on the merit of State proposals and suggest areas for appropriate reconsideration. These comments belong to the category of informal guidelines for appropriate follow-up in the final proposals of the Annual Plan of the concerned State.

Planning Commission also issues guidelines before the beginning of any Five Year Plan as to the classification of expenditure for the next plan period. In tune with the said tradition, the Planning Commission has also issued guidelines for Classification of Expenditure for the Twelfth Five Year Plan (2012-17). It is reproduced as below:

"The following guidelines may be observed for classification of expenditure relating to the Twelfth Five Year Plan in respect of State Plan

A. Plan Expenditure

The Plan expenditure is under the Central Plan or State Plan. The Central Plan consists of Central Sector Schemes and Centrally Sponsored Schemes. The Central Assistance to State Plan supports some State Plan schemes. The States also have their own schemes under State Plan financed from their own resources. For the Twelfth Plan, the emphasis needs to be on completion of on-going schemes and projects as well as upgradation of existing capital assets before starting new projects. The new projects may be taken up only after a certain minimum number of partially completed/on-going projects are brought to completion. These need to be indicated while presenting the plan proposal. This, however, does not entail a completion of all such existing schemes/projects that on present consideration are not seen to be the most desirable from the point of available technical options and/or economic principles. Such Schemes/Projects may be discontinued/shelved/weeded out in the course of review to be undertaken prior to the formulation of the Twelfth Five Year Plan. All outlays proposed under each category of Plan expenditure, viz., Central sector, Centrally Sponsored and State Plan would be classified as Ongoing and New Schemes. The Ongoing Schemes are in turn divided into sub-categories. The brief description is given as follows:

I. Ongoing Schemes

(i) Mandated by Legislation

Outlays connected with all ongoing Plan programmes/projects/ schemes such as MGNREGA which have been mandated by legislation and, therefore, need to be continued.

(ii) Social Security Transfers

Outlays connected with regular social security transfers such as old age and disability pensions, scholarships and other social insurance schemes.

(iii) Schemes/Projects for Completion

Outlays connected with all Plan programmes/projects/schemes in project mode and defined objectives which have been sanctioned in the Eleventh Plan or earlier, and which have not been completed as on 31-03-2012. These may fall into following categories:

(a) *Projects/Schemes due for completion in the Twelfth Plan or beyond as per the approvals*: These can be included as Plan projects.

(b) *Projects/Schemes due for completion by the end of the Eleventh Plan in which less than 10 per cent of the approved outlay as on 31-3-2012 will be spent*: These projects should be separately identified for weeding out/shelving/dropping or converging/transferring to the private/joint sectors, or PPPs as the case may be. Projects initiated prior to the Eleventh and where less than 20 per cent of the approved outlay for the project has been spent, so far, may be similarly treated.

(c) *Projects/Schemes due for completion by the end of the Eleventh Plan in which more than 75 per cent of the work has been completed*: These projects are to be indicated separately for accelerated completion. The revised estimates of time and costs and the phasing out are also to be included.

(d) *All other projects/schemes not falling into the above three categories*: States and Ministries are to review afresh such projects for the Twelfth Plan as per the guidelines applicable for any new proposal. These should not be included as ongoing projects.

(iv) Other Schemes with Same or Changea Mandate

Outlays connected with all other ongoing schemes which may be continued with same or changed mandate with the approval of Planning Commission.

II. New Schemes

Development programmes/projects/schemes on capital/revenue account that have been cleared for inclusion in the Twelfth Plan, in principle or otherwise, or for which an investment decision has been taken or is in the process of being taken by the concerned authority as per the applicable guidelines.

B. Committed Non-Plan Expenditure (Arising from Eleventh Plan)

The items of expenditure/outlays incurred in the current (Eleventh) Plan that are to be treated as committed non-plan expenditure are as follows:

(i) All expenditures connected with operation and maintenance of development schemes completed during the five-year period ending 31-3-2012.
(ii) In case of development schemes spilling over, a portion of the assets may have already been created or services/ facilities established. Operation and maintenance of such assets or services/facilities is to be treated as committed non-plan expenditure.
(iii) In the case of programmes/schemes/activities involving phased coverage, the expenditure on field staff of the phase already covered, along with expenditure on headquarters staff, is to be treated as committed non-plan expenditure.
(iv) All expenditures connected with maintenance of existing institutions and establishments will be treated as non-plan committed expenditure.
(v) In the case of programmes/schemes and activities which are of a recurring or continuing nature such as Health, Education, Water Supply and Sanitation and so on, the expenditure on staff in position as on 31-03-2012 should be treated as committed Non-Plan expenditure.
(vi) Normal or current operation and maintenance costs of all existing revenue generating assets are to be treated as a part of committed Non-Plan expenditure. Wherever transfer of Plan to non-plan under committed expenditure involves continuance of staff, the need has to be examined carefully

and full justification has to be given for any proposed continuance of staff.

The committed expenditure non-plan liability is to be borne by the Central Government in respect of Central Sector Schemes and by the State Governments in respect of State Plan Schemes and Centrally Sponsored Schemes. Such expenditure will be taken to the Non-Plan side of the budgets of Centre and States.

C. Selective Use of Plan Funds for Maintenance of Existing Assets

In an effort to improve the productivity of existing capital assets, and efficiency of resource use during the Twelfth Plan, selective use of Plan Funds, normally not exceeding 15 per cent of the Plan budgetary support may be used for critical repair, maintenance and renovation activities.

D. Presentation of Plan Outlay

Outlays for Central Plan should have two parts—Budgetary Support (BS) and Internal and Extra-Budgetary Resources (IEBR) of the Public Sector Enterprises (PSEs) of the concerned Ministries. The IEBR includes internal resources (retained surplus, depreciation, carry forward surplus of previous year net of loan repayments to GoI, non-plan capital requirements, net increase in margin for working capital, etc., and domestic and external long term borrowings which are available for plan outlays of the PSEs.

The Plan outlays for PSEs should include outlays for the following:

(i) Outlays on ongoing projects, which were slated to be completed in the Eleventh Plan, where substantial work is over, but are incomplete. These "Spill-over" projects should be given priority;
(ii) Outlays on ongoing projects, which are slated for completion in Twelfth Plan or beyond;
(iii) Outlays for "upgradation/expansion" which lead to addition or extension of capacity;

(iv) Outlays for "modernization/balancing investments" leading to improvement in productivity/performance/capacity utilization;

(v) Outlays to replace worn-out or over aged capital stock to be broadly classified as "Replacement investment";

(vi) Other new projects that have been cleared for inclusion in the Twelfth Plan, in principle or otherwise, or for which an investment decision has been taken or is in the process of being taken by concerned authority as per the applicable guidelines.

The Central Plan outlay should contain information on Ongoing and New Schemes in the manner described in Section I on Plan expenditure separately for Central Sector and Centrally Sponsored Schemes along with "Capital" and "Revenue" components for each of the programmes/schemes. The Ministries/Departments of the Central Government should also describe it separately. The quantification of revenue outlay should be done carefully with reference to the committed expenditure already provided under the non-plan side. Particular emphasis is to be placed on providing for maintenance outlays in committed Non-Plan expenditure as discussed above.

The Ministries/Departments should separately send Proposals for State Plan Schemes (also called ACA Schemes) to Planning Commission with the same details and presentation as discussed above for Central Plan outlay. The resources for State Plans should also include Budget support (financed from States' own resources, borrowings and central assistance), the IEBR of States' PSEs and the IEBRs of local bodies. The broad principles for IEBR as well as Plan outlays for PSEs of the State may be similar to what has been stated above for the Central PSEs.

The State Plans of different States should also follow the similar pattern of presentation in respect of their State Plan Schemes. The existing sectoral allocation may also be followed. The States' share for centrally sponsored schemes also needs to be provided under the respective scheme/sector as per the concerned guidelines and as per the information to be provided to them by subject divisions/State Plan Divisions/Ministries on the continuance of ongoing CSS and State Plan Schemes and new schemes."

II. Guidelines in relation to Assessment of Financial Resources for the Annual Plan

Assessment of financial resources is a prerequisite for annual planning. The projected assessment of resources availability for the next Annual Plan is made by the Finance Department of the State Government at the first instance. It is also independently worked out by the Financial Resources Division of the Planning Commission. The final projected resources are then worked out after interactive discussions between the Finance Department of the State and the Financial Resources Division of the Planning Commission. For a useful and productive discussion, a discussion format in the form of guidelines has been structured by the Planning Commission. The Financial Resources Division of the Planning Commission is vested with authority to issue guidelines in relation to assessment of Financial Resources for the Annual Plan of the States. The guidelines require the States to comply with them. A typical example of such Guidelines issued by the Financial Resources Division of the Planning Commission for the Annual Plan 2012-13 is given below:

"Official level discussions for the assessment of financial resources for the Annual Plan 2011-12 of States have to be completed by December 2011. During these discussions, review of the Actual Resources 2009-10 and 2010-11, Latest Estimates of the Resources realized for the Annual Plan 2011-12 will be made and resources for the Annual Plan 2012-13 estimated.

2. Earlier, based on discussion in the Working Group on State's Financial Resources, Planning Commission has intimated vide letter No. 3/3/2011-FR dated 11th October, 2011 the broad assumptions to be followed in estimating various items of resources and expenditure for the Twelfth Plan. The State governments, however, are requested to estimate resources for Annual Plan 2012-13 on the basis of current economic situation.

3. The Finance Department may be aware of the five Formats and four Statements in which estimates of financial resources of the States, *inter alia*, for the current Plan, *i.e.*, 2011-12 were presented. It is proposed to make use of the same set of formats and statements to assess the resources for the Annual Plan 2012-13, and the latest estimates of resources realized so far for the current Plan. However, the State governments will also be required to fill up the columns in the two tables, appended as Tables I and II, for certain crucial indicators of the fiscal performance of the States and progress and estimates of Plan expenditure

against the Plan Outlay respectively. Both the estimates of resources of the Annual Plan for 2012-13 and the latest estimates of resources realized for the current Plan may be indicated at current prices along with the projections of the resources for the Twelfth Plan (2012-2017) at 2011-12 prices as indicated in each of the formats and statements. Since it is proposed to compile data at the national level on the basis of information furnished by the State governments, uniformity in presentation is of utmost importance. Information on all items indicated in the forms supplied may, therefore, be required to be furnished. No column may be interchanged or left out. Wherever there is any deviation from the items/descriptions in the format and/or statement as the case may be, an explanatory footnote may please be provided. Duly filled-in formats and statements along with the relevant information and footnotes, if any, may be forwarded in soft as well as hard copies. Since an analytical note is to be prepared on the basis of information furnished by the States, it may be ensured that requisite information reaches us not later than 25th November, 2011.

4. Estimates of financial resources for the Annual Plan 2012-13 should be made keeping in view the objective to realize approved projections of the scheme of financing for the Twelfth Plan. The aggregate level of borrowings, States' Own Funds, etc., should also be estimated proportionate to the Twelfth Plan projections keeping in view the requirements under State's FRBM Act.

5. *Balance from Current Revenues (BCR)*: The following guidelines should be followed while estimating various components of Revenue Receipts and Non-Plan Revenue Expenditure (NPRE) for arriving at the Balance from Current Revenues (BCR).

- *State's Share in Central Taxes*: State's share of Union tax revenues may be retained at the current year's level as indicated in the Union Budget of 2011. This figure will be suitably revised in accordance with the Union Budget for 2012-13.
- *State's Own Tax Revenues (SOTR)*: States may at their own discretion project the level of SOTR. Growth of these revenues should not normally be less than the nominal growth of State Domestic Product (SDP) factored into estimates. Only increase in SOTR as a result of normal buoyancy should be indicated in Form III. Any increase in SOTR expected as a result of deliberate action, rate revision, etc., should be indicated under Additional Resource Mobilization (ARM) in Form I by the States.

- *State's Own Non-Tax Revenue (SONTR)*: Growth in a State's Own Non-Tax Revenue (SONTR) over the current year's level may be worked out using nominal SDP growth. Projections in excess of this level may become necessary if user charges of departmental undertakings are designed to eventually recover the cost of services.
  Provided. Surplus in SONTR on account of deliberate effort, rate revision, etc., should be indicated as ARM in Form II. The policy of recovering at least Non-Plan Revenue Expenditure on irrigation, water supply and sewage, power, transport and other departmental undertakings must be pursued diligently. As in the past, contribution from lotteries may be indicated under SONTR in Form II on **net** basis. In case of departmentally managed irrigation projects, gross receipts for major and medium irrigation should be indicated, along with working expenditure (O&M expenditure) and interest charges and the **net** figure should be computed on this basis. For power and transport projects undertaken departmentally, **net** contribution should be calculated and indicated only on the receipts side of the (NPRR).
- *Non-Plan Grants from the Centre:* All grants awarded by 13th Finance Commission are Non-Plan Grants. However, for the purpose of resources estimation, Ministry of Finance has classified certain grants as Plan grants. Non-Plan Revenue Deficit Grant, Performance Incentive Grants, Disaster Relief Grants (including for capacity Building), Local Bodies Grants (General Basic + General Performance + Special Area Basic Grants), Grants-in-aid for Water Sector and Grants-in-aid for maintenance of Roads and Bridges as recommended by the Thirteenth Finance Commission (ThFC) may be taken under Non-Plan Grants (NPG) from the Centre under NPRR. Grants-in-Aid for State Statistical System should be taken at half of the total recommendation by the ThFC as first instalment under NPG for 2012-13 projection. All other ThFC grants except that for State-Specific Needs, Elementary Education, Maintenance of Forests, Incentive for issuing UID, District Innovation Fund, Renewable Energy and Reduction in Infant Mortality Rate as recommended by ThFC [which are to be taken as Plan grants in the scheme of financing in Form (I) should not be taken as Non-Plan Grants from the Centre. Non-Plan Grants outside the purview of the Finance Commission may be included under "Others" depending

on the likelihood of realizing these inflows and an explanatory footnote provided.

- *Non-Plan Non-Developmental Revenue Expenditure:* This reflects expenditure on General Services covering the following four broad categories:
  - (a) *Interest Payments*: The level of interest payments may be calculated by States on the basis of the expected debt stock at the end of the current year. Debt stock may be appropriately adjusted for changed interest regime and FRBM requirements. Regarding the inflow of loans, the ceiling for a given fiscal year would be determined in accordance with the FRBM legislation of the State concerned. Depending upon the likely mix of these additional net borrowings during the current year, debt stock may accordingly be worked out at the end of the current year and projection of Interest Payable thereon may be made. Other measures actively contemplated to achieve targets fixed under respective State Fiscal Responsibility Acts, wherever applicable, may also be indicated in a footnote.
  - (b) *Pensions*: To estimate pension payments, care should be taken to build in the impact of revision of Dearness Allowance (DA), the retirement profile of State employees, changes in the retirement age and the commutation formula. State governments may furnish the method used for pension calculations separately. Reforms contemplated or already undertaken for pension programmes of employees may be indicated.
  - (c) *Salaries*: Salaries should be estimated taking into account increments on basic pay and two instalments of DA, etc. Due care may be taken to give a consistent data on salary in BCR Table (Form II) and Fiscal Indicators Table (Table I). Any deviation may be supported by an appropriate footnote. Month-wise total salary break-up should be provided separately.
  - (d) *Others*: This largely includes establishment expenses like office expenses, TA and DA, POL, purchase of motor vehicles, etc. Expenditure on these items may be estimated after detailed scrutiny of actual requirement and keep projections in line with the historically attained growth rates.

- *Non-Plan Developmental Expenditure*: This reflects expenditure on social and economic services covering salaries and other expenditure. Estimation of the salary component can be done using the approach indicated earlier. For estimating the non-salary component, care should be taken to make adequate provision for maintenance expenditure on material and equipment. The specific level of budgetary support recommended by the regulatory commission of the State should be indicated and provided as expenditure on the Non-Plan side.

6. *State's Own Resources (SOR):* State's Own Resources cover non-debt and debt receipts. The former comes under State's Own Funds (SOF) and the latter under State Government's Borrowings. The main constituents of SOF are BCR, Miscellaneous Capital Receipts (net), Plan grants from Finance Commission, Contribution of PSEs, and the resources of Local Bodies (both urban and rural). The main ingredients of the latter are: State Provident Funds (Net), Loans against Small Savings, Open Market Borrowings (Net), Negotiated Loans from Financial Institutions and Receipts from Bonds and Debentures. Guidelines for estimating the BCR for the Annual Plan 2011-12 have already been given above. The following points should be given due attention while estimating other items of the SOR:

- *Resources of State PSEs*: State Plan outlays include outlays of departments and public enterprises. Resources of enterprises should be assessed in terms of internal and Extra-Budgetary resources, including borrowings. Internal and extra-budgetary resources (IEBR) of State power and transport utilities are assessed separately and included as separate items in the resources of States. State Governments should bring net Plan resources of State owned power generation, transmission and distribution boards, companies and corporations under this category as they are assessed during discussions with the Energy and Transport Divisions of Planning Commission. IRs of other major State owned companies and corporations could also be assessed and put under the resource estimates. IRs of SEBs and SRTCs may be assessed taking tariff at current levels and expenditure for 2012-13 estimated with 5 per cent inflation or applying factors, which the Board or Corporation may consider suitable to take care of increase in input cost, O&M and remuneration. Additions to normal revenues of SEBs and SRTCs on account of tariff and fare revisions expected may be indicated as additional resource mobilization. State governments may aim at raising adequate non-tax revenue to meet at least O&M expenditure on the irrigation sector.

- *Resources of Urban and Rural Local Bodies*: Resources of Local Bodies both Urban and Rural should include Internal Resources, Extra-budgetary Borrowings and Budgetary Support as per the details provided in the Statements III and IV.
- *Plan Grants by 13th FC*: Grants for State-Specific Needs, Elementary Education, Maintenance of Forests, Incentive for issuing UID, District Innovation Fund, Renewable Energy and Reduction in Infant Mortality Rate as recommended by 13th FC should be taken as Plan resources under States' Own Funds (SOF).
- *Miscellaneous Capital Receipts (Net)*: Estimates of MCR (Net) may be provided by States on the basis of past experience. Detailed information regarding entries against the head Public Accounts and Recoveries of Loan and Advances is essential. A comprehensive note on the head Public Accounts and Recoveries of Loans and Advances should also be sent separately.
- *Net Accretion to State Provident Funds*: An important source of financial resources for States is net accretion to the State Provident Fund (SPF). States may estimate this on the basis of past experience for estimating net accretion. Such estimates should be consistent with the estimated level of salaries and salary levels of grants to grant-in-aid institutions, which make Provident Fund contributions to the State Government's Public Account. If DA impounding has been integrated into the forecasted net accretion to SPF, it should be appropriately specified. Projected net receipts from the SPF for the Annual Plan 2012-13 may be aligned to Eleventh Plan projections.
- *Loans against Small Savings*: States may on past experience estimate receipts from loans against small savings for the Annual Plan 2012-13. They should be aligned with Twelfth Plan projections.
- *Open Market Borrowings (OMB)*: Market borrowings (net) may be retained at the current year's level (excluding one time additional OMB, if any, allocated by the Planning Commission

to States) for Annual Plan 2012-13. The figures for State's share in open market borrowings (net) will be suitably revised as and when firm figures in this respect are made available by the Ministry of Finance, Government of India.

- *Negotiated Loans and Other Finances*: Plan loans for socially oriented sectors from Life Insurance Corporation of India (LIC) and General Insurance Corporation (GIC), loans from NABARD, IDBI, etc., fall under the category in Negotiated Loans and other finances. As firm figures are not yet available, States may retain the estimates for NABARD loans at the current year's level. No amount should be indicated against Plan loans from the LIC where State governments or their agencies and corporations have defaulted in loan repayment to LIC as difficulties have been experienced by defaulting States to get funds released from some institutions. In case of negotiated loans raised by Public Sector Enterprises (PSEs) from developmental institutions appropriate amounts based on past experience and future plans may be provided in the estimates. If any amount is included under "Others", details may be clearly given. Loans expected to be raised by power utilities from PFC, REC and banking institutions should be shown under this category. It is requested that institution-wise borrowing under negotiated loans may be listed out to further indicate it to the Ministry of Finance for considering concurrence under Article 293(3) of the Constitution. It may, however, be reiterated that the approval of Planning Commission will not be required for *interse* re-appropriation under this category of borrowings.
- *Bonds and Debentures*: States have been estimating substantial capital receipt inflows through debentures and bonds, although actual realization tends to be lower. These may be assessed taking into consideration administrative bottlenecks at the State level, the efficiency of State undertakings and capital market conditions, including the prevailing rate of interest. Institution-wise details of bonds and debentures to be issued may also be furnished.
- *Adjustment of Opening Balance*: For the purpose of projection of resources adjusted opening balance may also be indicated.

7. *Central Assistance*: This includes the grants under Normal Central Assistance (NCA), Additional Central Assistance for Externally Aided

Projects (ACA for EAPs) and ACA for special and other programmes based on the Gadgil formula. Item-wise allocation under Central Assistance *except* ACA for EAPs may be retained at current year's level and one time ACA and SPA allocated for the current Plan be excluded from the projections. ACA for EAPs may be projected by the State on the basis of their on-going and proposed projects.

8. As in the past, the following sub-groups have been constituted to assist in the estimation of resources of States and their public enterprises. These are:

(a) Subgroup on State Electricity Boards (SEBs),
(b) Subgroup on State Transport Corporations (SRTCs), and
(c) Subgroup on Externally Aided Projects (EAPs).

Finance departments are aware that Power and Energy Division, Transport Division and State Plans Division of the Planning Commission will organize meetings of the subgroup under their respective charge and furnish to Financial Resources Division, before or during resource discussions, their report and also the estimates of financial resources separately under the above items. State may, however, project the resources under these three items based on their preliminary estimates. All unusual estimates deviating from the past trends may please be substantiated with explanatory notes citing justification for such deviations. In case the Finance departments are in need for any clarification on the above guidelines, the same may be sought immediately from Financial Resources Division in Planning Commission or from the concerned subject division(s)'.

III. Guidelines in relation to the Normal Plan Assistance for States

At paragraph 7 on Guidelines in relation to assessment of Financial Resources for the Annual Plan, it has been mentioned about the components of Central Assistance and that the normal Plan Assistance is governed by the modified Gadgil Formula. It would be worthwhile to discuss the said formula in brief.

Gadgil Formula for Distribution of Central Assistance for State Plans

Prior to Fourth Five Year Plan, the allocation of Central Assistance to the State Plans was based on a schematic pattern and there was no definite formula for allocation. For an objective and transparent formula for allocation of Central assistance for State plans, a formula known as Gadgil formula was evolved in 1969 which was adopted for distribution of plan assistance during the Fourth and Fifth Five Year Plans. This formula was modified in 1980 and the modified formula became the basis for allocation during the Sixth and Seventh Five Year Plan. The modified formula was again revised in 1990 and formed the basis for allocation of Central Assistance for 1991-92 only. Following representations, the formula was further revised in 1991. The Gadgil Formula (1991) is known as Gadgil-Mukherjee Formula and has been in operation since the Eighth Plan period.

The main features of the formula are the following:

(i) From the total Central assistance, set apart funds required for externally aided schemes.

(ii). From the balance, provide reasonable amounts for Special Area Programmes, viz:
  (a) Hill Areas;
  (b) Tribal Areas;
  (c) Border Areas;
  (d) N.E.C.
  (e) Other Programmes.

(iii) From the balance, give 30 per cent to the Special Category States.

(iv) Distribute the balance among the Non-Special Category States as per the following criteria and weights:

	Criteria	Weight (%)
1.	*Population (1971)*	60
2.	*Per Capita Income*	25
	(a) 'Deviation' method-covering States with per capita SDP below the national average	20
	(b) Distance method-covering all States	5
3.	*Performance*	7.5
	(a) Tax effort; (b) Fiscal Management; and (c) Progress in respect of national objectives.	
4.	*Special problems*	7.5

Under the criterion of the progress in respect of national objectives, the approved formula covers four objectives, viz., (i) population control

Approved Normal Central Assistance (NCA) as per Gadgil Formula for 2009-10 and 2010-11

(Rs. in crores)

Sl. No.		2009-10	2010-11	2009-10	2010-11
Special Category Sates		*Loans and Grants/ Grants*			
1.	Arunachal Pradesh	969.48	1066.49	872.53	959.84
2.	Assam	2388.61	2627.63	2149.75	2364.87
3.	Himachal Pradesh	1181.03	1299.21	1062.93	1169.29
4.	Jammu & Kashmir	2339.94	2574.09	2105.95	2316.68
5.	Manipur	714.04	785.49	642.64	706.94
6.	Meghalaya	593.23	652.6	533.91	587.34
7.	Mizoram	683.52	751.91	615.16	676.72
8.	Nagaland	722.71	795.02	650.44	715.52
9.	Sikkim	460.97	507.1	414.88	456.39
10.	Tripura	1008.03	1108.9	907.23	998.01
11.	Uttaranchal	1165.97	1282.84	1049.37	1154.38
	Total (11 SCS)	**12227.53**	**13451.98**	**11004.79**	**12105.98**
Non-Special Category					
1.	Andhra Pradesh	1752.50	1952.03	525.75	585.61
2.	Bihar	3258.70	3561.97	977.67	1068.59
3.	Chhattisgarh	809.38	869.57	242.82	260.87
4.	Goa	124.35	148.73	37.30	44.62
5.	Gujarat	1092.75	1216.97	327.83	365.09

(Contd.)

(Contd.)

(Rs. in crores)

Sl. No.		2009-10	2010-11	2009-10	2010-11
6.	Haryana	488.41	597.10	146.52	179.13
7.	Jharkhand	969.14	1043.57	290.74	313.07
8.	Karnataka	1228.84	1358.13	368.65	407.44
9.	Kerala	882.64	993.10	264.79	297.93
10.	Madhya Pradesh	2032.78	2264.60	609.83	679.38
11.	Maharashtra	1926.16	4142.40	577.85	642.72
12.	Orissa	1784.89	1784.90	535.47	535.47
13.	Punjab	585.48	759.70	175.64	226.71
14.	Rajasthan	1682.71	1871.33	504.81	561.40
15.	Tamil Nadu	1647.65	1826.07	494.30	547.82
16.	Uttar Pradesh	5791.17	6374.53	1737.35	1912.36
17.	West Bengal	2132.70	2132.70	639.81	639.81
Total (17 NSCSs)		**28190.46**	**30893.40**	**84557.13**	**9268.02**
TOTAL STATES (28)		**40417.9**	**44344.49**	**19461.92**	**21374.00**

Source: website of the Planning Commission.

and maternal and child health; (ii) Universalisation of primary education and adult education; (iii) on-time completion of externally aided projects; and (iv) success in land reforms. Weights have been assigned separately for each of these within the overall weight of 7.5 per cent as under:

	Items	*Weights*
(a)	Tax policy	2.5%
(b)	Fiscal management	2.0%
(c)	National Objective	3.0%
(i)	Population control	1.0%
(ii)	Elimination of illiteracy	1.0%
(iii)	On-time completion of Externally aided projects	0.5%
(iv)	Land reforms	0.5%

In respect of Special problems, there were no specific criteria, and it was left to the Planning Commission to use its discretion in the allotment.

Based on the website of the Planning Commission a table is given below mentioning the kind of assistance released to the States on the basis of the Gadgil-Mukherjee Formula as on 18.11.2010.

4

Issues under State Planning

The concept of Planning has come into being to find out intelligent solution to various shortcomings in the quality of life and also to build up appropriate infrastructural base for up-scaled and sustainable quality of it. It is, therefore, important to identify issues that are crucial for planning. The planning issues for the National Plan and State Plan are almost identical in that both of them address macro items from wide range of focus. However, the national focus and State focus tend to vary. National focus has country dimension as centre of planning. It transcends consideration beyond boundaries and assesses the future vision and role of the country in the midst of the comity of nations. Issues linked with trade and commerce, external market behaviour, the expansion in the frontier of knowledge, science and technology, etc., are factors that strongly impact the national planning process. The great diversity in the development scenario of the country, plural socio-cultural behavioural status and disparity in the levels of economic and social status are also factors that are taken into consideration in national planning. Additionally, the inclusive development among the States of India together with varying status of human development require the national planning to address the issue of equity in a more robust and transparent form. A watchdog body in the forum of National Development Council (NDC) also examines all these issues for final approval of a national Five Year Plan. The core issue of State planning is, however, to address national issues as relevant for the State and to address State-specific issues, and ensure planning and implementation solution on them. The State-specific sectoral planning issues will thus be discussed hereunder:

1. Eradication of Poverty

Eradication of Poverty together with improvement of quality of life is the primary objective of planning at the State level. For addressing poverty related issues, it is necessary to have comprehensive idea about the current poverty scenario in the State. Normally, the States of India do not undertake poverty estimation at their levels. The Planning Commission as the Nodal agency in the Government of India undertakes periodical estimation of poverty status for the States. The method used for estimation of poverty is known as Expert Group Method. Based on this method, the State-wise rural and urban poverty lines for the year 2004-05 were identified using the Consumer Price Index of Agricultural Labourers for rural poverty lines and Consumer Price Index for Industrial Workers for urban poverty lines and are given in Table 4.1.

Subsequent to the release of large sample survey data on household consumer expenditure of 61st Round, two different consumption distributions for the year 2004-05 have been obtained. The first relates to consumption data collected using 30-day recall period for all items. The second relates to distribution of consumer expenditure data collected using 365-day recall period for five infrequently purchased non-food items, namely, clothing, footwear, durable goods, education and institutional medical expenses and 30-day recall for other items. These two consumption distributions have been identified as Uniform Recall Period (URP) consumption distribution and Mixed Recall Period (MRP) consumption distribution respectively. Based on the Expert Group methodology, the Planning Commission estimated poverty in 2004-05, using both URP and MRP, the State-specific percentage and number of poor in rural and urban areas as given in Tables 4.2 and 4.3.

There has taken place a growing criticism on various counts on the official estimates of poverty released by the Planning Commission. In view of this, Planning Commission set up an expert group under the chairmanship of Professor Suresh Tendulkar to examine the issue and suggest a new poverty line and estimates. The Expert Committee submitted its report in December 2009.

The Committee recommended that whereas the urban poverty line, as adjusted for inflation, continued to be reasonable, the rural poverty line had become too low because the method of indexing was inadequate and the rural poverty line should be raised. The Tendulkar Committee did not anchor the poverty lines on a normative calorie intake basis. In fact the Committee explicitly recommended delinking poverty from

Table 4.1: State-Specific Poverty Lines in 2004-05 (Rs. per capita per month)

Sl. No.	*State/Union Territories*	*Rural*	*Urban*
1.	Andhra Pradesh	292.95	542.89
2.	Assam	387.64	378.84
3.	Bihar	354.36	435.00
4.	Chhattisgarh	322.41	560.00
5.	Delhi	410.38	612.91
6.	Goa	362.25	665.90
7.	Gujarat	353.93	541.16
8.	Haryana	414.76	504.49
9.	Himachal Pradesh	394.28	504.49
10.	Jammu & Kashmir	391.26	553.77
11.	Jharkhand	366.56	451.24
12.	Karnataka	324.17	599.66
13.	Kerala	430.12	559.39
14.	Madhya Pradesh	327.78	570.15
15.	Maharashtra	362.25	665.90
16.	Orissa	325.79	528.49
17.	Punjab	410.38	466.16
18.	Rajasthan	374.57	559.63
19.	Tamil Nadu	351.86	547.42
20.	Uttar Pradesh	365.84	483.26
21.	Uttarakhand	478.02	637.67
22.	West Bengal	382.82	449.32
23.	Dadra & Nagar Haveli	362.25	665.90
	All India	**356.30**	**538.60**

Source: website of the Planning Commission.

calorie norms, but they concluded that the calorie intake at the new poverty line they had recommended was broadly in line with the new FAO norms (see Table 4.4).

The recommendations of the Tendulkar Committee with the higher rural poverty lines were accepted by the Planning Commission resulting in increased percentage of the poor in 2004-05 from 27.5 per cent of the total population to 37.2 per cent. In a related court case the Hon'ble Supreme Court expressed reservations about the poverty line fixed by the Planning Commission at the national level at 2004-05 prices and directed that the Commission "may revise norms of per capita amount looking to the price index of May 2011 or any other subsequent dates".

Pursuant to the directions of the Court, the Planning Commission recomputed the Tendulkar poverty line for June 2011 on the basis of the inflation during the interim period only. This yielded a poverty line of about Rs. 4,824 for a family of five in urban areas and about Rs. 3,905

Table 4.2: Number and Percentage of Population Below Poverty Line by States, 2004-05 (Based on URP-Consumption)

Sl. No.	States/UTs	Rural		Urban		Combined	
		Percentage of Persons	No. of Persons (Lakhs)	Percentage of persons	No. of Persons (Lakhs)	Percentage of Persons	No. of Persons (Lakhs)
(1)	(2)	(3)	(4)	(5)	(6)	(7)	(8)
1.	Andhra Pradesh	11.2	64.70	28.0	61.40	15.8	126.10
2.	Arunachal Pradesh	22.3	1.94	3.3	0.09	17.6	2.03
3.	Assam	22.3	54.50	3.3	1.28	19.7	55.77
4.	Bihar	42.1	336.72	34.6	32.42	41.4	369.15
5.	Chhattisgarh	40.8	71.50	41.2	19.47	40.9	90.96
6.	Delhi	6.9	0.63	15.2	22.30	14.7	22.93
7.	Goa	5.4	0.36	21.3	1.64	13.8	2.01
8.	Gujarat	19.1	63.49	13.0	27.19	16.8	90.69
9.	Haryana	13.61	21.49	15.1	10.60	14.0	32.10
10.	Himachal Pradesh	10.7	6.14	3.4	0.22	10.0	6.36
11.	Jammu & Kashmir	4.6	3.66	7.9	2.19	5.4	5.85
12.	Jharkhand	46.3	103.19	20.2	13.20	40.3	116.39
13.	Karnataka	20.8	75.05	32.6	63.83	25.0	138.89
14.	Kerala	13.2	32.43	20.2	17.17	15.0	49.60
15.	Madhya Pradesh	36.9	175.65	42.1	74.03	38.3	249.68
16.	Maharashtra	29.6	171.13	32.2	146.25	30.7	317.38
17.	Manipur	22.3	3.76	3.3	0.20	17.3	3.95
18.	Meghalaya	22.3	4.36	3.3	0.16	18.51	4.52
19.	Mizoram	22.3	1.02	3.3	0.16	12.6	1.18
20.	Nagaland	22.3	3.87	3.3	0.12	19.0	3.99

(Contd.)

Table 4.2—(*Contd.*)

(1)	(2)	(3)	(4)	(5)	(6)	(7)	(8)
21.	Orissa	46.8	151.75	43.3	26.74	46.4	178.49
22.	Punjab	9.1	15.12	7.1	6.50	8.4	21.63
23.	Rajasthan	18.7	87.38	32.9	47.51	22.1	134.89
24.	Sikkim	22.3	1.12	3.3	0.02	20.1	1.14
25.	Tamil Nadu	22.8	76.50	22.2	69.13	22.5	145.62
26.	Tripura	22.3	6.18	3.3	0.20	18.9	6.38
27.	Uttar Pradesh	33.4	473.00	30.6	117.03	32.8	590.03
28.	Uttarakhand	40.8	27.11	36.5	8.85	39.6	35.96
29.	West Bengal	28.6	173.22	14.8	35.14	24.7	208.36
30.	A & N Islands	22.9	0.60	22.2	0.32	22.6	0.92
31.	Chandigarh	7.1	0.08	7.1	0.67	7.1	0.74
32.	Dadra & Nagar. Haveli	39.8	0.68	19.1	0.15	33.2	0.84
33.	Daman & Diu	5.4	0.07	21.2	0.14	10.5	0.21
34.	Lakshadweep	13.3	0.06	20.2	0.06	16.0	0.11
35.	Pondicherry	22.9	0.78	22.2	1.59	22.4	2.37
	ALL-INDIA	28.3	209.24	25.7	807.96	27.5	3017.20

Source: website of the Planning Commission.

Table 4.3: Number and Percentage of Population Below Poverty Line by States, 2004-05 (Based on MRP-Consumption)

Sl. No.	States/UTs	Rural		Urban		Combined	
		Percentage of Persons	No. of Persons (Lakhs)	Percentage of Persons	No. of Persons (Lakhs)	Percentage of Persons	No. of Persons (Lakhs)
(1)	(2)	(3)	(4)	(5)	(6)	(7)	(8)
1.	Andhra Pradesh	7.5	43.21	20.7	45.50	11.1	88.71
2.	Arunachal Pradesh	17.0	1.47	2.4	0.07	13.4	1.54
3.	Assam	17.0	41.46	2.4	0.93	15.0	42.39
4.	Bihar	32.9	262.92	28.9	27.09	32.5	290.01
5.	Chhattisgarh	31.2	54.72	34.7	16.39	32.0	71.11
6.	Delhi	0.1	0.01	10.8	15.83	10.2	15.83
7.	Goa	1.9	0.13	20.9	1.62	12.0	1.74
8.	Gujarat	13.9	46.25	10.1	21.18	12.5	67.43
9.	Haryana	9.2	14.57	11.3	7.99	9.9	22.56
10.	Himachal Pradesh	7.2	4.10	2.6	0.17	6.7	4.27
11.	Jammu & Kashmir	2.7	2.20	8.5	2.34	4.2	4.54
12.	Jharkhand	40.2	89.76	16.3	10.63	34.8	100.39
13.	Karnataka	12.0	43.33	27.2	53.28	17.4	96.60
14.	Kerala	9.6	23.59	16.4	13.92	11.4	37.51
15.	Madhya Pradesh	29.8	141.99	39.3	68.97	32.4	210.97
16.	Maharashtra	22.2	128.43	29.0	131.40	25.2	259.83
17.	Manipur	17.0	2.86	2.4	0.14	13.2	3.00
18.	Meghalaya	17.0	3.32	2.4	0.12	14.1	3.43
19.	Mizoram	17.0	0.78	2.4	0.11	9.5	0.89
20.	Nagaland	17.0	2.94	2.4	0.09	14.5	3.03

(Contd.)

Table 4.3—(*Contd.*)

(1)	(2)	(3)	(4)	(5)	(6)	(7)	(8)
21.	Orissa	39.8	129.29	40.3	24.30	39.9	153.59
22.	Punjab	5.9	9.78	3.8	3.52	5.2	13.30
23.	Rajasthan	14.3	66.69	28.1	40.50	17.5	107.18
24.	Sikkim	17.0	0.85	2.4	0.02	15.2	0.87
25.	Tamil Nadu	16.9	56.51	18.8	58.59	17.8	115.10
26.	Tripura	17.0	4.70	2.4	0.14	14.4	4.85
27.	Uttar Pradesh	25.3	357.68	26.3	100.47	25.5	458.15
28.	Uttarakhand	31.7	21.11	32.0	7.75	31.8	28.86
29.	West Bengal	24.2	146.59	11.2	26.64	20.6	173.23
30.	A & N Islands	16.9	0.44	18.8	0.27	17.6	0.71
31.	Chandigarh	3.8	0.04	3.8	0.36	3.8	0.40
32.	Dadra & N. Haveli	36.0	0.62	19.2	0.16	30.6	0.77
33.	Daman & Diu	1.9	0.03	20.8	0.14	8.0	0.16
34.	Lakshadweep	9.6	0.04	16.4	0.05	12.3	0.09
35.	Pondicherry	16.9	0.58	18.8	1.34	18.2	1.92
	ALL-INDIA	21.8	1702.99	21.7	682.00	21.8	2384.99

Table 4.4: Final Poverty Lines and Poverty Head Count Ratio for 2004-05

State	*Poverty Line (Rs.)*		*Poverty Headcount Ratio (%)*		
	Rural	*Urban*	*Rural*	*Urban*	*Total*
Andhra Pradesh	433.43	563.16	32.3	23.4	29.9
Arunachal Pradesh	547.14	618.45	33.6	23.5	31.1
Assam	478.00	600.03	36.4	21.8	34.4
Bihar	433.43	526.18	55.7	43.7	54.4
Chhattisgarh	398.92	513.70	55.1	28.4	49.4
Delhi	541.39	642.47	15.6	12.9	13.1
Goa	608.76	671.15	28.1	22.2	25.0
Gujarat	501.58	659.18	39.1	20.1	31.8
Haryana	529.42	626.41	24.8	22.4	24.1
Himachal Pradesh	520.40	605.74	25.0	4.6	22.9
Jammu & Kashmir	522.30	602.89	14.1	10.4	13.2
Jharkhand	404.79	531.35	51.6	23.8	45.3
Karnataka	417.84	588.06	37.5	25.9	33.4
Kerala	537.31	584.70	20.2	18.4	19.7
Madhya Pradesh	408.41	532.26	53.6	35.1	48.6
Maharashtra	484.89	631.85	47.9	25.6	38.1
Manipur	578.11	641.13	39.3	34.5	38.0
Meghalaya	503.32	745.73	14.0	24.7	16.1
Mizoram	639.27	699.75	23.0	7.9	15.3
Nagaland	687.30	782.93	10.0	4.3	9.0
Orissa	407.78	497.31	60.8	37.6	57.2
Pondicherry	385.45	506.17	22.9	9.9	14.1
Punjab	543.51	642.51	22.1	18.7	20.9
Rajasthan	478.00	568.15	35.8	29.7	34.4
Sikkim	531.50	741.68	31.8	25.9	31.1
Tamil Nadu	441.69	559.77	37.5	19.7	28.9
Tripura	450.49	555.79	44.5	22.5	40.6
Uttar Pradesh	435.14	532.12	42.7	34.1	40.9
Uttarakhand	486.24	602.39	35.1	26.2	32.7
West Bengal	445.38	572.51	38.2	24.4	34.3
All India	446.38	578.8	41.8	25.7	37.2

Source: website of the Planning Commission.

for a family of five in rural areas. This estimate is on the basis of the 2004-05 poverty lines updated for inflation and not on the basis of NSSO consumption expenditure data in 2011. When converted into a daily per capita figure, it results Rs. 32 for urban areas and Rs. 26 for rural areas. There has been a lot of public outpourings on the current poverty line (based on the Tendulkar Committee recommendations), as worked out by the Planning Commission which has actually been redrawn well above the historical line. Further, the Tendulkar poverty line is not meant to be an acceptable level of living for the *'aam aadmi'*. It is actually the standard of living of those at the poverty line in 2004-05.

The importance of poverty line lies in selection of TPDS, in the adoption of national food security coverage and to allocations of other social safety-net programmes. The macro-level percentage of poverty estimation is a mechanism through which equity in selection of schemes and allocations of central resources are channelised. From planning angle, this is a given fact and the objective of the planners is to eradicate current level of poverty as much as possible so as to reflect it in the reduction of poverty status of the State. The reduction of the poverty status by itself is also an indicator of the success of the planning efforts in the State.

Status of BPL

For planning at the State level, the micro-level data on poverty status on households is important which is popularly known as Below the Poverty Line (BPL) lists. Below the Poverty Line is an economic benchmark and poverty threshold used by the Central Government to identify economically disadvantaged individuals and households in need of government assistance and aid. It is determined using various parameters which vary from State to State and within States. The estimation of poverty gives an aggregate picture of the poverty status of the country and also for the States. While such findings do have immense policy implications for the country or for the States, the BPL is the document based on which poverty eradication programmes would have to be actually structured at the micro-level. The BPL is a tool for programme implementation. All rural and urban poverty related programmes in our country is based on targeted programme intervention to bring down level of poverty. Because of equity attached with the BPL, it is accepted as a high valued document. However, it is not always possible to have a defect-free BPL list because of village politics and murkier role of political parties. As a result, ineligibles very often manage to enjoy subsidized programme benefits at the expense of the very poor, poor and people on the margin. While efforts are on at the grass roots level to have error-free and validated BPL, the analytical study of the List connected with specific programme is the other important consideration. Further, from operational angle, it is necessary to see that such list does not remain as permanent even after successful execution of related schemes. It needs to be concurrently updated by interactive process based on programme benefits provided by other tier of the panchayats to those included in the BPL list. The analytical study and its related input is an important consideration while planning at the State and also at the decentralised level. The district specific BPL list has thus come up as a focal point to address poverty eradication programmes by the decentralised local bodies through planning efforts of related schemes.

2. Minimum Needs Services Issues

Basic minimum standard of life for all sections of people has been the planning concern of the country since the Fifth Five Year Plan. The Chief Ministers Conference held in July 1996 endorsed the seven basic minimum services as of paramount importance in securing a better quality of life for the people, especially those residing in rural areas. The seven basic services identified for priority attention were:

- 100 per cent coverage of provision of safe drinking water in rural and urban areas;
- 100 per cent coverage of primary health service facilities in rural and urban areas;
- Universalisation of primary education;
- Provision of Public Housing Assistance to all shelterless poor families;
- Extension of Mid-Day Meal Programme in primary schools, to all rural blocks and urban slums and disadvantaged sections;
- Provision of connectivity to all unconnected villages and habitations; and
- Streamlining of the Public Distribution System with focus upon the poor.

The programme has undergone generational changes both in programme nomenclature, in its content and also in delivery of services but the essence of minimum basic services is that it has all the fundamentals for inclusive plan, tailored as it is with equity issue of human development. These primary areas have to be kept in the upfront at every planning exercise at the State level.

3. Human Development

Human Development has been defined in the Human Development Report 1970, as the process of enlarging the range of people's choices. The basic purpose of planning in the context of human development is to enlarge people's choices. In principle these choices are infinite and can change over time. The objective of human development is again to create an enabling environment for people to enjoy long, healthy and creative lives. Human development depends on intervention on three key areas namely, building human capabilities, enhancement of freedom and achieving outcomes.

Human Development (HD) has now become almost synonymous with Millennium Development Goals (MDGs) and the performances in the MDGs determine the status of HD of the country. The MDGs are an agreed set of goals that international community set for itself at the UN Millennium Summit 2000. It encompassed universally accepted human values and rights such as freedom from hunger, the right to basic education, the right to health and responsibility to future generations. The MDGs, as set for implementation and monitoring, are as follows:

Goal 1: Eradicate extreme poverty and hunger
Goal 2: Achieve universal primary education
Goal 3: Promote gender equality and empower women
Goal 4: Reduce child mortality
Goal 5: Improve maternal health
Goal 6: Combat HIV/AIDS, malaria and other diseases
Goal 7: Ensure environmental sustainability
Goal 8: Develop a global partnership for development.

Source: UNDP.

Human development in the MDGs strives to secure improvement in areas of Livelihood, Education, Health and other social sector areas. These are also the areas on which State planners take periodical planning exercises. During such annual exercises, the latest publication on status of human development needs to be consulted. Usually, such benchmark status is available in the State Human Development Report (SHDR). The SHDR is a statement of the level of achievements in its HDI and highlights the strong and weak areas of its economic and social development. It enables to track down the need of programme correction to make good of the human development deficit. In States where SHDR has not been published or where it has been published long ago, the current macro status as revealed in the National Human Development Report (NHDR) 2011 need to be consulted as a benchmark to meet the related deficit in its human development achievement. Further, for understanding the deficit of human development, MDG Report published by the Ministry of Programme Implementation, Government of India need also to be consulted. Additionally, decentralised data are also available under District Human Development Reports (DHDR) of the State which may be very useful in addressing human development deficit areas in the State. The Million Development Report 2010 published by United Nations and periodical fact-sheets of international bodies like UNDP, UNICEF, UNFPA and others may also be useful as reference background materials. The State specific deficits in these areas need to be addressed by focused programme intervention and monitoring.

Incidentally, improving the HD status of the State is also a joint and shared responsibility of all programme partners including the rural and urban local bodies. Planning is an important forum where actionable response is needed to ensure its ultimate outcome. Thus, the issue of varying degree of achievements in Human Development at the State level *vis-à-vis* the MDG destination has to be consciously addressed by realistic planning. On this area of Human Development, the State Planners need also to work out its planning connectivity with decentralised local bodies. Such local bodies are usually empowered with human development related functions. Out of the twenty nine items of the Eleventh Schedule of the Constitution for the Panchayats, the following items fall directly under Human Development:

- *Livelihood*
  (i) Poverty Alleviation Programme (Sl. No. 16);
- *Primary Education*
  (i) Education including Primary and Secondary Education (Sl. No. 17).
- *Primary Health*
  (i) Health and Sanitation including hospital, primary health centres and dispensaries (Sl. No. 23),
  (ii) Family welfare (Sl. No. 24).

Other Social Sector items:

(i) Women and child development (Sl. No. 25),

(ii) Social welfare, including welfare of the handicapped and mentally retarded (Sl. No. 26),

(iii) Welfare of the weaker sections, and in particular, of the Scheduled Castes and the Scheduled Tribes (Sl. No. 27).

Similarly, out of the eighteen items under the Twelfth Schedule, the following items on Human Development fall directly under the Municipalities:

- *Livelihood*
  (i) Urban Poverty Alleviation (Sl. No. 11);
- *Primary Education*
  (i) Promotion of cultural, educational and aesthetic aspects (Sl. No. 13);
- *Primary Health*
  (i) Public health, sanitation conservancy and solid waste management (Sl. No. 6);
- *Other Social Sector Items*
  (i) Safeguarding the interests of weaker sections of society, including the handicapped and mentally retarded (Sl. No. 9),
  (ii) Slum improvements and upgradation (10).

The march towards MDGs becomes smoother if all partners work in unison with shared responsibility and commitment from planning to implementation.

4. Employment

From human development angle, access to gainful employment is an essential condition to earn livelihood and economic well-being. This is equivalent to exercising economic rights in a market democracy. This fundamental consideration has been in the uppermost consideration in India's planning efforts since independence. Generation of productive and gainful employment on a sustainable basis to absorb growing labour force has been the avowed objective of our Five Year Plans. Employment performances over the years have, however, not been able to absorb the new entrants into the labour force. The policy initiatives have, therefore, been to absorb incremental labour force along with surplus labour from the agricultural sector into the non-agricultural areas in the organized and unorganized sector for productive and gainful employment. This basic policy has to remain unchanged till some more time on ground of economics. However, employment elasticity of private organised sector to employment generation is quite modest representing around 2.5 per cent of all jobs. The burden for largest number of new jobs falls in the Small and Medium Enterprises (SMEs) which contribute the vast majority of private sector jobs as well.

Based on this framework, employment planning issue during State planning needs to revolve around new generation of skill and knowledge based SMEs which have enough employment potentiality and elasticity. Additionally, Self-employment programmes with tied up skill development and credit linkage need priority attention. Based on mapping of the existing Self-employment programmes, dedicated programmes based on new generation of skill and knowledge are also other exciting issue for State planners. Further, a sizable section of rural and urban livelihood depends on wage employment. Planning for such revolving type of wage employment on area approach and ensuring inter-connectivity of employment availability throughout the better part of the year is the other issue that State planning needs to address comprehensively. Finally, from inclusive consideration, gender aspect and the case of economically backward citizens are also to be factored in while planning on the employment area in the State.

5. Infrastructure

India happens to be one of the fastest growing economies in the world with an upsurge in investment and robust macro-economic fundamentals. Its growth potentialities could be unleashed in full if the infrastructure facilities are improved to meet the growing demand of the economy. Thus, the provision of quality and efficient infrastructure services is essential to realize the full potential of the growth impulses surging through the economy. Infrastructure is the pillar of development and shapes the very foundation for the basic character of the economy. Infrastructure has nation specific, State specific and district specific requirements connected as it is with basic structure of related sectors at major, medium and minor level. While infrastructure for national economy is concerned with requirement for mega project having multiplier impact on the economy, the requirement for infrastructure at the State level is to build up foundation for State level projects of different sectors.

The most distinct part of physical infrastructure development is the development of road network across the country. The road network consists of Expressways, National Highways, State Highways, Major District Roads, Other District Roads and Village Roads. While the Central Government has set ambitious plans for upgradation of National Highways, Expressways, Development of ring roads, bypasses, grade separators, service roads, etc., under different modules of NHDP, the State Highways, Major District Roads, Other District Roads and Village Roads belong to the responsibility of the State.

The road vision of the State is intimately connected with the projected as well as the current development scenario of the State. Further, the infrastructural support of road networks at the district level is concerned with livelihood and social development. All these infrastructural supports are not mutually exclusive and there exists inherent connectivity among the layers of infrastructure. All of them in aggregate terms determine the infrastructure base of the national economy. Such infrastructural base has also short term, medium term and long term focus and requires upgradation with generational changes in the development scenario. The aspects of connectivity, interdependence and generational changes have to be kept in the upfront at the stage of planning.

The infrastructural issues relating to energy, transport and other social infrastructures have been discussed separately.

6. Water

Water has emerged as a new focused issue on State planning. Gone are the days of abundant and relatively comfortable water resources position. The exponential growth of water demand from both traditional and not so traditional sources has been rapidly turning into a supply constraint scenario. The demand for adequate water as a basic human right has added further dimension. The competitive claim of water by agriculture (India's net irrigated area is still less than 50%), Industries of various descriptions (both water intensive and water based), Power sector (both hydel and thermal), Municipalities and other institutions from Nature's grid of water are bound to increase at a much higher rate. Concurrently at the same time, supply side is being seriously affected by regular shrinkage of catchments in the hills, declining and uneven rainfall status, shrinking carrying capacity of the river beds and reservoirs, warming up of the climate and its consequent impact on lesser volume on surface water reservoirs, over-use of groundwater resources, absence of commensurate corrective restoration programmes and its concurrent monitoring, non-recycling of water wastes and the like. The high point on planning on water related issue is making a balance between demand and supply.

In understanding the water scenario, it is to be kept in mind that according to an estimate of the Water Resources Ministry, India's per capita availability of water is around 1,545 m^3 a year in 2011 including non-personal consumption, such as irrigation and is below the international threshold of 1,700 m^3 a year. India is home to 17 per cent of the world's population but has only 4 per cent of fresh water. Further, according to the UN-adopted Falkenmark Water Stress Indicator, the most widely cited measure of water scarcity is national per capita availability which indicates water stress conditions. According to the World Bank and UNICEF estimates, 30 per cent of rural Indians lack drinking water supply and only 7 States have full drinking water access in rural areas. The Industry uses 6 per cent of freshwater and will double its usage in 10 years. Water is most crucial for the agriculture sector that supports two-thirds of all Indians and uses 90 per cent of total water supply. The country currently uses 829 billion m^3 of water every year, which is approximately the size of Lake Erie, the fourth largest of the five Great Lakes in North America. By 2050 the demand for water is expected to cross the 1.4 trillion m^3 mark. Groundwater recharge, a critical source to enhance supply has remained sporadic and neglected.

In this connection it would be appropriate to keep in the upfront that India allocated Rs. 100 crore during the 11th Five Year Plan for water recharge, of which Rs. 61 crore has been utilized so far. The Planning Commission has now proposed an accelerated water recharge project in all States during the next Five Year Plan period to scale up conservation.

While addressing water issue, the related State planning body needs also to address (i) Quantity, (ii) Accessibility, (iii) Quality and (iv) Sustainability aspects, specially with reference to drinking water. Further, following emerging scenario need to be given appropriate consideration:

(i) Shifting of the focus from spot water sources to a regime of micro-piped drinking water supply to serve the dual purpose of quality (arsenic free) of water and inclusive centred delivery of water services.

(ii) The water supply sources—both surface and groundwater—are dynamic in character and calls for periodical verification. GIS based watertable maps need to be periodically published for appropriate programme correction. Climatic change has also to be factored in.

(iii) For big cities and its satellite towns, the water source-points are common. The feasibility of sharing water from a Water Grid on a cost sharing basis may be explored.

(iv) Information network on the quality of water and infrastructure facilities on water testing qualities are to be put in place.

(v) The water retention capacity of big reservoirs built in the bygone years need to be augmented where re-excavation would be more cost effective on consideration of economies of return of additional water from such investment.

7. Climate

Climate change is now the most defining challenge of mankind. It is a process of long term change of weather pattern. Such climatic change has already set in and beginning to transform life pattern on earth. Seasons are shifting, temperatures are climbing and sea levels are rising. Some of the damage consequences of climate change, which impact on our life and our surroundings may be short listed as below:

- High temperature
- Changing landscape
- Increasing risks of drought, fire and flood
- Stronger storms and increased storm-damage
- Rising seas
- Wildlife and biodiversity loss
- More heat related illness and diseases
- Economic loss

In the context of our rural economy, the impact of climate change on agriculture is very crucial. Agriculture is highly sensitive to climate variability such as drought, floods, severe storms and other seasonal stresses. Climatic change impacts agriculture instantly including its effects on crops, livestock, weeds, pests, pathogens, etc. Despite technological advances such as improved variety of seeds and irrigation system, weather does play a significant factor on availability of water—both surface and groundwater and affects other crucial soil properties. As a matter of fact, the effect of climatic change on agriculture is related to variabilities in local climate rather than global climatic pattern. Consequently, assessment of climatic change on each local area is very important. The effect of climatic change on agriculture may take place in several ways as below:

(i) productivity in terms of quantity and quality of crops;
(ii) agricultural practices, through changes of water use and agricultural inputs such as herbicide, insecticide and fertilizers; and
(iii) environmental effects, in particular in relation to frequency and intensity of soil drainage, soil erosion and crop diversity.

The upshot of the above discussion is that climate change has assumed critical planning issues in the area of mitigation and adaptation and the State planners need to address them based on local level variability status of climate change. It may be worthwhile to mention that climatic change related issues are not mere planning issues; it transcends beyond that as it impacts the living environment of the local area. Very soon it might turn out as a robust challenge for the State and also for the decentralised bodies for possible eruption of climatic unrest in some sensitive locations of the State and also pose a key governance issue. Climatic change planning is meant to prevent and mitigate such disaster at near future.

8. Gender Issues

Gender has emerged as an important planning issue at all levels of planning connected as it is with inclusiveness, empowerment and the MDG. However, no structured Gender Plan as such has come into being either at the national level or at the State level except under the State Annual Plan where it is required to submit Women Component in Annexure IXA (financial) and IXB (physical) to the Planning Commission. Capturing such components does not automatically lend itself to a creditable Gender Plan.

At the Government of India level, for preparation of "Gender Budgeting" for the Budget 2012-13, all the Ministries are required to prepare the statement which reflect the quantum of public expenditure earmarked for (a) women specific programmes (100% provision); and (b) pro-women allocations (at least 30% provision) for gender neutral programmes reflecting the specified percentage provisions. It would be desirable for the States to take them as guide while planning Gender Plan in the State, enlarge the programme coverage and then take up its budgeting at the appropriate time. At such Gender Plan of the State, programmes under TSP ans SCSP may be included along with those covered under minority development programmes for wholesome coverage.

In this context it would be relevant that the following items bearing overarching impact on the lives of women need to be included under Gender Plan in the State in appropriate manner:

Livelihood

(i) Wage employment related dedicated schemes for the women;
(ii) Self-employment and market linked initiatives for the women;
(iii) Skill development and skill based employment for the women; and
(iv) Pension for the aged and the old age home for the women.

Education

(i) Gender gap in literacy;
(ii) Residential facilities for girl students in educationally backward districts;
(iii) Book grant, merit scholarship etc. for economically backward girl students;
(iv) Required toilet and boundary facilities in schools; and
(v) Vocational education and vocational counselling centre for the girls.

Health

(i) Pre-natal and Post-natal care including new born care;
(ii) Stoppage of female foeticide and implementation of Preconception and PNDT Act;
(iii) Adolescent health care;
(iv) Nutrition care on life cycle basis; and
(v) HIV and AIDS related issues.

Social Sector

(i) Network of crèches;
(ii) Prevention of child marriage and dowry;
(iii) Institutional care for the destitute and the women in distress; and
(iv) Counselling care networks for domestic violence, trafficking, migration of women, harassment in work places and other regulatory issues.

9. Tribal Sub-Plan (TSP) and Scheduled Caste Sub-Plan (SCSP)

The welfare of the Scheduled Castes and the Scheduled Tribes has been an important area on planning and the Planning Commission has been addressing this issue for long under the State Plan. The Tribal Sub-Plan (TSP) as a planning strategy has been taken up since 1974 to ensure adequate flow of plan resources for the development of Scheduled Tribes while the Special Component Plan for Scheduled Castes (SCP) has been in force since 1979-80 to ensure proportionate flow of plan resources for the development of Scheduled Castes. The SCP has been renamed as Scheduled Caste Sub-Plan (SCSP) since 2006.

Tribal Sub-Plan (TSP)

Historically, the Tribal Community remained cut off from the mainstream development activities. With the launching of the First Five Year Plan in our country, the first serious efforts to initiate development programme for the tribal community took place in 1955 in the form of Special Multipurpose Development Blocks. However, dedicated programmes were needed exclusively for the tribal community and as a result the concept of Tribal Development Block having more than 50 per cent of tribal population came into being during the Second Five Year Plan. It was, thereafter, realised that the Tribal Development Blocks to be a focal point for the welfare of the Scheduled Tribes need to be integrated with overall planning efforts of the State. The concept of Tribal Sub-Plan (TSP) thus came up during the Fifth Five Year Plan which required that within the State Plan there need to have dedicated programmes for the Scheduled Tribes of the State for their economic and social development. Such dedicated programmes taken up under TSP also receives Special Central Assistance (SCA) from the Central Government along with Central Sector programme support. Additionally, the Constitution of India required under Article 275(1) to meet the cost of schemes for the purpose of promoting the welfare of the Scheduled Tribes in the State or raising the level of administration of the Scheduled Areas therein to that of the administration of the rest of the areas of the State. The grants-in-aid so received are also taken into account for the available fund for TSP.

The Planning Commission has stipulated that required flow of outlay for TSP should correspond with the percentage of the ST population in the State. However, this turned out to be mechanical exercise and the Planning Commission during the terminal year of the Tenth Plan revised it to ensure that scheme-specific aggregate outlays on TSP are at least equal to percentage of ST population in the State. The overarching objective of the TSP is to ensure inclusiveness of the ST population in the planning process and improve their human development status.

The focus under TSP has always been to meet the development deficit in general, however, the variations on status of human development of ST *vis-à-vis* the average status of the citizens are also important issues for planning considerations. The TSP programmes are in the nature of additionality; the ongoing general programmes are to proceed as usual with one rider that there has not to take place any duplication efforts and that distinct visibility for each of the programmes has to be ensured. The scope of programme convergence, wherever feasible, may, however, be attempted upon.

In terms of priorities in the TSP, all types of education—primary, upper primary, secondary, higher secondary, higher education, vocational education, etc., occupy important place. The gender gap and factors responsible for low level of achievement are to be addressed.

The format of presentation of TSP has been discussed in detail at Annexures VA and VB.

Special Central Assistance to Tribal Sub-Plans (SCA to TSP)

The Special Central Assistance to Tribal Sub-Plans (SCA to TSP) is provided by the Ministry of Tribal Affairs to the State Government. The SCA is additive to State Plan efforts for tribal development and forms part of TSP strategy. Funds under this programme are released for demand based employment-cum-income generation activities and the infrastructure incidental thereto, for Scheduled Tribes below the poverty line, thereby raising their economic and social status, including that of the Particularly Vulnerable Tribal Groups.

The important features of the SCA to TSP are the following:

- 70 per cent of the SCA are to be used for primary schemes supporting family/self-help groups (SHGs)/community-based employment and income generation in sectors such as Agriculture/Horticulture, Land Reforms, Watershed Development, Animal Husbandry, Ecology and Environment, Development of Forests and Forest villages, etc., and 30 per cent for the development of infrastructure incidental thereto;
- Priority to the neglected Scheduled Tribes living in forest villages and synchronization of the programmes with Joint Forest Management (JFM);
- Preparation of long term area specific micro plans for ITDAs/ ITDPs; and

- 30 per cent of beneficiaries are to be women.

Scheduled Caste Sub-Plan (SCSP)

The Scheduled Caste Sub-Plan (SCSP) since evolved in 1979 is aimed at:

(a) Economic development through beneficiary oriented programmes for raising their income and creating assets;
(b) Basti-oriented schemes for infrastructure development through provision of drinking water supply, link roads, house-sites, housing, etc., and
(c) Educational and Social development activities like establishment of primary schools, health centres, vocational centres, community halls, women work place, etc.

The Scheduled Caste Sub-Plan envisages to channelise the flow of outlays and benefits from all the sectors of development in the Annual Plans of States at least in proportion to their population both in physical and financial terms. The State governments exercise their quantification as 'Divisible' and 'Non-Divisible' components. Effective quantification is made only from the 'Divisible' component scheme-wise.

The broad criteria for categorisation of any scheme as SCSP or TSP are as follows:

(a) Only those schemes should be included under SCSP or TSP which ensure direct benefits to individuals or families belonging to Scheduled Castes or Scheduled Tribes; and
(b) Outlay for Area oriented schemes directly benefiting Scheduled Caste hamlets/villages having more than 40 per cent Scheduled Castes or Scheduled Tribes population shall be included in SCSP or TSP, as the case may be.

The existing guidelines further require to:

(i) earmark funds under SCSP/TSP from the State Plan outlay, at least in proportion of percentage of SC and ST population as per Census, 2001.
(ii) place funds earmarked for SCSP under a separate Minor Head '789' and for TSP under Minor Head '796' below the

functional Major Head/Sub-Major Heads to ensure their non-divertibility.

The Task Force recently constituted by the Planning Commission recommended Criteria for categorizing Plan Expenditure under SCSP and TSP in the following manner:

Plan outlay and expenditure falling under the following two broad categories will be eligible for being classified in SCSP/TSP:

(i) Expenditure on Poverty Alleviation and individual beneficiary oriented schemes, e.g. MGNREGA, IAY, NRLM, SGSRY, PMEGP, etc.; and
(ii) Expenditure on other schemes which is incurred in: (a) SC and ST concentration areas respectively, i.e., in the villages, blocks and districts having more than 40 per cent SC/ST population respectively, and largely benefiting such villages, blocks and districts, and in other areas, but which demonstrably benefits SCs/STs respectively.

It has been recommended that the extent to which plan expenditure in the above-mentioned categories may be classified under SCSP/TSP may be determined on the basis of:

(i) The extent of coverage of SCs/STs respectively, in poverty alleviation and beneficiary-oriented schemes (actual coverage in the case of ongoing schemes, and estimated coverage, in the case of new schemes),
(ii) (a) All plan expenditure under other schemes in SC/ST concentration areas respectively to the extent its benefits go to such areas only; and
(b) Plan expenditure in 'other schemes' in non-SC/ST concentration areas, to the extent the schemes demonstrably benefit SCs/STs respectively.

Wherever flow of benefits of a scheme to SCs/STs, to some extent, is not in doubt but its quantification, based on hard data, is difficult, the appropriate extent for each such project/institution/scheme may be determined by the Central Tripartite Committee.

The format of presentation of SCSP has been discussed in detail at Annexures VIA and VIB.

Special Central Assistance (SCA) for SCSP

The Ministry of Social Justice and Empowerment (M/SJ&E) provides 100 per cent grant under the Central Sector Scheme of SCA to SCSP as an additive to SCSP to the States/UTs to fill the critical gaps and vital missing inputs in family oriented income generating schemes with supporting infrastructure development so as to make the schemes more effective. The objective of the SCA is to provide additional support to Below Poverty Line (BPL) SC families to enhance their productivity and income. SCA could also be utilized for infrastructural development in the blocks having 50 per cent or more of SC population. SCA is released to these States/UTs on the basis of the following criteria:

(i) SC Population of the States/UTs—40 per cent.
(ii) Relative backwardness of the States/UTs—10 per cent.
(iii) Percentage of SC families in the States/UTs covered by Composite Economic Development Programmes in the State Plan to enable them to cross the poverty line—25 per cent.
(iv) Percentage of SCSP to the Annual Plan as compared to SC population percentage of the States/UTs—25 per cent.

10. Monitoring Issues Relevant to Planning

The Planning Commission very often sets targets for the States of India to ensure that the implementation process of the Five Year Plan is on the right track. The targets are set for the State as a whole. It is meant for the Line Departments of the government and other partners in the State. Accordingly, during its planning process the State needs to disaggregate them among its Line Departments, DPCs and other programme partners. It is a fact that such a target setting from top is against the very spirit of decentralisation and the basis of these target setting is not always above inconvertible logic. However, the reaching the targets with combined efforts of all programme partners would stand in good stead to reach the avowed goals of Five Year Plan of the State and the country. Based on this spirit of accommodation, it is worthwhile to address these targets on the basis of realities as available in the district and set provisional targets for them to achieve the same.

It is in this spirit that the Planning Commission set monitoring targets for the Eleventh Five Year Plan for the States of India. The moot point in relation to these targets is that these targets are to be taken as planning issue and address them adequately in course of planning itself. State specific targets for seven States for the Eleventh Plan are shown in Table 4.5 by way of an example.

11. Monitorable Items—Twenty Point Programme—2006

Another monitorable item that qualifies for planning issue at the State level is the Twenty Point Programme. The Twenty Point Programme 1986 has been restructured in 2006 in conformity with the priorities of the Government. It consists of 20 points and 66 monitorable items. Out of 66 items, 25 items are monitored on monthly basis and the remaining on annual basis. It aims to the benefit of the rural and urban people. The Twenty Points and number of monitorable items under each category are indicated below:

1. Poverty Eradication (6 items),
2. Power to the People (3 items),
3. Support to Farmers (5 items),
4. Labour Welfare (4 items),
5. Food Security (1 item—3 components),
6. Housing for All (2 items),
7. Clean Drinking Water (2 items),
8. Health for All (8 items)
9. Education for All (2 items)
10. Welfare of Scheduled Castes, Scheduled Tribes, Minorities and OBCs (10 items)
11. Women Welfare (2 items)
12. Child Welfare (2 items).
13. Youth Development (3 items)
14. Improvement of Slums (1 item)
15. Environment Protection and Afforestation (3 items)
16. Social Security (2 items)
17. Rural Roads (1 item)
18. Energization of Rural Area (6 items)
19. Development of Backward Areas (1 item)
20. IT enabled e-Governance (2 items).

For the purpose of ranking the performar.ce of States under TPP-2066 on monthly basis, the following 15 items are taken into consideration:

Table 4.5: State-Specific Monitorable Targets for the Eleventh Five Year Plan

	Bihar	*Madhya Pradesh*	*Uttar Pradesh*	*Rajasthan*	*Chhattisgarh*	*Jharkhand*	*Orissa*
(i) Adjusted Additional Jobs (ii) Jobs needed (iii) Difference	(i) 4936764 (ii) 5777606 (iii) 840842	(i) 5167944 (ii) 4405955 (iii) 761989	(i) 12312892 (ii) 111554438 (iii) 1157454	(i) 3984290 (ii) 4695431 (iii) 711142	(i) 2089766 (ii) 1490527 (iii) 599240	(i) 2126120 (ii) 2228551 (iii) 102431	(i) 2056073 (ii) 3457021 (iii) 1400948
IMR	61 to 29	79 to 38	72 to 35	67 to 32	60 to 29	49 to 24	77 to 37
MMR	371 to 123	279 to 126	517 to 172	670 to 148	379 to126	371 to 123	358 to 119
TFR	4.3 to 2.2	3.8 to 2.4	4.4 to 2.8	3.9 to 2.2	3.8 to 2.4	4.3 to 2.2	2.6 to 1.9
Malnutrition	54.4 to 27.2	5 5.1 to 27.6	51.7 to 25.9	50.6 to 25.3	55.1 to 27.6	54.4 to 27.2	54-4 to 27.2
Anaemia	63.4 to 31.7	54.3 to 27.2	48.7 to 24.4	48.5 to 24.3	54.3 to 27.2	63.4 to 31.7	63.0 to 31.5
Sex Ratio	942 to 950	932 to 940	916 to 924	909 to 917	975 to 983	965 to 973	953 to 961
School Drop Out	78.03 to 27.85	46.81 to 16.08	42.84 to 17.96	68.50 to 29.47	46.81 to 9.95	78.03 to 29.70	61.72 to 31.99
Literacy Rate	46.96 to 64.04	63.72 to 84.50	56.23 to 77.20	60.43 to 79.57	64.69 to 86.16	53.52 to 70.56	63.10 to 83.96
Gender Gap	26.6 to 17.4	25.8 to 16.3	26.6 to 13.4	31.9 to 25.6	25.5 to 15.6	28.4 to 23.0	24.8 to 15.1

Source: N-11016/4(6)/2005-PC, Planning Commisssion.

1. Food Security:
   (i) Targeted Public Distribution System,
   (ii) Antodaya Anna Yojana;
2. Rural Housing—Indira Awaas Yojana;
3. EWS/LIG Houses in Urban Areas;
4. Rural Areas:
   - Accelerated Rural Water Supply Programme;
5. Immunisation of Children;
6. Sanitation Programme in Rural Areas;
7. SC Families Assisted;
8. ST Families Assisted;
9. Universalisation of ICDS Scheme;
10. Functional Anganwadis;
11. Afforestation:
    (i) Area Covered under Plantation—Public and Forest Lands;
    (ii) Number of Seedlings planted on—Public and Forest Lands;
12. Rural Roads—PMGSY;
13. Rajiv Gandhi Grameen Vidyutikaran Yojana;
14. Energising Pump Sets; and
15. Supply of Electricity.

All these monitorable items are indicators of outreach of plan initiatives in the State and are also important from assessing its overall plan performances. It is important that State Government gives due emphasis on these monitorable items at the stage of planning itself and considers them as important and serious planning issues.

12. Planning Issues under Sectors of Planning

Planning Commission requires the State Plan to be presented under eleven sectors. The sectors represent specified development functions and each of the sectors represent important areas of State planning. The planning issues for each of the sectors are distinct and different from one another though there may be commonalities of issues among some sectors. In each sector there exists some planning issues which are almost universal in character and forms in a way a kind of grammar for each sector. With the change of every Five Year Plan and the resultant change of the status of sectoral development, the core issues and focus of sectoral planning changes. However, the basic issue remains almost the same even under the new format of Five Year Plan. Further, because of diversity of the planning environment and plural status of State development indicators, core sectoral planning issues are also different from one State to another along with intensity of its focus. In this section, general and basic issues relating to sectoral planning are addressed in brief. The State specific sectoral issues are to be added for the concerned State. However, the new issues of planning for the 12th Plan will be discussed separately.

(A) Planning Issues for Agriculture and Allied Sectors

Agriculture and Allied sectors is the backbone of the economy and provides platform to the growth and sustenance to the secondary and tertiary sectors. The planning issues of this sector are numerous and varied. It includes Rice, Wheat, Pulses, Oilseeds, Cotton, Agro forestry, Horticulture, Medicinal Plants, Fisheries, and Dairy, etc. It covers soil testing, farm services, organic farming, seeds, technology, marketing, input supply, extension services, credit and institutional support, agri-clinic, cooperatives, etc. It has to deal with varying nature of monsoons, floods, drought and erratic behaviour of the market and work out damage limitation exercise. It has to work on balance production in between cereals, pulses, oilseeds, fibre and other horticultural crops having regard to net agricultural land area under cultivation. This sector focuses on issues connected with Food for all, Fish for all, and Milk for all. Production, productivity, diversification and sustainability are some other important issues of this sector.

(B) Planning Issues for Rural Development

Rural development shapes the rural economy of any State. It covers a host of listed sub-sectors like Drought Prone Area Programme (DPAP), Desert Development Programme (DDP), Integrated Wasteland Programme, DRDA Administration, Promotion of SHG, Rural Employment covering Swarnajayanti Gram Swarozgar Yojana (SGSY), Sampoorna Gram Rozgar Yojana (SGRY), National Food for Work./ National Employment Guarantee Programme, Land Reforms related programmes and Programmes on Community Development and Panchayats are also included. The sub-sectors are programme based.

The planning issues of this sector are varied and most crucial for the State economy. The essential requisite for planning for rural development is to have clear picture about the profiles of the poors of the State. The size and composition of BPL including its district-wise disaggregation are important. The knowing the details of land character and natural resources endowments are also relevant. Based on above, intervening issues connected with extent of improvement of drought prone areas, desert related problem, and treatment and making use of wasteland also come up. Issues connected with wage employment and self-employment and items connected with the implementation of Flagship and other programmes are also important planning items. It is required to address access, choice, capability and participation together with inclusive issues.

(C) Planning Issues for Special Area Programmes

Special Area Programme is an operational strategy to address sustainable development of a relatively backward area. Such backward area could be the geographical location such as hilly areas, border areas and the like. It could also relate to forest fringe backward areas inhibited by the Scheduled Tribes. The existing budgetary allocation of Line Departments seldom addresses special needs of such areas as a result of which development deficit of such areas are not adequately addressed. Under Special Area Programme, diverse needs for removing development deficit are addressed with dedicated schemes and fund.

The planning issues in this area centre around bridging the gap of deficit *vis-à-vis* the State average or the national average of development. Identification of deficit areas together with availability of schemes of the Line Departments and its resources has to be done first. The planning under Special Area Programme needs to address thereafter either with additional programme/scheme requirement over ongoing schemes or plan for new initiatives for uncovered areas with required fund. Usually, such new initiatives are taken under infrastructure development and it has to be ensured that planning takes care of quality and future considerations of infrastructure as well. Further, such initiatives need also to take care of the special needs of social inclusion through social service sector. For ensuring visible outcome, depending on the nature of project, it would be relevant to take up schemes which could be completed within the planning year or within national Five Year Plan, as the case may be, to show demonstratable result. Additionally, planning exercise needs to take care of inter-connectedness of various programmes and schemes and addresses convergence wherever it is desirable and possible.

(D) Planning Issues for Irrigation and Flood Control

Irrigation system is the lifeline for the agricultural crops. The planning issues in relation to irrigation need to be segregated under Major and Medium irrigation, Minor irrigation, AIBP, Command Area Development and Flood Control.

The planning for Major and Medium irrigation is concerned with the completion issue of ongoing schemes at the first instance. A large number of major as well as medium projects including AIBP have been continuing for long years without completion, with its gestation period varying in between 15 to 20 years for major projects and 5 to 10 years for medium projects. The spill over projects, quite a substantial number of them under State funded programme are needed to be completed at the earliest. Linked with it is the canal network that has not been significantly developed even in cases where the irrigation project has been completed. The older completed projects have also been showing faster than projected siltation requiring desiltation programme to commence early and the general picture of maintenance of distribution channels is also not good. Further, utilization of irrigation potential created has also been rather poor. The water use efficiency of the present level is around 30–40 per cent and the gap between Irrigation Potential Created (IPC) and Irrigation Potential Utilized (IPU) has been increasing steadily over time. There has also been inadequate or complete absence of involvement of water users through Water User Associations (WUAs).

Minor irrigation is the backbone of irrigation system in any State. The areas under agriculture not covered under the major or the medium irrigation system are usually taken up under minor irrigation. Planning issues on minor irrigation system relate to extension of net minor irrigation areas. It is also concerned with the necessity, desirability and extent of intervention in different modes in different places for different crops by either with high capacity deep tube well, medium capacity deep tube well, low capacity deep tube well, shallow tube well, river lift irrigation and open dug wells or a combination of them. The command areas, utilisation of potentials, economic use of water, the groundwater resources as currently mapped and its extraction status are other considerations. Since groundwater is the main source of water, special emphasis is needed on obtaining an accurate picture of groundwater resources, including a comprehensive mapping of aquifers at a watershed scale, with their storage and transmission characteristics. Setting up of Water User Associations (WUAs) and the nature of its involvement for economic water use and water rate collection are other issues.

(E) Planning Issues for Energy

Energy is a critical input for production and rapid growth of GDP. Twelfth Five Year Plan envisaged a GDP growth rate of 9 per cent per year and it will require energy supply to grow at around 6.5 per cent per year between 2010-11 and 2016-17.

The Twelfth Five Year Plan begins with a backlog of still-to-be completed power projects of various installed capacities across the States. The most important task is, therefore, to ensure completion of such projects with minimum time run with all resources support. However, the States will require taking up new power projects to meet growing power demand. Before planning for new thermal power project, the issue of tied-up coal supply linkage and financial health of the utilities has to be resolved. In addressing further capacity addition, efforts are to be made to expand energy from clean energy sources. The share of new renewable energy in total commercial energy use at this juncture in the country is around 10 per cent with conventional hydro-electricity accounting for another 22 per cent. The share of new and renewable energy including wind power generation and solar thermal and solar photovoltaic modes needs to be expanded with improved capacity utilisation in the overall energy basket. Connected with power supply is also the issue of energy efficiency in all electrical appliances which need to be effected through replacement of inefficient agricultural pumps by efficient pumps in phased manner.

Transmission and distribution loss is one of the weakest links in the power system. The current losses of distribution utilities before accounting for State subsidy are approximately Rs. 70,000 crore. Continuation of losses on this scale is simply not viable. This needs adequate intervention.

With the change of economy, human expectation, lifestyle and also the production system in the rural areas, the access to energy together with consideration of equity and inclusiveness has assumed great importance. Adequate attention to Rural Electricity including connections to all villages and free connections to BPL families are now priority items of planning.

(F) Planning Issues for Industry and Minerals

Industry and Minerals under State Planning include Small Scale Industries, Handlooms/Powerlooms, Handicrafts, Sericulture/Coir/Wool, Food Processing Industries, Other Industries and Minerals. Planning issues under Small Scale Industries relate to common service facility centre, cluster development programme, orientation and entrepreneurship development programme, incentive for setting new industrial enterprises, credit and loan to Village and Small Industries, Quality Control, modernisation and marketing issues, etc. While these issues are common for other sub-sectors, distinct planning issues also exist for them. Under Handicrafts, skill development programme, participation in Handicrafts fair, export promotion for Handicrafts, Urban marketing outlets, Handicrafts museum, Financial Assistance to Handicrafts artisans/co-operatives, pension to Old Aged Handicrafts artisans, etc., are also relevant. For coir sub-sector, Training centre for manufacture of coir products is important. For Handloom sub-sector, diversification of products, export oriented production, market promotion of handloom products, linkage with Fashion technology, financial assistance to handloom weavers, welfare and social security of handloom weavers are some of the dedicated planning issues. Modernisation issue of powerloom sub-sector and diversification of its products are also important. Under Sericulture, planning issues include high yielding varieties of mulberry crop, rearing inputs/appliances, maintenance and multiplication of basic silkworm seeds, improvement of post-cocoon sector through development of reeling/twisting technology for silk yarn, cultivation of eri and muga and related training, sericulture cluster scheme, etc.

The food processing industries as a sunrise sub-area has immense potentialities for growth. Planning issues include identification of projects, raw materials availability, escort services relating to finance, shed, electricity, etc., marketing and exportable opportunity, product development, skill training, modernisation, anchoring facilities with the Ministry of FPI, Government of India, APEDA, NHB, etc., infrastructure for food producing industries including Food Park, cargo complex for perishable goods, Quality control, cold storage and refrigerated transport, joint venture, research and development, etc.

Minerals of minor variety come within the orbit of State Planning. The planning issue relates to explore such minerals, examine its potential usefulness, scope of converting those into marketable commodities and address all issues connected therewith for converting them into trade and services.

(G) Planning Issues for Transport Sector

Rapid growth of the economy and its competitiveness is dependent on commensurate road network and efficient transport system. Transport sector planning at the State level covers Minor Ports, Civil Aviation, Roads (including PMGSY) and Bridges, Road Transport and Inland Water Transport. Of these items, the planning issue relating to Roads and Bridges is crucial as it shapes the infrastructural base of the State. Apart from planning for integrating linked road network with National Highways Development Programme, the planning for extension and quality upgradation of State highways is also equally important. Development of major district roads, rural roads and connectivity with unconnected habitations through PMGSY is other item for planning. Further, prioritisation of upgradation, the status of sanctioned schemes and likely time schedule of completion are also important issues of planning.

A number of State governments organises Road Transport with PSUs with plan fund for operation and extension. Issues connected with utilisation, vehicle productivity, load factor, staff-bus ratio, staff productivity, etc., come up for discussion. Additionally, road safety issue, rescue aid posts, road safety education, etc., also feature as planning issues. Further, expansion and modernisation of Bus Stations is also equally important.

An alternative transport avenue through Inland Water Transport has got momentum in recent times. Location, feasibility, construction of jetties, floating jetties, fleet of launch, steamer, etc., together with economies of it are areas for planning decision.

(H) Planning Issues for Science, Technology and Environment

This is the fast spacing sector assuming overarching leadership for the sustainable development of the State. All sub-components are equally important. It covers Scientific Research, IT&E-Governance, Ecology and Environment and Forestry and Wildlife. Under Scientific Research, the planning issues pertain to promotion of scientific research for fulfilment of socio-economic needs of the State, popularization of science and technology through different mediums and forums, pilot schemes from lab to land, setting up of remote sensing centre for providing updated data on natural resources, extension and practical application of science and technology in rural areas, etc. For IT&E-Governance sub-sector the planning issues relate to government portals, e-governance, related capacity building, dedicated portals like telemedicine, Agriculture portal, etc., establishment of software technology park and NeGP. Under Ecology and Environment, some of the important issues cover environmental awareness, environmental research, environmental pollution, disposal of solid and hazardous wastes, conservation of bio-diversity, climate change related issues, etc. Forestry and Wildlife sub-sector needs to address issues on extent of forestry coverage, forest resource survey, forest consolidation, forest protection, JFM and improvements of parks and gardens, urban forestry etc.

(I) Planning Issues for General Economic Services

Tourism is the most important development functional item under General Economic Services. The Tourism profile of States varies sharply depending on richness of its geographical diversity, its religious heritage and infrastructural network on its tourist establishments and support structure. The planning issues for Tourism thus centre around all aspects linked with promotion of Tourism. The provisioning of tourist accommodation for different economic categories of tourists, related road networks down the line, promotion of transport facilities, diversified and innovative recreational avenues and other related support services. Promotion of heritage tourism, eco-tourism, circuit tourism, rural tourism, religious tourism, tea tourism, health tourism, etc., are some areas for planning for diversification. Public-private partnership and incentive schemes for promotion and extension of tourism are other issues for planning.

Another important area under General Economic Services is Civil Supplies. Here the planning issue relates to creation of infrastructural facilities for Public Distribution Supplies. At the stage of planning of PDS, distance factor and location of Scheduled Tribes in far away forest fringe areas need appropriate consideration.

Different departments of the State Government undertake programmes on Census, Surveys and Statistics. Similarly, for the establishment of Weights and Measures, planning issues include norms and basis for expansion of infrastructural network and adoption of state of art of modern technology. Finally, under component of District Planning Committee, issues on its strengthening and funding, including those of the Panchayats and the Municipalities, await appropriate consideration.

(J) Planning Issues for Social Services

The big area of Social Services is directly linked with inclusive and human development. While all the components of this sector are equally important, the planning issues of major components are discussed hereunder in this segment.

1. General Education

(a) Elementary Education

The planning issues on School Education are concerned with enlarged access, comprehensive enrolment, full retention, zero dropouts and also to address on facilitation of quality of education besides addressing inclusive issue by gender, social groups and regional locations. Another important area is to work on medium term monitorable targets in terms of average years of schooling and for providing quality elementary education up to Class VIII to all children in the age group of 6-14 years as per RTE Act mandate. The planning for effective delivery mechanism for implementation of various schemes/programmes is another big issue. Further, another important issue is to work on convergence with other schemes in place for progressively universalizing Early Childhood Care and Education (ECCE) for all children in the age group of 4-6 years with high priority to disadvantaged regions. Additionally, it has to address RTE harmonized Sarva Shiksha Abhiyan, MDMS and various Literacy Programmes for achieving the Millennium Development Goals (MDGs) and improvements/restructuring of literacy programmes and increasing transparency and accountability.

(b) Literacy and Adult Education

The Census figures give the latest update of the literacy scenario of the State and also its gender-wise position across the districts. It also gives the literacy status of SC, ST and OBCs. Based on literacy deficit, the State has to plan for a sustainable threshold level of literacy. The planning issues cover measures for faster reduction in illiteracy in the State with emphasis on gender, regional and social dimensions (including alarming deficit of literacy for women belonging to ST and OBCs of different descriptions) and also incentivizing the districts to achieve 100 per cent literacy during the Twelfth Plan period.

(c) Secondary Education

The planning issues for secondary education are to make good quality education available, accessible and affordable to all young persons in the age group of 14-18 years. Accordingly, it has to be addressed for universal access to secondary education with a GER of 100 per cent, enhancing retention of children in secondary classes and achieving the target of 75 per cent GER in Higher Secondary Classes by 2017. For that the GER targets of 100 per cent in secondary education (grades IX-X) and 75 per cent in higher secondary education (grades XI-XII) are set to be achieved by the end of the Twelfth Plan period and the required average increase in the size of the GER per annum would have to be calculated both at the secondary and higher secondary levels.

(d) Higher Education

The planning issues for Higher Education cover expansion of the higher education sector in all its modes of delivery to increase the Gross Enrolment Ratio (GER) in higher education to 21 per cent by Twelfth Plan and 30 per cent by the year 2020. Further, institutional base of higher education (including technical, professional and vocational education) by creating additional capacity in existing institutions, establishing new institutions and Non Government Organizations/civil society has to be expanded. For inclusion of women and socially deprived communities including differentially-abled persons, opportunities have to be created for higher education. Additionally, for removing higher education divide in unserved and underserved areas, access to higher education need to be provided by setting up of institutions at such areas. Additionally, improved research facilities in universities and colleges need also to be strengthened.

2. Technical Education

The Planning issues under Technical education relate to Skill development for enhancing employability of the youths. It is concerned with promotion of the quality of technical education by investing in infrastructure and faculty, promoting academic reforms, improving governance and institutional restructuring. It includes introduction of the right skills to meet the challenges of knowledge based market economy. Based on the identification of the skill gaps in different sectors, it is required to address by setting up of finishing schools, offering courses for enhancing employability and student-centric Training Support. Further, Planning issues also include Research and Innovation, Technology-enabled learning, strengthening state technical institutions and skills and employability. Additionally, creating a skilled workforce to meet the global economic needs is also a greater planning objective of this sector.

3. Sports

National Sports Policy 2001 gives an overall direction for the achievement of two main objectives, viz., broad-basing of sports and excellence in sports, as these two objectives cover the entire gamut of the promotion and development of sports in the country. For realization of these objectives, all stakeholders, viz., Central Government, State Government, sports bodies have to work in tandem.

Since 'Sports' is a State subject under entry No. 33 of List-II (State List) of the Seventh Schedule of the Constitution of India, the primary responsibility for promotion and development of sports is that of the States both for creation/development of sports infrastructure and sports facilities in the States and nurturing and training of the identified talent. Incidentally, allocation for sports sector by the States is less than 0.50 per cent of their State Plans.

The Planning issues relating to sports cover mass participation in sports including physical education, promotion of excellence in sports including coaching upgradation and infrastructure, Sports Sciences, Sports related developments on Health, Physical Fitness and Nutrition.

4. Youth Services

The planning issues for Youth Services are multi-disciplinary in character. It has to encourage young persons for their support, participation and involvement in the process of development of the State. It has to seek ways and means for the youth training for self-employment. It has to provide opportunity to the youth for economic and social development and also provide opportunity for taking part in Adventure Programme. Finally, it has to provide such other programmes for building character of the youth.

5. Art and Culture

Art and Culture is again a multi-disciplinary area of planning. Usually, a good number of departments address this area depending on its core functional areas. It may be the Information and Cultural department, Higher education department, Hill affairs department and SC/ST Welfare department of the state. It relates to setting and upgradation of Museum, Research centres, Archives, and Digitisation of reference media records. It may be for construction, renovation or setting up of folk culture centre,

Theatre/Drama/Dance Academy, Cultural Complex, Art Gallery, Heritage related initiatives, etc.

6. Medical and Public Health

The planning issues on Medical and Public Health centre around reduction in child and maternal mortality, universal access to public services for food and nutrition, sanitation and hygiene, universal access to public health care services, integrated comprehensive primary health care with emphasis on services addressing women's and children's health and universal immunization, prevention and control of communicable and non-communicable diseases, including locally endemic diseases, population stabilization, gender and demographic balance, revitalize local health traditions and mainstream AYUSH and promotion of healthy lifestyles. It is also concerned with increase in healthcare infrastructure, human resources and provision of health services, specifically to women, children and the rural population of the country. It is also to address strengthening community processes and community ownership of public health services and improved delivery of Reproductive and Child Health and Nutrition services. Improved performance of the disease control programmes and their integration with the rest of the health sector is also issue of planning.

7. Water Supply and Sanitation

The Planning issues for Water Supply relate to, among other things, ensuring provision of safe and adequate drinking water supply to all uncovered, partially covered and quality affected habitations in the rural areas of the State and also to all schools and anganwadis to have access to safe drinking water.

It also includes enabling GPs/VWSCs to plan, manage, operate and maintain local water sources and water supply under participatory integrated water resources management and keep surveillance on their drinking water sources, water supply and initiate corrective action to have contaminants free water. Further, it also has to address equity related concern to give high priority in coverage of habitations with high SCs/STs and minority population. It has also to address high cost treatment technologies for tackling arsenic and fluoride contamination to development of alternative sources in respect of arsenic and alternate sources/dilution of aquifers through rainwater harvesting for tackling fluoride contamination.

In regard to Sanitation programme, the planning priority at the State level is on rural sanitation programme because of its low coverage. For that end, the Total Sanitation Campaign (TSC) programme needs to be outreached extensively. For school sanitation and Anganwadi centres, the TSC programme has also to be used effectively. For urban sanitation, comprehensive sanitation coverage has to be made and make use of dedicated schemes under JNNURM and UIDSSMT. Finally, as per the Eleventh and the Twelfth Schedules of the Constitution, sanitation is also the constitutional responsibility of the Panchayats and also of the Municipalities. In planning sanitation under State Plan, this fact may also be taken into consideration for focusing on role of Line Department in given areas *vis-à-vis* those of the Panchayats and Municipalities.

8. Housing

The planning issue under Housing in the State plan is to increase the affordable and low-rent housing to different categories of citizens and the speeding up of slum demolition. Similarly, in rural areas, it has the objective to assist BPLs to build up their own rural homes with State assistance and to move into their permanent house. Further, police housing is also an important item to take care of rental housing needs associated with their nature of jobs and of its transferable character. Additionally, the State has also to plan for rental accommodation of its employees at different locations.

9. Urban Development

Urban planning is a highly technical and administrative subject. The planning issues vary with nature of the urban locations. It is different for Metropolitan city, other city, district town or for any satellite town. Broadly speaking, there are common issues which include Infrastructure, Land Use and Environment Development, Social and Livelihood Development, Municipal Institutional Strengthening, Livelihood and Poverty Alleviation, Local Economic Development, Healthcare Services Delivery Improvement and Primary Education Development Plan and the like.

After the 74th Amendment, depending on the nature of devolution, the role of the Municipalities has also increased considerably. All the districts do now have Urban Plans. During the course of Urban Planning at the State level it has to take into consideration inputs from those decentralized urban plans also. Further, under Article 243ZE of the Constitution of India, the Metropolitan Planning Committee has also been empowered with planning function and to prepare the draft Metropolitan development plan. Such draft Metropolitan development plan has to be appropriately taken into consideration during the process of urban planning for the State. In a way, there has to have linkages, synergies and convergence between the Urban Plan for the State Annual Plan and the decentralized urban plans. In absence of horizontal and vertical linkage and connectivity, the Urban Plan of the State would lose its wholesome character.

10. Information and Publicity

The planning issue for the Information and Publicity relates to dissemination of the plans and programmes of the State. It includes generation of awareness on socially relevant subject. The creation of information network and dedicated portal are other issues that have to be addressed.

11. Development of SCs, STs, OBCs

The planning issues on development of SCs, STs. OBCs have been extensively discussed earlier. The development deficit of SC, ST and OBCs has to be addressed under three counts: (a) by intervention of planned schemes by the nodal department of SC/ST/OBC, (b) by intervention of planned schemes of other line departments through SCSP and TSP, and (c) by other special programmes of the Central Government/ Planning Commission.

12. Labour and Employment

The overarching planning issues under Labour and Employment are labour welfare, productivity, living standards of labour force and social security. It has also to address rehabilitation of Bonded Labour and prevention of child labour. Further, skill upgradation through suitable training is also to be planned for raising the living standards of the work force and achieving higher productivity. Employment generation of both men and women workers in different productive sectors is another area of planning.

13. Social Security and Social Welfare

Social security and social welfare provide a minimal level of well-being and social support to identified socially disadvantaged section of citizens. The planning issues depend on the nature of disadvantages and the categories. It covers old age pension, family benefit programme, the special needs for the physically and mentally challenged persons including hearing handicapped (Deaf and Dumb), and visually handicapped (Blind). It needs to address disability specific vocational training, arranging institutional linkages for credit and marketing outlets, and also disability pension for old age. The planning for mentally challenged persons has also to be more elaborate requiring special medical and personal care associated with it at every stage of their living.

14(i). Empowerment of Women

The gender related planning issues have been discussed earlier. It centres around creating an environment through positive economic and social platform for full development of women to enable them to realize their full potential, equal access to participation and decision making of women in social, political and economic life of the nation, equal access to women to health care, quality education at all levels, career and vocational guidance, employment, equal remuneration, occupational health and safety, social security and public office, etc., mainstreaming a gender perspective in the development process and building and strengthening partnerships with civil society, particularly women's organizations.

Empowerment of Women has thus emerged as an important planning issue at all levels of planning connected as it is with inclusiveness, empowerment and the MDG.

(ii) Welfare and Development of Children

The welfare of children is the most important area for inclusive development. The central focus of planning for the children is to develop a healthy generation capable of meeting the challenges for tomorrow by way of providing uniform services of supplementary nutrition, immunization, health check-up, referral services, non-formal pre-school education, nutrition and health education. The planning issue is, therefore, to build up the foundation of nutrition, health and mental preparedness of the children to enter formal educational world of tomorrow. ICDS is now covered both in the rural and also in the urban areas and it would be imperative to plan for its six components severely and collectively to ensure that there does not exist unresolved issues for programme implementation. Further, institutional care and protection for disadvantaged children, Street children, prevention and control of juvenile social maladjustment are some other areas that need to be appropriately planned for.

15. Nutrition

Nutrition is a multidisciplinary subject; it relates to low dietary intake because of poverty and low purchasing power, high prevalence of infection because of poor access to safe drinking water, sanitation and health care; and poor utilisation because of available facilities due to low literacy and lack of awareness. The planning issues for nutrition security relate to availability of food through strengthening of PDS, improving purchasing power through food for work programme (e.g., NAREGA, etc.), food supplementation through ICDS, Midday Meal Programme. etc., and also addressing micronutrient deficiencies and adverse health consequences of undernutrition, infectious diseases and unwanted pregnancies. It also includes nutrition care for the adolescents and the aged. Further, NFHS data has to be the subjects of programme intervention and planning. The most recent figures available from NFHS-III are to be used as base-line for planning. No further figures have since been generated. The proportion of children under weight below the age of three is 40.4 per cent (NFHS III). The proportion of severely underweight is 15.8 per cent (NFHS III). 52 per cent of underweight children were among Underweight mothers (BMI<18.5). Malnutrition is highest in Madhya Pradesh, where 60 per cent of the children were underweight and 27 per cent severely underweight; followed by Bihar and Jharkhand (56%), Meghalaya (48%) and Orissa (40%). Stunting was at 44.9 per cent with severe stunting at 22 per cent. The State of Uttar Pradesh has shown the highest proportion of children stunted (56.8%), followed by Bihar (55.6%), Chhattisgarh (55.9%) and Gujarat (51.7%). The proportion of children under wasting is 22.9 per cent (NFHS III), and severe wasting is 7.9 per cent (NFHS III). Malnutrition is consistently much higher in SC and ST families. All these issues have to be addressed during nutrition planning.

(K) Planning Issues for General Services

Under General Services the most important item for planning is infrastructural development of different Jails (now called correctional homes). Usually, infrastructure development of Jails is taken care of by the central grants received from the awards of the Finance Commission. However, the State governments undertake construction of new Correctional Homes, construction of staff quarters and barracks, and introduce promotional and welfare programmes like vocational training and rehabilitation of the inmates outside the orbit of the Central grant and plan for the same. The planning issue in this context is to see the rationality and extent for inclusion of such components under State Plan for improvement of correctional homes.

Public Works relate to construction of government buildings falling under different departments including those meant for the district administration of the State. It has also to decide on expansion of infrastructural facilities for court buildings to facilitate proper justice delivery system with fund made available under the related centrally sponsored scheme. The planning issue in this connection is to assess the number of schemes that can be taken up, the status of incomplete schemes, possible completion schedule, the existence of required technical support staff, etc. It also requires ascertaining the requirement of counterpart fund for CSS programmes.

The importance of Administrative training both at induction level and also at the in-service level has gone up requiring expansion of such facilities with state of art of modern technology. Periodical upgradation and improvement, both in respect of infrastructural facilities and course content, is required to be made with resources under State Plan.

13. National Five Year Plans and Decentralised Issues

Planning is a dynamic and continuous process. The planning scenario of the country undergoes generational changes with every Five Year Plan. Accordingly, there comes with every new Five Year Plan new approaches, newer objectives and also revisit of priorities with different emphasis on sectoral provisioning. It tends to address emerging planning concerns of the time and the related realities. The approval of the new Five Year Plan by the National Development Council gives it a mandate for its implementation by the Central Government and also by all the State governments. It is also a mandate applicable to all decentralised planning bodies in the country. The State planners need to work on planning issues for the Line Departments and for the decentralised local bodies in partnership with DPCs. Planning issues relevant to the State and planning issues relevant to decentralised local bodies are required to be settled with due and close interactions based on the status of devolution obtaining in the state.

(A) Eleventh Five Year Plan

The core planning issues of the Eleventh Five Year Plan meant for the Central Government, State Government and the decentralised local bodies have been as follows:

(a) *Accelerating Growth*

- Target average growth rate of 8.5 per cent.
- Agricultural growth rate to be raised to 3.9 per cent.
- Industry Services growth rates above 9 per cent.

(b) *Inclusive Development*

- Empowerment through education.
- Comprehensive strategy for better health.
- Rural infrastructure.

(c) *Bridging Divides*

- Poverty and employment.
- Rural-urban divide.
- Balanced regional development.
- The left behind: SCs, STs, Minorities and others.
- Gender balancing.

(B) Planning Issues of the Twelfth Plan

Based on the Approach Paper of the Twelfth Five Year Plan, the core planning issues, as indicated below, need to be taken up for interactive discussions with the DPCs for shared responsibilities. For productive interactions on the matter, it would be necessary to undertake sector-wise mapping of planning issues meant for the State and those belonging to the devolved functional responsibilities of the decentralised local bodies and then decide on them.

The planning issues for the Twelfth Five Year Plan can be broadly divided under the following components:

- Enhancing the Capacity for Growth.
- Enhancing Skills and Faster Generation of Employment.

- Managing the Environment.
- Markets for Efficiency and Inclusion.
- Decentralisation, Empowerment and Information.
- Technology and Innovation.
- Securing the Energy Future for India.
- Accelerated Development of Transport Infrastructure.
- Rural Transformation and Sustained Growth of Agriculture.
- Managing Urbanization.
- Improved Access to Quality Education.
- Better Preventive and Curative Health Care.

5

Role of the State Planning Board, the Planning Department and the Finance Department

The nodal authority of State planning varies from State to State. In some States, the State Planning Board takes the lead role in preparing the State Plan while in others the Planning Department enjoys the pivotal position. In some States, the Finance Department of the State also acts as the Planning Department as plan finance is closely linked with State planning. Despite regional diversity, any of these three government units perform almost similar functional role in respect of State planning. The role clarification of such units is very important as it has significant bearing on the process of planning.

Unlike District Planning Committee, the State Planning Board is neither a constitutional body nor a statutory authority. It usually comes into existence under a notification issued by the Planning Department of the State. The ostensible purpose of creating the State Planning Board is to obtain quality advice on areas of planning from subject matter specialists appointed as Members and also from the Deputy Chairman/Chairman of the State Planning Board. Normally, the government notification spells out the functional role and areas of operations of the State Planning Board and in most cases also the terms of the Members and the allocated areas of subject to them. The usual *modus operandi* of intervention by the SPB is through dialogue, interactions, reviews, workshops and the like with the appropriate level of functionaries in the concerned department of the government. The role of the SPB is always advisory in nature. It is the Minister of the Line Department who takes the final decision on matters connected with planning on the related subject area. Incidentally, this is an area where there does not exist clear understanding in role relationship between the SPB and the Ministers of the Line Departments. The powers and authority of the Minister of a Department follow from the Rules of business published under Article 166(3) of the Constitution of India. Accordingly, as per the said Rules of Business, the concerned Ministers are empowered to perform both the planning and implementation responsibilities of the related areas of the Ministry along with all incidental issues connected therewith. As the Department of Planning is also invested with principal planning functions of the State, the usual norm is to address and settle finally the whole issue of State Planning in the forum of a Cabinet meeting. It is for the simple reason that no statutory role is envisaged for the SPB.

Based on this framework, it would be relevant now to focus on the business of planning and role of the above units:

(a) Role of the State Planning Board

The SPB is the apex planning body in the State represented by experts in the related discipline. The high knowledge profile of Members of SPB is the gravitating point to secure command and respect on all issues connected with planning in the relevant discipline. The role of SPB may be divided under the following broad heads:

On Approach: The Approach of the Five Year Plan of the country is designed at the national level by the Planning Commission, while the Approach of the Five Year Plan of the State is worked out, in conformity with the national approach, by the State Planning Board. Based on overarching national priorities as reflected in the national plan, the State Planning Board finds out emerging priorities in the State that needed to be addressed in course of the next Five Year Plan in tandem with national priorities. These relate to growth specific State target, on areas of development deficit, on reprioritisation of social sector intervention or on upgrading the infrastructural support base. It includes all issues with inclusiveness like rural-urban divide, pockets of backwardness, securing access on dedicated programmes for ST/SC and other backwards, women, children and the like. It may reset all the human development related initiatives based on current level of human development indicators. The disaggregation of State level monitorable targets for the decentralised planning bodies could be other areas for intervention of the State Planning Board.

On State Planning: The Approach to the Five Year Plan is needed to be adequately reflected in projection of outlay in the Five Year Plan document and also on Annual Plan of the State. The SPB while working on the State Five Year Plan usually organises Working Groups on several sectors with specialists in the related area for taking an objective and professional view in the context of the given field scenario and the State vision. Such Draft Reports are taken up for further interactions with related Line Departments and other stakeholders, including the Finance Department for appropriate comments and views. After due accommodation of views and responses, the draft of the Five Year Plan is then placed for further comments, if any, to the concerned Members of the SPB. The Final draft is thereafter placed at the full meeting of the SPB for decision.

From the very initial stage of planning exercise on the Annual Plan, the Line Departments need faithfully to follow the planning vision and priorities as embodied in the said Approach of the Five Year Plan, its further elaboration through a slew of programmes and schemes on the document of the Five Year Plan and adopt the same as guidance while formulating the Annual Plan of the Department. The routine guidelines issued by the Planning Commission on the eve of each of the Annual Plans have also to be given appropriate consideration. Settling priorities of the Annual Plan on emerging realities and earmarking required resources for its implementation is an important work area for the State Planning Board. The SPB is also required to see that unmet gaps in programme coverage are duly addressed and that inclusive growth is manifestly visible in its coverage. The adequate provisioning on schemes meant for SCSP, TSP, OBC and women are also to be ensured.

Some of the State governments also require that merit and proposals of big project/scheme under State Plan involving substantial plan fund, say above Rs. 20 crore, need to be professionally examined at the level of SPB and issues notification to that effect. Such schemes can only be undertaken as a scheme under State Plan after clearance of the SPB has been made available. Investment clearance thus happens to be one of the important functional responsibilities of the SPB in some State. It is for the same reason that role clarification of the SPB cannot be set in quantitative terms. Based on diversity and planning culture obtaining in the State, the functional role of the SPB evolves. It takes a State-specific character.

On Monitoring: There exists almost identical approach in respect of monitoring of plan schemes by the concerned SPB. The commonality in monitoring functions of all the State Planning Boards centres on the process of programme implementation and its periodical update.

Accordingly, all the SPBs undertake periodical reviews on programme performances of Line Departments and suggest on-line corrections. The monitoring inputs of a particular quarter happen to be reference benchmark for subsequent review and all such inputs are also used at the time of interactions of the Annual Plan exercises with the Line Departments.

On Decentralisation: It is a fact that the District Planning Committee is a constitutional body while the State Planning Board is neither a constitutional nor a statutory body. However, the State Planning Board being the apex planning body in the State enjoys superior hierarchical position above the District Planning Committee which is also linked in some manner with State planning. The SPB is the advisory body of the State in all areas of planning including district planning. By virtue of positioning such pivotal role, the State Planning Board enjoys natural advisory authority on plan related matters over the District Planning Committee and to all rural and urban local bodies. Such advisory role is, however, limited to the extent of interacting on State vision, State priorities and the need for inclusive growth approach at the decentralised levels. It does not have any role to interfere with local level planning. As per the constitutional mandate, the planning at the local government level is the responsibility of the concerned Panchayat and the Municipality while the District Planning Committee consolidates the plans prepared by the Panchayats and Municipalities into draft development plan. Unlike the State Plan, the Constitution of India has not mentioned of any authority requiring approving the District Plan nor has it mentioned the process how the Draft District Plan would be transformed into the District Plan. In some States, for example, in West Bengal, the Draft District Plans are required to be submitted to the Planning Department who is required in turn to obtain the views of the State Planning Board before returning the same to the District Planning Committee with its views.

On National Development Council: The SPB is the automatic nodal point for firming up State government's views on issues/agenda to be discussed at the NDC. The considered opinion of the SPB needs to be placed before the Chief Minister for its appropriate use.

(b) The Role of the Planning Department

The Planning Department in the State is the nodal department for planning under the Rules of Business in the State. It interacts with the Planning Commission, the State Planning Board, with the plan implementing departments in the State and also with all the district planning committees of the State and others. Important letters and circulars of the Planning Commission, Ministries of the Central Government and Departments of the State Government and others like the UN, World Bank, DFIED, etc., on plan related issues are acted upon by this department and shared with others. As a nodal department on State Plan, it organises periodical meeting on formulation of State plan with Line Departments, prepares Draft State Plan in consultation with the State Planning Board, presents the State's Annual Plan in the Planning Commission, firms up State representatives in the Working Groups' meeting in the Planning Commission, undertakes periodical performance appraisal of the Annual Plan, etc. The department is also responsible for interacting with the Planning Commission on fixation of firm date for finalisation of the agreed outlay of the Annual Plan in between the Deputy Chairman of the Planning Commission and the Chief Minister of the State. After the agreed outlay for the Annual Plan has been so made available, it is also required to communicate department-wise final Plan outlay for the purpose of annual budget preparation.

The Planning Department is the nodal department for matters connected with National Development Council and all follow-up issues incidental thereto. It usually prepares agenda-wise comments in consultation with the SPB and places the matter before the Chief Minister for its finalisation. Thereafter, the same is got printed by the department for its use in the NDC meeting. Any follow-up meeting at the State level or dissemination of the decisions of the NDC is also done by the Planning Department.

The Planning Department is also the nodal point for decentralisation plan of the State. Its jobs include providing planning guidance through circulars, meetings, seminars and workshops, creation of infrastructural support, releasing of incidental fund for plan formulation and the like. This department is also responsible to interact and coordinate with the Department of Panchayats and Rural Development for Panchayat Plans and with the Municipal Affairs Department for Municipal Plans. It also receives Draft District Plans, organises comments from the SPB and sends back the Draft District Plans with comments of the State Government.

The Planning Department is also required to interact closely with the Finance Department on plan finance related issues connected with the Annual Plan, Plan budget issues, periodical release of Plan fund, booking of Plan expenditure on quarterly basis and Accountant General's verified Annual Plan expenditure and so on. Together with the Finance Department, it is also required to attend plan finance meeting connected with Annual Plan taken by the Member-Secretary of the Planning Commission. The Finance Department is required to act upon Annual Plan outlay communicated to the Line Departments by the Planning Department.

(c) Role of the Finance Department

The Finance Department of the State is the most important partner department for State planning. The resources meant for State planning is dealt and controlled by the Finance Department of the State. Because of confidential nature of State finances as its subject, the Finance Department deals it directly with the Planning Commission and the Department of Expenditure, Government of India. This department of the State is required to submit those in five Formats and in four Statements in which estimates of financial resources of the State for the current Annual Plan are to be explained for facilitating interactions on plan finance for the next Annual Plan. A number of meetings takes place with them to firm up projected fund availability including External Aided Projects (EAP) for the Annual Plan. As a matter of fact no productive discussion on possible size of the proposed Annual Plan can be taken up at the State level unless an indication on plan resources is made available to the Planning Department by the Finance Department. The Planning Commission is aware of this fact and also of the time lag usually taken to firm up plan finance and making it available to the Planning Department. Least the State annual planning process does suffer on this count, the Planning Commission mentions in its Annual Plan related guidelines that the level of the Centre's Gross Budgetary Support for the Annual Plan would be settled at a later date. However, the State *may* go ahead with the preparation of the Draft Annual Plan on the basis of 10 per cent enhancement over the Central Support given to the State during the current Annual Plan and availability of resources may be calculated accordingly at the drafting stage. Be that as it may, inputs about possible resources on plan finance is crucial for tentative interdepartmental allocation having linkage with intersectoral outlay and the role of Finance Department of the State is very important in this regard. As a matter of fact the Finance Department is repository of all issues connected with plan finance and no discussion either with the Planning Commission or with the plan implementing departments in the State is possible without the active participation of the Finance Department at every stage. The plan outlay for the Annual Plan of the State is settled based on the lead role played by the Finance Department in the consultative process with the Member-Secretary of the Planning Commission and later during the Deputy Chairman and Chief Minister level of interaction.

For filling up the Annexure of the Draft State Plan document, it has to indicate actual expenditure against plan schemes taken up in earlier years. The relevant data can be accessed from the audited books of the Accountant General of the State. Since such audited figures are usually available with the Finance Department of the State, the plan implementing departments very often collect the same from the Finance Department of the State.

The agreed outlay for the Annual Plan, as arrived at in the meeting between the Deputy Chairman of the Planning Commission and the Chief Minister of the State requires to be budgeted before the onset of the next financial year. The plan implementing departments of the State submits their plan proposals, as earlier communicated by the Planning Department, to the Finance Department in a different format with accounts code as approved by the Accountant General of the State. The scheme specific financial outlay, when budgeted by the Finance Department, becomes operationally meaningful for its release.

The financial health of many of the State governments is not uniformly very sound. In situation of unsteady financial health, the release of plan finance becomes very critical. At that stage, the release of plan fund is also controlled by the Finance Department of the state based on priorities as worked out in the government. Additionally, the Finance Department also enjoins the right to oversee the spending of plan fund with prudence and in time. Accordingly, it also undertakes monitoring of plan expenditure independently at its level.

6

Planning Role of the Line Departments of the State

The State Plan is an aggregation of plans prepared by the Line Departments entrusted with planning function. At the State level, there is normally one to one correspondence between the number of departments in the State Government and the number of plan implementing departments. However, in some cases where the nature of functions of such department is purely regulatory, the department may have only Non-Plan component. The areas of planning of Line Departments are, however, determined in respect of items covered for them in the State List and Concurrent List (Seventh Schedule of the Constitution-State List and Concurrent List) and the Rules of Business published by the State Government under Article 166(3) of the Constitution. The Rules of Business enumerates in detail the functioning areas of the Line Departments and also the empowered area of planning. The enumeration of detailed functions precludes the possibility of encroachment and confusion in respect of planning and implementation.

The clear delineation of functions is also very important for deciding which department is to function as the nodal department in the State. Once a department becomes the nodal department on the given subject, it automatically becomes also the focal point for interactions with the Central Ministries or the Planning Commission on the related subject. An illustration might be relevant in this area. In some States, irrigation issues are administered by two departments: major irrigation by the Irrigation and Waterways Department and minor irrigation by the Minor Irrigation Department. Similarly, Nutrition is administered by three departments: Social Welfare Department (ICDS), Health Family Welfare

Department (nutrition related care) and School Education Department (Mid-Day Meal). The nodal focal point for representing the State on Water related issues or on Nutrition with the concerned Central Ministry is an area that requires resolution at the State level. Further, based on delineation of functions, the concerned department also becomes automatic choice for administering Centrally Sponsored Scheme or Central Sector Schemes, when implemented by the State Government.

The State Plan is an aggregation of plans prepared by plan implementing departments. The quality of the State Plan depends on the quality of such Plans of individual departments. The national priorities, State priorities, human deficit areas, development deficit in the region, inclusive growth, etc., are all to be addressed by such departments. Such departments are required to prepare departmental Annual Plan in two modes: (i) in terms of format of planning functions for the Annual Plan proposals to the Planning Commission; and (ii) in terms of accounting code for budget after the plan proposals have been approved by the Planning Commission.

The planning functions have been designed by the Planning Commission of India under eleven sectors which are further divided and sub-divided under major heads and minor heads. The minor heads of development in the ultimate analysis represent the character of development function. The plan implementing departments have to focus on such developmental function both at the time of its planning and also at the stage of implementation. It is always possible that two or more departments may address a common development function or a particular department may address more than one development functional area. There is, however, no scope of conflict of interest as the developmental function accommodates enough space for all programme partners. Further, the Rules of business ensure that there would not take place any collusion of programme implementation as the boundary of functional jurisdiction of each department is well defined. However, there is scope and need for co-ordination and convergence among the programme partners within a developmental functional area.

Another very important point worth remembering in this connection is that in case of having more than one department for a development functional area, plan proposals of a department presented under that developmental function area are added with plan proposals from other Line Departments on such developmental function area. The aggregated outlay represents the total of proposed outlay on that developmental function area for the State Plan and accordingly posted in the statistical statement of Annexure. In such scenario it does not reflect proposed outlay for any particular department. Needless to mention, the name of the scheme/(s) cannot be discerned from that aggregated picture of development function.

The Planning Commission stipulates that Annual Plan of the State need to have adequate provision for Tribal Sub-Plan (TSP) and Scheduled Caste Sub-Plan (SCSP) having regard to the size of ST/SC population in the State. The Plan implementing departments need to earmark required outlay to address to the special needs of the ST/SC under TSP/SCSP to meet the development deficit in this area. Additionally, though there is no Sub-Plan for women, all schemes intending to address women issues and women development need to be covered adequately to improve gender dimension of the Annual Plan.

Now, as soon as the plan proposals are approved by the Planning Commission, those are required to be budgeted for the next financial year. The plan implementing departments are required to know at this stage the extent of approved outlay for the proposed scheme/(s) from the Planning Department of the State and propose for its budget approval. The plan scheme proposals of the Line Department under the heads of development, as approved by the Planning Commission, are then repackaged under heads of accounts and submitted to the Finance Department of the State for adoption under Budget. The plan proposals become meaningful only when its budget proposal secures approval of the State Legislative Assembly. The budgeted Estimate for the scheme in question is the starting point to release fund for implementation of plan scheme.

The Plan implementing departments are required to ensure proper execution of schemes with prudence and in time having regard to the intended outreach in a transparent manner. The human development related requirements of enlarging access, widening choice, enhancing capability and improving participation, as relevant under the schemes, have to be put in place. The broader issue of inclusiveness has to be addressed during implementation also. Further, while filling in Annexure 2, the plan implementing departments have to mention physical targets in quantifiable terms. At the stage of implementation, it has to be seen that not only the physical outputs are achieved but also ensure that it transcends in the generation of outcome. The outcome is the last mile destination for the essence of any quality plan scheme. In ensuring such outcome, the departments are required to monitor closely and put in place concurrent evaluation, wherever required. The department also needs to capture them under Annual Report for record keeping and also for dissemination.

Another area that deserves attention is to ensure that planning is not reduced as a seasonal affair. All plan related schemes have local specific dimension, it may as well have national and international ramifications. Some of such schemes are counterpart schemes of the global agenda or of the national agenda. The theoretical understanding of the premises and its periodical updating is very important and that high valued spirit needs to be the driving focus during implementation.

Finally, in matters relating to district plans, the plan implementing departments have other decisive roles. In States where devolution of functions has taken place under Article 243G for the level of Panchayats and for the Municipalities under Article 243W in a very clear format, the functional role of Line Departments under the district plan is rather limited. In that situation it has virtually no role except to honour the sanctity of devolved responsibility of such local bodies and share the district component of its own departmental plan schemes with the DPC for information and reference. Additionally, the department has to see if there is scope for convergence of the departmental district sector schemes with the schemes of the local bodies and to way forward convergence when there is such a possibility. Further, in case some of the line departments have assigned particular plan scheme to a particular tier of Panchayats or the Municipalities it is incumbent for them to inform the size of fund availability at the time of plan exercises for the related local bodies. In most of the States in the country, however, devolution has not taken place in the manner enshrined under Article 243G or 243W and the role of the local bodies that emerged is completely different—and the resultant roles of the DPC are also completely different. In such situations the levels of Panchayats and the Municipalities perform the role of agency functions of the departments but usually pass it for devolution. Such local bodies formulate Annual Plan with the schemes of the departments and include them as their own in their Annual Plan. This practice in many parts of the countries has been corrupting the constitutional provision of devolution and standing as roadblock to the growth of local bodies to discharge the intended devolved responsibilities.

Planning Commission has been emphasizing the importance of preparation of District Plans and their incorporation into State's Annual Plan and Five Year Plans. As a matter of fact, Planning Commission has also issued Guidelines for the preparation of District Plans and suggested incorporation of District Plans in the State Annual Plan. It is in this very context necessary to examine the nexus between the State Plan and the District Plans, and also the role of Line Departments under the scheme of Seventy Third and Seventy Fourth Amendments of the Constitution.

(i) The Planning Role of Line Departments in the District

There exists understanding variations on the role of the Line Departments of the Government working in the District and their relation in the District Plan. The District Plan, under Article 243ZD, is a consolidation outcome of plans prepared by the Panchayats and the Municipalities. Legally speaking, there is no scope for the plans of the Line Departments of the State Government to be part of such District Plan. On the basis of devolved functional items out of the Eleventh Schedule under Article 243G or out of the Twelfth Schedule under Article 243W, the Panchayats and the Municipalities are to plan on them and then submit it to the DPC. Similarly, as per Rules of Business, under Article 166(3) of the Constitution of India, the Line Departments of the Government are also to plan and implement schemes as are covered under List-II and List-III of the Seventh Schedule and submit to the Planning Department of the State for following it up with the Planning Commission. There is no constitutional provision for the Panchayats or the Municipalities to plan for items of the line departments covered under List-II and List-III of the Seventh Schedule. Thus, there exist parallel planning authorities in any district for performing two distinct types of planning functions. However, the items planned under List-II and List-III of the Seventh Schedule by the Line Departments are outside the consolidation function of the DPC and hence are not part of the District Plan. The exclusion of planning efforts of the Line Departments in the district from the purview of the constitutionally mandated District Planning Committee make the entire District Planning exercise less wholesome. From planning angle, those planning efforts are needed to be captured and made part of the District Plan. This is a critical area of reforms under District Plan and needs to be addressed early.

Be that as it may, the Line Departments of the district are to perform its constitutional obligation to plan for areas of the districts for items as are covered under List-II and List-III of the Seventh Schedule and empowered to them under Article 166(3) of the Constitution. This duality of planning has to exist for some more time till clarity on these areas take place and also till well defined functional devolutions are put in place for the tiers of the Panchayats and the Municipalities.

(ii) The Relationship between the District Plans and the State Plan

There is also variation of understanding on the relation between the District Plans and the State Plan. The popular perception is that the State Plan is the summation of district plans. This symbiotic relationship between the State plan and the District plans is based on an ideal premise where the State Government disaggregates the total plan outlay among its districts on some defined norms and asks the concerned District Planning authority to plan for them. The District Plans, thus emerged, would add up to the State Plan. This ideal premise is hardly available or practicable in real-life situation. As a matter of fact, it is just not possible to have any separate Planning authority at the district level to plan for subjects meant for State Government departments nor it is permissible for any district planning authority to plan for State level projects spanning over a number of districts. Another way of looking at the issue is that at the end of the day, irrespective of the authority of plan formulations, all plans meant for the districts have necessarily to add up to the total of the State Plan outlay. This is a truism and a very simplistic way of looking on the subject. Besides, it does not factor in planning functions as a premise for arriving at such views. The basic point that remains to be resolved is whether all draft plans prepared at the level of the Constitution mandated District Planning Committees would have any linkage with the State Plan. The answer is linked with the niceties of planning and the State Government's constitutional responsibility on State Plan and its budgeting.

The State Plan embodies in general the planning efforts on items included in State List and Concurrent List under the Seventh Schedule of the Constitution. More specifically, it covers items of the Line Departments in the State Plan as per notification issued under the Rules of Business of Article 166(3) of the Constitution of India. The District Plan, on the other hand, reflects a consolidated picture of plans prepared by the Panchayats and the Municipalities for devolved items under the Eleventh and the Twelfth Schedule of the Constitution respectively. In other words, the planning responsibilities of the departments of a State Government are different from the planning responsibilities of the tiers of the Panchayat and the Municipalities. Thus, jurisdiction over functional items is important and it finally determines the areas on planning. Incidentally, empowerment on defined subjects on areas of planning has led to the emergence of planning rights over them in favour of Line Departments of the State Government, on three tiers of the Panchayats in the rural areas or to any municipality in the urban areas. Such planning rights cannot be delegated or usurped by any other planning authority. It is for the same reason that the DPC cannot arrogate to itself the planning rights either of the Panchayats or the Municipalities nor can it subsume the planning rights of the State Planning departments.

Now the jurisdiction of the planning rights of the Panchayats and the Municipalities is limited to devolved items only. It does have neither the mandate nor the competency to plan for items included under State List or Concurrent List. It is for the same reason that plans of such rural and urban local bodies, as consolidated into the District Plan, need not be looked upon as sub-sets of the State Plan. The planning areas are distinct and different for the State and for each of the tiers of the Panchayats or for the Municipalities.

There is, however, inherent linkage between schemes of the State plan with schemes of the decentralised plans on development functional area. Productive interactions in between such schemes in defined development area in a time format broaden planning vision and shared perception are instrumental in reordering planning priorities and revisiting its sectoral allocation. Such planning connectivity enriches sectoral planning and activates programme convergence to achieve desired outcome. The nature, scope and character of State Plan and District Plans are, however, different as per constitutional provision.

As mentioned earlier, the State Plan, in ideal setting, could have been an amalgamation of all items included in the District Plans and also those included in the Plans of the Line Departments of the State Government. However, this ideal setting of amalgamation is not possible for other valid reasons also. Unlike resources meant for the State Plan, the District Plans, in most cases, are not prepared on the basis of firm resources. Further, own resources of the Panchayats and the Municipalities, however big or small as it may be, happen to be very significant components of resources for local level planning. Such resources are not usually taken into consideration for computing resources meant for the State Plan. Additionally, in absence of real devolution in most States, the items in the District Plans also include projected fund for assigned schemes in favour of the Panchayats or the Municipalities, which incidentally have already been booked by the concerned plan implementing departments in their departmental State Annual Plan. There is real danger of double counting on this crucial area. On top of it all, there is no provision in the Constitution of India requiring the Planning Commission either to approve or to disapprove of District Plans and, therefore, incorporation of such District Plans within State Plan would amount to seeking Planning Commission's approval in a round about way which is not permissible under the constitutional mandate. The State Plan, in real terms, is the aggregation of the plans of the Line Departments only. The Planning Commission approves this aggregated State Plan Outlay of Line Departments, presented under Major or Minor heads of development, after due process of assessment of State resources, Working Group discussions in the Planning Commission with the Secretaries of the Line Departments only and finally after Deputy Chairman and Chief Minister level of interactions. The State Plan, as approved by the Planning Commission, is also required to be approved by the State Cabinet before taking it up for budgeting by the State. The State Plan becomes functional from the next financial year after it is so budgeted.

The District Plans in the Constitutional scheme of things on the other hand are, required to be sent to the State Government as per Article 243ZD (4) *ibid.* Such District Plan comes back to the concerned District Planning Committee with State Government's comments, if any. There is no scope to accord Cabinet approval or approval by any department of State government on such District Plans. There is also no scope to follow up the budgeting exercise either by the State Government or by the DPC. The responsibility of budgeting its Annual Plan lies with the related unit of the tier of Panchayats as provided under the State Panchayat Act or with the Municipalities under the State Municipal Act. The District Planning Committee is required only to send back the State Government's observations, if any, on the Draft Annual Plan to all units of Panchayats and Municipalities for appropriate action. The respective local bodies, after due consideration of such observations, then approve its plan and take measures to budget for them. The procedural format for plan approval and its budgeting is also different for each tier of the Panchayat or the Municipalities. It is an independent function not connected in any way with the budgeting of the State Plan. In the circumstances, it would not be fair to hold that State Plan is an aggregated version of District Plans of any State. The District Plans are in fact by its own nature functionally different and in no way qualify to be sub-sets of the State Plan.

7

Sectoral Planning and the Partnership Role of concerned Line Departments

The Planning Commission has a dedicated format for presentation of the State Plan. Such presentation has to be in eleven sectors. Sectors represent defined development functions. Under each sector there exists layer of major and minor heads of development indicating respectively development functions at that heads of development. The genesis of this heads of development is that schemes *per se* are definitely important; but from planning angle the most important consideration is the development function and the inherent merit for taking up such schemes to address that development function and its identified development deficit. The schemes are designed to contribute meaningfully for generation of output for that defined development functional area. In other words, planning efforts boil down to improve the current status of any development functional area represented by related sector, major head and minor head of development through selection of schemes. This is the overarching consideration for sector-wise planning under State Plan.

Further, the format of presentation in terms of heads of development gives an aggregated picture of development functions in the State Plan. It does not reveal individual planning efforts of Line Departments unless it is specifically so structured. In case, however, there exists a single department for any development functional area, the proposed schemes and the accompanying outlay reflect the planning efforts of the individual department on the said development functional area as well. It would be relevant to mention that the existence of multiple departments in a sectoral area in the Annual Plan document and the need to refer sometimes department-wise planning efforts by the State representatives at the

Working Group discussions is one of the reasons why this format of plan presentation is not very popular among government functionaries. Department-wise outlay may, however, be easily worked out by interacting with the Planning Department of the State Government before the Working Group discussions. Be that as it may, the format of the State Plan reflects aggregated picture of development functions—not department-wise outlay. From planning point of view, such presentation is in tune with the basic principle of planning.

Generally speaking, the spirit of sectoral planning is seldom adequately discussed in the forum of the State Planning Board or seriously practised in the government departments in the State. While it is true that the individual plan implementing departments are accountable in respect of plans so designed by them, such plan by itself is bound to be qualitatively more focused and productive when it is validated with the sectoral vision of the related heads of development. There is, however, no quick-fix method how to go about it. It would be useful to have clear idea about the fellow Line Departments, working in the same development area, nature of their programme intervention, its geographical location and the scope and extent of possible convergence among the schemes with such partner departments. The lead role for a sector level interactive session may be taken by the head of the major partner or could be anchored by the head of the Planning Department as well. Programme partner departments need to have shared sectoral vision, its programme coverage, its programme linkage and the strength and weakness in the working area and focused area of mutual support. The crucial area of co-ordination is another area that is also very relevant. The *modus operandi* would have to be in terms of dialogue, interactions and exchange of notes. An illustration might be given in this regard. The warehousing network could be meaningful when it is so planned with regard to prospects of the crop husbandry programme. Similarly, agricultural marketing programme intervention has one to one correspondence with the present and future prospects of crop husbandry programme and horticulture programme. Apart from sectoral partners, cross sectoral partners also matter in the formulation of quality planning and its outcome. An illustration may be given. Planning for agriculture under minor head Crop Husbandry depends on cross sectoral support from the Irrigation and Flood Control sector and also Energy sector. Unless the irrigation planning efforts are linked with agricultural schemes on spatial consideration, the very essence of planning would lose its relevance. Similarly, drawing of power connectivity lines is linked with energization of pump sets for irrigation for agriculture.

The big area of dialogue and interaction among sectoral partners lie in the Social Services sector. It is primarily a sector that shapes inclusive growth and human development. This sector also addresses unmet development needs for Scheduled Castes and Scheduled Tribes. Human development deficit in general and marginalised section in particular are areas of planning and programme intervention in this sector. The Tribal Sub-Plan and the Scheduled Caste Sub-Plan are also very important planning functions of this sector. Additionally, apart from owning localised sectoral vision, the national goal of the sector, the national and State level targets on Five Year Plan are other considerations that require interactive dialogue for sectoral planning for ensuring shared responsibility.

I. Sectoral Planning for Agriculture and Allied Activities

The Agriculture and Allied sector is to plan for food and nutrition support of the State. In planning for the sector it needs to work on Crop Husbandry, Horticulture, Soil and Water Conservation, Animal Husbandry, Dairy Development, Fisheries, Plantations, Food, Storage and Warehousing, Agricultural Research and Education, Agricultural Financial Institutions, Cooperation and Agricultural Marketing. The size of the population of the State, percapita foodgrains requirement, net agriculture land, irrigation potential availability, cropping intensity, current production, productivity and its incremental potentialities, etc., would all have to be factored in sectoral planning. There exist a large number of schemes through which programme support could be extended. For effective good planning, it would be useful to map all available programmes, schemes and resources—State schemes, Centrally sponsored programme (including all mission mode programmes), Central sector programmes (including BRGF, RKVY, etc.) and then find out how the related tied fund and schemes would have to be made use at different locations. In so doing, several aspects like agro zone, agro-climatic factors, soil map, soil fertility, district scenario, etc., have to be taken into account. Similarly, intra-sectoral connectivity, wherever needed, have to be addressed. The minor heads of development would then have to be addressed with schemes and proposed outlay.

In designing the sectoral planning for the Agriculture and Allied activities apart from the centrally sponsored schemes and the Central sector schemes (including Mission mode programmes), institutional schemes for funding agriculture related programme (such as those under

NABARD, Cooperatives, etc.) and State schemes etc. have also to be mapped, assess the current status of implementation, projected requirement of fund and its utilising potentialities and then settle the details of the schemes (including location, etc.) *vis-à-vis* the vision of the sector with proposed outlay with consideration of convergence, wherever possible. The requirement of counterpart fund from the State Plan outlay, if required, for centrally sponsored schemes may also be worked out at this stage.

While planning for the sector, spatial considerations and convergence factors have to be given due consideration as larger number of schemes are location specific and crop specific. Incidentally, these work areas fall under district sector schemes and depending on the nature of devolution, the nodal authority may be the Line Departments of the State posted in the district or the levels of the Panchayats. In absence of devolution, the levels of Panchayats are likely to be assigned the task of implementing some programmes/schemes in those States. Depending on the nature of nodal authority, the planning responsibility would emerge. Incidentally, for planning assistance for RKVY, there has to exist State Agriculture Plan and District Agriculture Plans. Since Planning is a serious job at the State level with futuristic vision in upfront, there is no short cut method to prepare the State Agriculture Plan mechanically by editing and aggregating District Agricultural Plans (DAPs) as suggested in the guidelines of RKVY. The vision and objectives of the State Agricultural Plan are distinct and different from the district specific approach of the District Agricultural Plans. It is, however, another matter that the district plans need to accommodate the State's long term vision and priorities in the respective district plans. In any case, there is necessity to have programme linkage between the State Agriculture Plan and District Agriculture Plans and these linkages have to be institutionalised during the planning stage.

Another area that is needed adequate importance is the quantification of physical targets. Scheme specific past achievement of targets and proposed targets for the next Plan is very important. These have to be worked out with extreme care and application of mind. There has to exist prudent justification on quantum of investment and its output.

Additionally, at this stage of planning, inclusive factors have to be addressed and plugged in the proposed programmes/schemes itself. Accordingly, it has to be planned for TSP and SCSP components and required percentage of plan outlay at the State level has to be booked for them. The proposed financial outlay for each scheme along with its physical targets have to be worked out. In this matter, the nodal department on SC/ST in the State may be appropriately consulted. Further, for inclusive consideration and also on requirement of Women Component in the Agriculture and Allied activities, dedicated schemes have to be worked out. It need not be a mechanical exercise but a serious exercise on planning to ensure how the gender divide in the Agriculture and Allied activities sector can be bridged by adopting women centric schemes. Proposed Financial Outlays along with target of its physical output has also to be settled. These have to be presented then in the Annexure designed by the Planning Commission.

II. Sectoral Planning for Rural Development

Rural development aims at finding ways to improve the rural lives with participation of the rural people. These fundamentals have to be kept in the upfront while planning for rural development. Here economic activities revolve around the primary sector and community development centred actions and initiatives are needed to improve the standard of living in the rural areas. While planning for rural development, development deficit in the structure of the rural economy and human development deficit in the quality of rural life are to be taken into consideration. However, as per sectoral design of the State Plan, not all areas can be taken up under the Rural Development Sector. Only a set of programmes/schemes under defined heads of development can be planned to improve physical features of the rural economy and also for improving the quality of life. Incidentally, some of the programmes meet both the objectives at the same time.

Depending on physical features of the land, Drought Prone Area Programme (DPAP), Desert Development Programme (DDP) and Integrated Wasteland Programmes are to be taken up in the related area. While initiating planning for such programme, the NRDMS data are to be obtained to pinpoint location and nature of schemes. A good number of schemes of various descriptions working in the livelihood sector like National Food for Work./National Employment Guarantee Programme/ NEREGA/National Rural Livelihood Mission (NRLM), etc., also address improvement on physical features. While planning for them, spatial considerations and convergence factors have to be given due consideration. Incidentally, these work areas fall under district sector schemes and depending on the nature of devolution, the nodal authority may be the line departments of the State posted in the district or the levels of the Panchayats. In absence of devolution, the levels of Panchayats are likely to be assigned the task of implementing the programmes/schemes in those States. Depending on the nature of nodal authority, the planning responsibility would emerge.

In respect of livelihood support programmes, a large number of schemes are available for planning. These include Promotion of SHG, Rural Employment covering Swarnajayanti Gram Swarozgar Yojana (SGSY), Sampoorna Gram Rozgar Yojana (SGRY), National Food for Work/National Employment Guarantee Programme/NAREGA/National Rural Livelihood Mission (NRLM), etc. These programmes address both the wage employment and to a great extent self-employment programme including capacity building. For client-specific livelihood option, it is required to know the kind of schemes being implemented in those rural areas by the departments of SC/ST/Minorities/Others on self-employment related works and to map them up for possible back-up reference. The most important reference is, however, the BPL. For scheme-specific programme planning, the BPL has to be studied, analysed and then planned for the beneficiaries. Here again, devolution is very important and depending on the nature of devolution in the State, the nodal authority could be any tier of Panchayats or that such tier of Panchayats might be entrusted with the responsibility for implementing them.

Another aspect relating to planning in the livelihood area is adherence to human development issues. These relate to enlarging access, expanding choice, enhancing capability and widening participation. By planning on each of the segments, it would be possible to ensure inclusiveness and also the quality of human development from the premise of livelihood component.

Land Reforms related developmental programmes and programmes on Community Development and Panchayats would vary from one State to another on ground of diversity in the States of India. However, there could be common programme as well like digitisation of cadastral maps and linking it to ROR. In any case, based upon the State specific situation, the related items are to be planned and included as a part in this sectoral plan.

In designing the sectoral planning for the Rural Development, it is required to have the complete list of all centrally sponsored schemes, central sector schemes, institutional schemes of the funding institutes and all State schemes having connectivity with rural development along with current location and outlay. Further, current status of implementation of the departmental State schemes, projected requirement of fund and its utilising potentialities, etc., are needed to plan for details of the schemes (including location, etc.) *vis-à-vis* the larger vision of the sector for settling scheme-specific proposed outlay with due consideration of convergence wherever possible. The requirement of counterpart fund from the State Plan outlay for centrally sponsored schemes may also be worked out at this stage. Another area that is not adequately given importance is the quantification of physical targets. Scheme specific past achievement of targets and proposed targets for the next plan is very important. These have to be worked out with extreme care and application of mind. There has to exist prudent justification on quantum of investment and its output.

Additionally, at this stage of planning, inclusive factors have to be addressed and plugged in the proposed programmes/schemes itself. Accordingly, it has to be planned for TSP and SCSP and required percentage of plan outlay has to be booked for them. The proposed financial outlay along with its physical targets has to be worked out for defined schemes. In this matter, the nodal department on SC/ST in the State may be appropriately consulted. Further, for inclusive consideration and also on requirement of Women Component in the Rural Development sector, dedicated schemes have to be worked out. It need not be a mechanical exercise but a serious exercise on planning to ensure how the gender divide in the Rural Development sector can be bridged by adopting women centric schemes. Proposed Financial Outlays along with target of its physical output has also to be settled. These have to be presented then in the Annexure designed by the Planning Commission.

III. Sectoral Planning for Special Area Programmes

Special Areas Programmes are taken up in the State to address pockets of backwardness and pronounced development deficit in defined locations. Under Special Area Programmes, a number of dedicated schemes are taken up to ameliorate relative backwardness of certain functional areas and lift it up at least to the level of State average. Accordingly, intensive planning efforts are to be made through designated schemes. For sectoral planning to be pragmatic and meaningful, it would be useful to ascertain the planning efforts of other agencies working in the area, nature of their programme intervention and the volume of its investments. The scheme mapping of such other initiatives would enable to assess the needs for additive nature of intervention and investment under Special Area Programme. Currently, the important national programmes that are available for such interventions under State Plan include (a) Hill Areas Development Programme, (b) Border Area Development Programme,

(c) Backward Region Grant Fund (Backward Districts/Area Fund), (d) Grants under proviso to *Article* 275(1), (e) Special Central Assistance to Tribal Sub-plan, (f) Integrated Action Plan (IAP), and (g) Others.

All the national programmes meant for special area planning are not universally applicable for the States of India. The programmes have been designed to meet special needs of defined backward regions. The States have, however, inherent right to initiate new/other programmes for State-specific backward areas and capture them under special area planning. An illustration will make it clear. Sunderban development in West Bengal happens to fall under State sponsored special area programme as it is meant to address relative development deficit there. It is needed to be captured it here, under the head of development—Others. Similar such State sponsored special area programmes of the State need to be captured, under head—Others.

In designing the focused sectoral planning and to avoid duplication of programme efforts, it is reiterated once again that complete list of all centrally sponsored schemes, Central sector schemes and State schemes having connectivity with development on those areas along with outlay are to be mapped before commencement of actual planning. Further, current status of implementation of the ongoing schemes, projected requirement of fund and its utilising potentialities, etc., are also needed to plan for details of the schemes along with its requirement of next year's outlay. At this stage, due consideration on convergence may be given wherever possible. The requirement of counterpart fund from the State Plan outlay, if required, for centrally sponsored schemes may also be worked out at this stage. Another area that is needed adequate importance is the quantification of physical targets. Scheme specific past achievement of targets and proposed targets for the next plan is very important. These have to be worked out with extreme care and application of mind. There has to exist prudent justification on quantum of investment and its output.

Additionally, at this stage of planning, inclusive factors have to be addressed and plugged in the proposed programmes/schemes itself. Accordingly, it has to be planned for TSP and SCSP components and required percentage of plan outlay has to be booked for them. The proposed financial outlay for each scheme along with its physical targets has also to be worked out. In this matter, the nodal department on SC/ST in the State may be appropriately consulted. Further, for inclusive consideration and also on requirement of Women Component in the Special Areas sector, dedicated schemes have to be worked out. It need not be a mechanical exercise but a serious exercise on planning to ensure how the gender divide in the Special Areas sector can be bridged by adopting women centric schemes. Proposed Financial Outlays along with target of its physical output has also to be settled. These have to be presented then in the Annexure designed by the Planning Commission.

IV. Sectoral Planning for Irrigation and Flood Control

Water resources planning and Irrigation planning are interconnected. Water resources planning is in fact a bigger concept encompassing balance of conservation of water resources and its uses by multiple number of clients from a dynamic and sustainable point of view. It is linked with implementation of the Water Policy of the Country/State. Irrigation planning is a sub-theme of water resources planning within the bounds of sectoral planning. Its targeted area of planning is Major and Medium Irrigation, Minor Irrigation, Command Area Development, AIBP and Flood Control (including Flood Protection work). It primarily aims at catering the needs of agricultural crops and also protecting it from flood damage.

The main purpose of Irrigation planning is to increase the irrigation potential of the State through variety of options. In earlier days, major and medium irrigation projects received priority consideration in planning because of possible larger irrigation potentials. However, time slippage, cost over-run, time schedule of land acquisition, rehabilitation and environmental cost do not permit it now as a priority option. As a matter of fact, AIBP has come into being to complete such incomplete major and medium irrigation projects in the country. The planning priority is now to be focused on completion of pending incomplete major and medium irrigation projects in the State. Incidentally, the Approach to the Twelfth Plan has mentioned about 553 spill over projects into the Eleventh Plan from previous Plan periods which have been waiting for completion. It may not be desirable at this stage to take up new major/medium irrigation schemes without completing the backlog. From cost economics angle, unit cost per unit of acreage from major/medium irrigation turns out to be higher than minor irrigation schemes and its gestation period is also longer. The priority focus needs now to shift on minor irrigation where benefits of irrigation reach out quickly. It is also inclusive friendly. Minor irrigation schemes mean those schemes whose cultural command area is 2000 hectares or less. It also includes high capacity deep tube well, medium capacity deep tube well, low capacity deep tube well, shallow tube well, river lift irrigation and open dug well. Based on the demands for agriculture and horticulture crops from defined areas and from also GIS based data on areas actually covered under irrigation, the irrigation planning needs to settle mode of extension of irrigation for the uncovered areas. The assistance of GIS is to be taken as a planning tool to ensure linkage between the cultivable areas and irrigation connectivity and also take care of underground water stress condition. Depending on the size of irrigation demand it will enable to adopt the correct choice of the mode of irrigation instruments. Apart from meeting customer centric irrigation and full use of irrigation potentialities, it will also address sustainable issue directly. Such mode of planning will also help to pinpoint areas requiring rain water harvesting structures. This will also facilitate correct location for field channel programme under Command area development programme.

Depending on flood data of previous years and flood prone sensitive areas, drainage and embankment protection are also required to be put in place for guarding against soil damage, crop loss and other areas of destruction. In view of changing nature of waterways, varying precipitation and climatic change factor, the flood scenario is now somewhat dynamic and different. The encroachment of drainage and traditional waterways also results localised flood and waterlogging which need also to be factored in for planning for flood protection.

In designing focused irrigation planning and to avoid duplication of programme efforts, it is required to have the list of all minor nature of irrigation initiatives through different centrally sponsored schemes (like NAREGA, BRGF, etc.), and State schemes (dug well schemes of agriculture department, water tank excavation/re-excavation schemes of the fisheries department and similar other schemes of the line departments) providing minor irrigation connectivity. Further, current status of implementation of the ongoing schemes, projected requirement of fund and its utilising potentialities, etc., are needed to plan for details of the schemes along with its outlay after due consideration of convergence wherever possible. The requirement of counterpart fund from the State Plan outlay, if required, for centrally sponsored schemes may also be worked out at this stage. Another area that is needed adequate importance is the quantification of physical targets. Scheme specific past achievement of targets and proposed targets for the next plan is very important. These have to be worked out with extreme care and application of mind. There has to exist prudent justification on quantum of investment and its output.

Additionally, at this stage of planning, inclusive factors have to be addressed and plugged in the proposed programmes/schemes itself.

Accordingly, it has to be planned for TSP and SCSP components and required percentage of plan outlay at the State level has to be booked for them. The proposed financial outlay for each scheme along with its physical targets have to be worked out. In this matter, the nodal department on SC/ST in the State may be appropriately consulted. Further, for inclusive consideration and also on requirement of Women Component in the Minor Irrigation sector, dedicated schemes have to be worked out. It need not be a mechanical exercise but a serious exercise on planning to ensure how the gender divide in the Minor Irrigation area can be bridged by adopting women centric schemes. Proposed Financial Outlays along with target of its physical output has also to be settled. These have to be presented then in the Annexure designed by the Planning Commission.

V. Sectoral Planning for Energy

Energy happens to be the most critical component for ensuring production and productivity in all sectors of the economy. Energy planning has two components: (i) Demand side component; and (ii) Supply side component. From its Demand side angle, the planning has to probe into the current demand, its immediate deficit and also to its emerging demand linked as it is with the behaviour of the State economy. Adequate care should be given to assess energy demand for power intensive industries in the immediate future. Prioritisation of such demands—sector-wise and planning for intervention of them is very important. Equally important is also the expanding demand assessment of the rural energy segment including critical input for energisation of agriculture pump-sets.

The supply side of the power planning hinges on expansion of capacity utilisation by way of timely completion of the ongoing projects. All resource supports have to be ensured at this stage. It needs also to address planning for expansion by way of creation of new facilities and also by improving energy efficiency of the system. In deciding on new facilities, the natural advantages of the State on ground of its geographical location and natural resources have to be given adequate considerations. In the event the State decides to augment its supply through thermal power utility, the State needs to address inputs related all issues including the tied-up coal block, water availability and environmental clearance. Further, the State needs to examine the potentialities of all options—nuclear, hydel, solar, wind, etc., to arrive at a balanced and optimal decision to increase its supply position. In the context of climatic change scenario, the need for adequate consideration for non-conventional sources of energy has tremendously increased. The National Solar Mission has come into being to enable the States to take advantage in this area.

Another critical area for sectoral Planning in Energy is in the area of transmission and distribution loss. Massive Aggregate Transmission and Commercial (AT&C) losses have crippled the financial viability of State Distribution Companies (SDCs). It would be useful to address this issue and take advantage of the Restructured APDRP (R-APDRP) where fund availability is contingent upon actual, demonstrable performance in terms of sustained reduction of AT&C losses. R-APDRP seeks to tackle the problem of unmetered supply and lack of proper data acquisition systems followed by system upgradation and modernisation of equipment.

Rural Electricity is an important segment under Energy Planning connected as it is with irrigation network for agricultural production. Additionally, the access to power is a big agenda for inclusive development and equity considerations demand spread and outreach of this facility to all villages as well. The RGGVY has been designed for electrification of over one lakh unelectrified villages and providing electricity connections to 2.34 crore rural households including free connections to BPL families. It should get appropriate reflection under Energy Plan.

While designing the sectoral planning for the Energy sector, it is needed that adequate importance is given for the quantification of physical targets. Scheme specific past achievement of targets and proposed targets for the next plan is very important. These have to be worked out with extreme care and application of mind. There has to exist prudent justification on quantum of investment and its output.

Additionally, at this stage of planning inclusive factors have to be addressed and plugged in the proposed programmes/schemes as far as practicable. Accordingly, it has to be accommodated TSP and SCSP components. Proposed Financial Outlays along with target of its physical output has also to be settled. These have to be presented then in the Annexure designed by the Planning Commission.

VI. Sectoral Planning for Industry and Minerals

The sectoral planning on Industry is connected with the functional role of the government in this area. The setting up of big industries by itself does not feature as planning responsibility of the State government. The role of the State government is to create investment-friendly environment in the form of infrastructural support and speedier clearance of all regulatory norms. The required infrastructural support includes facilitation of improved road network and transportation services, other communication services, housing, health and education facilities, easy availability of power, pool of skilled labour, etc. Creation of infrastructural facilities is a responsibility of the government through combined efforts of all related sectors and not solely the planning responsibility of this Industry and minerals sector. The State Government has promotional role in ensuring investment on various types of industries through the enterprising efforts of private sector by way of required tied-up infrastructural support. Such items of private initiatives, however, do not feature as items of work under the State Plan.

The planning for this sector is concerned with the micro, small and medium enterprises as defined under The Micro, Small and Medium Enterprises Development Act 2006 which has brought about complete change in the environment for village and small enterprises. As per the new Act, all units in the manufacturing sector with investment in plant and machineries above Rs. 25 lakh and machineries up to Rs. 500 lakh belong to the small-scale industries category. Those units with investment in plant and machineries below Rs. 25 lakh belong to the small-scale industries category. Enterprises in the service sector are also considered as an industry under the Act. In the service sector, the enterprises with investment on equipments above Rs. 10 lakh but below 200 lakh are treated as a small-scale enterprise. An enterprise with investment below Rs. 10 lakh is treated as Micro Enterprise. The planning support for the micro, small and medium enterprises has to cover escort services for setting up new units, formation of SHGs for promotion of micro, village and handicraft industries and development of marketing outlets, promoting the formation of industrial clusters, assisting the formation of ancillaries and downstream units, developing infrastructure for this sector through consolidation and expansion of cluster development approach, arranging for the flow of credit to SSI units, quality assurance, etc. It also includes common service facility centre, orientation and entrepreneurship development programme, incentive for setting new industrial enterprises, credit and loan to Village and Small Industries, Quality control, modernisation etc.

Under Handicrafts, skill development programme, participation in Handicrafts fair, export promotion for Handicrafts, Urban marketing outlets, Handicrafts museum, Financial Assistance to Handicrafts artisans/ co-operatives, pension to Old Aged Handicrafts artisans, etc., are to be planned. Similarly, for coir development, Training centre for manufacture of coir products and in Handloom sub-sector, diversification of products, export oriented production, market promotion of handloom products, linkage with Fashion technology, and financial assistance to handloom weavers, welfare and social security of handloom weavers have also to be planned. Modernisation issue of powerloom and diversification of its products are also important. Under Sericulture, high yielding varieties of mulberry crop, rearing inputs/appliances, maintenance and multiplication of basic silkworm seeds, improvement of post-cocoon sector through development of reeling/twisting technology for silk yarn, cultivation of *eri* and *muga* and related training, sericulture cluster scheme, etc., have also to be appropriately planned through dedicated schemes.

Due emphasis has to be given for the food processing industries in sectoral planning. It has to assess abundant and perishable agricultural and horticultural products as available in the State. Planning requires to identify right project, tie-up of raw materials availability, linkage with escort services relating to finance, shed, electricity, etc., marketing and exportable opportunity, product development, skill training, modernisation, anchoring facilities with the Ministry of FPI, Government of India, APEDA, NHB, etc., infrastructure for food processing industries including Food Park, cargo complex for perishable goods, Quality control, cold storage and refrigerated transport, joint venture, research and development, etc.

Minerals of minor variety come within the orbit of State Planning. The planning support for exploring such minerals, examining its potential usefulness, converting those into marketable commodities and addressing all issues connected therewith for converting them into trade and services has to be made.

In designing the sectoral planning for the Industry and Minerals, the availability of centrally sponsored schemes, Central sector schemes, institutional schemes of the funding institutes, State schemes, etc., have all to be mapped, assess the current status of implementation, if any, projected requirement of fund and its utilising potentialities and then settle the details of the schemes (including location, etc.) *vis-à-vis* the vision of the sector with proposed outlay with due consideration of convergence wherever possible. The requirement of counterpart fund from the State Plan outlay, if required, for centrally sponsored schemes may also be worked out at this stage. Another area that is needed adequate importance is the quantification of physical targets. Scheme specific past achievement of targets and proposed targets for the next plan is very important. These have to be worked out with extreme care and application of mind. There has to exist prudent justification on quantum of investment and its output.

Additionally, at this stage of planning inclusive factors have to be addressed and plugged in the proposed programmes/schemes itself. Accordingly, it has to be planned for TSP and SCSP components and required percentage of plan outlay at the State level has to be booked for them. The proposed financial outlay for each scheme along with its physical targets have to be worked out. In this matter, the nodal department on SC/ST in the State may be appropriately consulted. Further, for inclusive consideration and also on requirement of Women Component in the Industry and Minerals sector, dedicated schemes have to be worked out. It need not be a mechanical exercise but a serious exercise on planning to ensure how the gender divide in the Industry and Minerals sector can be bridged by adopting women centric schemes. Proposed Financial Outlays along with target of its physical output has also to be settled. These have to be presented then in the Annexure designed by the Planning Commission.

VII. Sectoral Planning for Transport

Of the six items under the sector, Minor Port and Civil Aviation do not pose serious planning items for the States in general. Minor ports come under concurrent list and because of lumpy nature of investment and other maritime connected factors, the port expansion is usually taken up by the Central Government. Civil Aviation is also the area falling under the Union list and only those incidental issues requiring to put in place for the setting up of any airport by the State fall under this sectoral planning.

Roads and Bridges are key areas of sectoral planning connected as it is with rapid growth of the economy and the road network for efficient transport system. Based on the road vision of the State, Perspective Road Plan in the State and also on consideration of connectivity with National highway and Express highway, the selection for new roads and upgradation of existing roads for State highways have to be taken up in the State Plan. With the increasing volume of transport load, new areas of overbridge construction might be inescapably necessary across the river and other waterbodies. All of these have to be included under sectoral planning under Roads and Bridges.

Further, in view of huge demand for unmet service needs on Roads and Bridges, transparent norms for prioritisation for new roads or for upgradation of existing roads from planning angle needs to be put in place and plan it accordingly. The status of sanctioned schemes and likely time schedule of completion of them have also to be taken into consideration for finalising sectoral plan on Roads and Bridges. Additionally, PMGSY, a Centrally Sponsored Scheme for connectivity of uncovered villages in the district road networks is also to be indicated under Roads and Bridges. The linkage between State roads and the road network of the Panchayats and the Municipalities have also to be addressed in course of this sub-sector level planning.

Almost all the States of India have taken up Road Transport as a part of social responsibility of the government. As a result, Road Transport Corporations have come into being with funding support of the State government. It thus becomes a subject under State plan. While planning for new fleet or for augmentation of road transport network, the economices of vehicle productivity, load factor, staff-bus ratio, staff productivity, etc., are to be taken up for consideration. Additionally, road safety issue, rescue aid posts, road safety education, etc., are also to be planned as relevant.

Inland Water Transport system has got momentum in recent times. Just like Road Transport Corporations, Inland Water Transport Corporations have come into being in several States. All issues similar to those of Road Transport Corporations have to be given due consideration. Additionally, location, feasibility, construction of Jetties, Floating Jetties, fleet of launch, steamer etc. together with economies of it are to be factored in for planning decision.

While undertaking sectoral planning for the Transport Sector it is also needed to give adequate importance in the quantification of physical targets. Scheme specific past achievement of targets and proposed targets for the next plan is very important. These have to be worked out with extreme care and application of mind. There has to exist prudent justification on quantum of investment and its output.

Additionally, at this stage of planning inclusive factors have to be addressed and plugged in the proposed programmes/schemes itself. Accordingly, it has to be planned for TSP and SCSP components and required percentage of plan outlay has to be booked for them. The proposed financial outlay for each scheme along with its physical targets have to be worked out. In this matter, the nodal department on SC/ST in the State may be appropriately consulted. Further, for inclusive consideration and also on requirement of Women Component in the Transport Sector, dedicated schemes may be worked out, as feasible.

These have to be presented then in the Annexure designed by the Planning Commission. Proposed Financial Outlays along with target of its physical output has also to be settled. These have to be presented then in the Annexure designed by the Planning Commission.

VIII. Sectoral Planning for Science, Technology and Environment

Planning for the sustainable agenda of the State Plan is primarily taken up under this sector. Under Scientific Research, socio-economic needs are to be taken up as core programme. Relevance of science and technology as a way for improving the quality of life of ordinary citizens is an important item for demonstration. Schemes for popularization of them need to be taken up through mediums and forums. Successful experimentation on socially relevant items has also to be taken out beyond laboratory and Pilot schemes on lab to land initiative taken up. The data need on updated status of natural resources have gone up and the importance of setting up of remote sensing centre has increased. It needs to come under State Plan. Further, for bridging the rural urban divide the extension and practical application of science and technology has to be spread in rural areas.

Under IT&E-Governance, government portals, e-governance, related capacity building, dedicated portals like telemedicine, Agriculture portal, etc., establishment of Software Technology Park and NeGP are to be taken up. Under Ecology and Environment, environmental awareness, environmental research, environmental pollution, disposal of solid and hazardous wastes, conservation of biodiversity, climate change related issues, etc., are to be planned for dedicated schemes.

The national goal to have a minimum of one-third of the total land area of the country under forest or tree cover is the prime planning concern. Improving the current forest cover of the State by and by and reaching ultimately the national goal of forest and land ratio is the objective for planning under Forestry and Wildlife under the State Plan. The increasing population density, non-availability of newer land and degradation of traditional forest land are some difficult areas. However, improving the forest cover has to take the route of planning for canopy cover improvement (intensification) and also extension of afforestation of degraded forest land (extension). The Approach to the Twelfth Plan suggested to take up forestry extension through afforestation of non-conventional forest areas adopting farm and agro-forestry approaches. While doing so fruit bearing species may be given due importance for the strengthening nutritional security of the rural population. Forestry and Wildlife also plans for forest resource survey, forest consolidation, forest protection, JFM and improvements of parks and gardens, urban forestry, etc. Appropriate schemes have to be planned and tie it up with CSS where the fund availability is considerable.

In designing the sectoral planning for the Science, Technology and Environment, the availability of centrally sponsored schemes, Central sector schemes and State schemes, etc., have all to be mapped, assess the current status of implementation, projected requirement of fund and its utilising potentialities and then settle the details of the schemes (including location, etc.) *vis-à-vis* the vision of the sector with proposed outlay with due consideration of convergence wherever possible. The requirement of counterpart fund from the State Plan outlay, if required, for centrally sponsored schemes may also be worked out at this stage. Another area that is needed adequate importance is the quantification of physical targets. Scheme specific past achievement of targets and proposed targets for the next plan is very important. These have to be worked out with extreme care and application of mind. There has to exist prudent justification on quantum of investment and its output.

Additionally, at this stage of planning inclusive factors have to be addressed and plugged in the proposed programmes/schemes itself. Accordingly, it has to be planned for TSP and SCSP components and required percentage of plan outlay at the State level has to be booked for them. The proposed financial outlay for each scheme along with its physical targets have to be worked out. In this matter, the nodal department on SC/ST in the State may be appropriately consulted. Further, for inclusive consideration and also on requirement of Women Component in the Science, Technology and Environment sector, dedicated schemes have to be worked out. It need not be a mechanical exercise but a serious exercise on planning to ensure how the gender divide in the Science, Technology and Environment sector can be bridged by adopting women centric schemes. Proposed Financial Outlays along with target of its physical output has also to be settled. These have to be presented then in the Annexure designed by the Planning Commission.

IX. Sectoral Planning for General Economic Services

Tourism planning depends on richness of geographical diversity and its religious and historical heritage. It is also closely linked with location of international and national heritage site in the State. It also depends on innovative set-up put in place for attraction of different interest groups and quality of infrastructural network including its tourist establishments and support structure. The provisioning of tourist accommodation for different economic categories of tourists, related road networks down the line, promotion of transport facilities, diversified and innovative recreational avenues and other related support services are to be planned and provided. Promotion of heritage tourism, eco-tourism, circuit tourism, rural tourism, religious tourism, tea tourism, health tourism, etc., are some areas meant for planning for diversification. Opening up of new tourists spot on public-private partnership and incentive schemes for promotion and extension of tourism are also items for planning.

Civil Supplies did not receive adequate planning importance over the years. As a result infrastructural network on Civil Supplies has not grown up across the States. The coming up of food-based programme like Annapurna, Antyodaya Anna Yoyana, TPDS and PDS have multiplied the importance of this area and the needed infrastructural set-up. The Operational framework of Food Security Act would call for a gigantic network of warehousing and PDS network at the State level, district level, block level and village level. The creation of infrastructural facilities and setting up modern outlets for Public Distribution Supplies is thus an urgent call on planning. While the planning for infrastructure of PDS, distance factor and location of Scheduled Tribes in far away forest fringe areas need appropriate consideration. Location of such PDS may be settled with the help of NRDMS/GIS. It also requires to plan for quality testing laboratories for foodgrains.

The right-based approach has led to the demand for transparency and quality of weight and measurement practices connected with consumer satisfaction. In keeping with changing time of rising expectation of quality in measurement, etc., it has to be planned for modernisation of the establishment of Weights and Measures, bringing in of new generation of infrastructural network and adoption of state of art of modern technology.

In designing the sectoral planning for the General Economic Services in an aggregate sense, the availability of centrally sponsored schemes, central sector schemes and State schemes, etc., have all to be mapped, assess the current status of implementation, projected requirement of fund and its utilising potentialities and then settle the details of the schemes (including location, etc.) *vis-à-vis* the vision of the sector with proposed outlay with due consideration of convergence wherever possible. The requirement of counterpart fund from the State Plan outlay, if required, for centrally sponsored schemes may also be worked out at this stage.

Another area that is needed adequate importance is the quantification of physical targets. Scheme specific past achievement of targets and proposed targets for the next plan is very important. These have to be worked out with extreme care and application of mind. There has to exist prudent justification on quantum of investment and its output.

Additionally, at this stage of planning inclusive factors have to be addressed and plugged in the proposed programmes/schemes itself. Accordingly, it has to be planned for TSP and SCSP components and required percentage of plan outlay at the State level has to be booked for them. The proposed financial outlay for each scheme along with its physical targets have to be worked out. In this matter, the nodal department on SC/ST in the State may be appropriately consulted. Further, for inclusive consideration and also on requirement of Women Component in the General Economic Services sector, dedicated schemes have to be worked out. It need not be a mechanical exercise but a serious exercise on planning to ensure how the gender divide in the General Economic Services sector can be bridged by adopting women centric schemes. Proposed Financial Outlays along with target of its physical output has also to be settled. These have to be presented then in the Annexure designed by the Planning Commission.

X. Sectoral Planning for Social Services

The Social Services sector is directly connected with the inclusive agenda of the Five Year Plan. It is also instrumental in furthering the spread of human development of the citizens. Its importance with the quality of life is immense and far reaching. The planning for Social Services is, therefore, of crucial importance in the overall planning of the State. All the components of the Social Services sector are discussed hereunder:

1. General Education

(a) Elementary Education

Education for all is the overarching policy framework for general education in the country. The planning for Elementary Education revolves around school education and literacy/adult education. A uniform structure of school education system, based on right based approach, as per RTE Act, has now to be the focal point of planning. The State has now to organise free and compulsory education to all children of the State in the six to 14 age group, arranged for a fixed student-teacher ratio, take measures for improvement in quality of education, and create School infrastructure to be improved in three years. Under school infrastructure, arrangements for drinking water and sanitation separately for boys and girls including the infrastructure for MDM have to be planned and put in place. The State has also to meet its proportionate cost from its plan resources. Further, for out of school students alternative schooling has also to be planned and outreached. The test of proper planning of RTE is to meet three cardinal principles, namely, access, equity and quality in all forms of elementary education. Further, it has to plan on convergence with other schemes for progressively universalizing Early Childhood Care and Education (ECCE) for all children in the age group of 4-6 years in high priority disadvantaged social groups and regions. Further, for 'Out of school' children, there has to be scope for taking up home-based innovative elementary education through multi-option programmes like day care centres, pre-vocational programme resource centres and community-based resource centres. Similarly, for older girls belonging to dropout and never enrolled, the educational needs may be met through the routine programme of bridge courses followed by mainstreaming into formal institutions through the format of SSA. Additionally, the National Programme for Education of Girls at Elementary Level (NPEGEL) needs to be focused on Blocks with low rate of Female Literacy and the design of the programme for girls in these Blocks could include any of the elements already stipulated in SSA like Remedial Teaching, Bridge Courses, Alternative Schools, Child Care Centres, and also plan for other measures to suit context specificities and local requirements.

Additionally, it has to address RTE harmonized Sarva Shiksha Abhiyan, MDMS and various Literacy programmes and achieve goal number 2 of universal primary education under MDG.

(b) Literacy/Adult Education

The Census figures give the latest update of the literacy scenario of the State and also its gender-wise position across the districts. The literacy rate of the country as per provisional figure of the Census, 2011 is 74.04 per cent in aggregate while the share of the males and females are respectively 82.14 per cent and 65.46 per cent. There are sharp variations on literacy among the States and also among the literacy status of SC, ST and OBCs. Based on literacy deficit, the State has to plan for a sustainable threshold level of literacy. Further, the State has to work on low literacy pockets and prepare a literacy map of the State to focus on SC, ST, females and other disadvantage groups.

Under Goal 4 of 'Education For All (EFA)', it is to aim at achieving 50 per cent improvement in the levels of literacy by 2015, especially for women, and equitable access to basic and continuing education for all adults. For that the State may proceed with its own schemes along with NLM which seeks to achieve this goal by imparting functional literacy to non-literates in the age group of 15-35 years. Apart from pre-determined levels of reading, writing and numeracy, functional literacy has to be organised for self-reliance, empowerment, skill development and imbibing values of national integration, conservation of environment, gender equity, and observance of small family norms.

(c) Secondary Education

The focus on secondary education planning is to make good quality education available, accessible and affordable to all young persons in the age group of 14-18 years. With this focus in mind, the following targets have to be set and plan for its achievement during the Twelfth Five Year Plan:

(a) Universal access to secondary education with a GER of 100 per cent;
(b) Enhancing retention of children in secondary classes; and
(c) Achieving the target of 75 per cent GER in Higher Secondary Classes by 2017.

If the GER targets of 100 per cent in secondary education (Grades IX-X) and 75 per cent in higher secondary education (Grades XI-XII) (as per SES GER in 2007-08 was 58.2 for Grades IX and X and 33.4 for Grades XI and XII) are set to be achieved by the end of the Twelfth Plan period, the required average increase in the size of the GER per annum between 2007-08 and 2016-17 would have to be around 5 percentage points both at the secondary and higher secondary levels. Given the average increase in the size of GER per annum between 2004-05 and 2007-08 (i.e. 2 percentage points each for GER at the secondary and higher secondary levels), the required change in the size of the GER at secondary and higher secondary levels (i.e., around 5 percentage points per annum) is rather high but have to be addressed in the context of other favourable factors emerging in this area. For advanced States, this may not pose any problem. However, for relatively backward States, this is a great challenge and also opportunity to surge ahead and achieve possible desired target as far as possible with heightened priority. Further, for the vision of the secondary education to make good quality education available, accessible and affordable to this category of students, it is necessary to provide a secondary school within a reasonable distance of five kilometres for secondary schools and 7-10 kilometres for higher secondary schools from their habitation. It should also provide for access to secondary education with special references to economically weaker sections of the society, the educationally backward, the girls and the disabled children residing in rural areas and other marginalized categories like SC, ST, OBC and Educationally Backward Minorities (EBM).

(d) Higher Education

The vision of higher education is to develop India as a knowledge society. This is also the shared vision for the States of India. The planning focus on higher education is, therefore, to improve and expand education in all sectors and eliminates disparities in access and lay greater emphasis on the improvement in the quality and relevance of education at all levels. In that very context, the adoption of State specific higher education planning is very crucial. It has to address curriculum reforms, vocationalisation, information technology, quality of research, networking and distance education. The other important planning initiatives include programmes for general development of universities and colleges, special grants for the construction of hostels for women, scholarships to students, scheme to provide interest subsidy on educational loans for professional courses to ensure that nobody is denied professional education. The use of ICT in education, promotion of research and quality education are other areas that require appropriate address.

In real terms it has to plan for expansion in all its modes of delivery to increase the Gross Enrolment Ratio (GER) in higher education to 15 per cent by 2011-12 and to 21 per cent by Twelfth Plan and 30 per cent by the year 2020. It has also to expand institutional base of higher education (including technical. professional and vocational education) by creating additional capacity in existing institutions, establishing new institutions. It has also to provide opportunities of higher education to socially deprived communities and remove disparities by promoting the inclusion of women and differently-abled persons. It is during planning stage that efforts are needed to remove regional imbalances in access to higher education by setting up of institutions in unserved and underserved areas.

2. Technical Education

The Vision of India's Technical Education is to realize India's human resource potential to its fullest with equity and inclusion. The three pillars of strategy for planning in Technical Education are expansion, inclusion and excellence. It has to be planned to empower our youths with the right skills to meet the challenges of knowledge-based market economy. Based on the identification of the skill gaps in different sectors, it has to be planned for setting up of finishing schools and offering courses for enhancing employability. The planning strategies for increasing employability factor need to be either faculty-centric or student-centric and have to cover Industry Institute Student Training Support, Industrial Challenge Open Forum, and Long Term Student Industry Placement, etc. The multi-various opportunities under National Skill Development Mission have to be appropriately tied up to meet skill deficiency in different sectors of the economy.

3. Sports

Given the two main objectives of National Sports Policy 2001, viz., broad-basing of sports and excellence in sports, the planning for sports has to concentrate on creation/development of sports infrastructure and sports facilities in the States as per sports related regional aptitude and proficiency. It has also to plan for nurturing and training of the identified talent and organise support and fellowship. It has also to address mass participation in Sports including physical education, promotion of excellence in Sports including coaching upgradation and infrastructure, Sports Sciences, Sports related developments on Health, Physical Fitness and Nutrition.

4. Youth Services

The planning for Youth Services has to cover multi-disciplinary subjects. In line with that of NYK, it has to encourage young persons and support their participation and involvement in the process of development of the State. The State has to plan for ways and means for the training of youth for self-employment. It has also to plan for vocational training including computer training and such other coaching centres as the State may consider appropriate. Besides, promotion of Science Club may be encouraged for the youths. The State has also to encourage the spirit of adventure and provide opportunity for promotion of adventure sports including mountaineering. Accordingly, Youth Hostels have to be setup for such locations in the State. Further, for facilitating social development youth festival may also be encouraged.

5. Art and Culture

Art and Culture is again a multi-disciplinary area of planning. Usually, a good number of departments usually address this area depending on its core functional areas. It may be the Information and Cultural department, Higher education department, Hill affairs department and SC/ST welfare department of the State. It relates to setting and upgradation of Museum, Research centres, Archives, Digitisation of reference media record. It may be for construction, renovation or setting up of Folk Culture Centre, Theatre/Drama/Dance Academy, Cultural Complex, Art Gallery, Heritage related initiatives, etc.

6. Medical and Public Health

The planning for Medical and Public Health has to focus on "Universal Essential Health Care" and put in place an operational framework. It has accordingly to synchronise three aspects: Public Health Systems for health promotion, disease prevention and health care delivery. Further, it has to make use and further build up and strengthen the system developed under NRHM to augment Human Resources. Since the major constraint is on availability of Human Resources, the planning efforts have to concentrate on setting up of more medical and other colleges specially in backward districts to increase availability of Nurses, ANMs and Paramedical staff. Creation of mid-level health practitioners is another focus area of planning along with capacity development through quality training and supportive supervision. Further, the existing primary health care system needs also to be strengthened based on availability of more health personnel and that priority has to be accorded to remote and inaccessible areas. Districts may, however, remain to be the focal point for improving the health services and accordingly the district level hospitals need to be strengthened to provide advanced secondary level health care. The scope for setting up a district level knowledge institute to provide quality training may also be addressed. Further, while the health needs of the rural areas need to be met as much as possible with the National Rural Health Mission, the health needs of urban poor may be addressed through National Urban Health Mission. In planning for the health sector, strong emphasis has also to be accorded on determinants of health like Nutrition, Water Supply and Sanitation.

For inclusive development, the scope of providing support and care at the community level is very important. This would broaden access to health through communication and enhance awareness to public health programmes. In this context, early screening of children for timely detection of disability and treatment along with disabled friendly design of health facilities would be needed. Additionally, with the advancement of life span, Geriatric care has also assumed considerable planning priority. Further, since IMR and MMR continue to remain on higher side, comprehensive planning has to be made for perceptible change in those areas. Accordingly, continued focus on reproductive and child health, communicable diseases and the growing non-communicable diseases have to be given. The health planning is very crucial in this area in the context of achieving the MDG No. 4 of 'Reduce child mortality, goal No. 5 of "Improve maternal health" and goal No. 6 "Combat HIV/AIDS, malaria and other diseases".

In designing the health planning, it has to be kept in mind that there exist a good number of schemes—centrally sponsored schemes, central sector schemes, EAP and State schemes, etc. All of them have to be mapped, focus on common areas for possible convergence within the system, assess the current status of implementation, projected requirement of fund and its utilising potentialities and then settle the details of the schemes (including location, etc.) *vis-à-vis* the vision of the sector with proposed outlay with due consideration of convergence wherever possible. The requirement of counterpart fund from the State Plan outlay, if required, for centrally sponsored schemes may also be worked out at this stage. Another area that is needed adequate importance is the quantification of physical targets. Scheme specific past achievement of targets and proposed targets for the next plan is very important. These have to be worked out with extreme care and application of mind. There has to exist prudent justification on quantum of investment and its output.

7. Water Supply and Sanitation

Water supply and sanitation are important basic needs affecting the quality of life and productive efficiency of the people. Water supply also falls under basic minimum needs programme and is, therefore, a much focused issue on State planning. In its planning context, it has to be remembered that days of abundant and comfortable water resources position do not exist any more. The exponential growth of water demand from both traditional and not so traditional sources has been rising rapidly and has turned it into a supply constraint scenario. The demand for adequate water as a basic human right has added further dimension. In this given scenario, the water supply planning is to be focused at the first instance on provision of safe and adequate drinking water supply in the rural areas and also in the urban areas. In this process equity aspect of coverage of SCs, STs and other Backward Castes need due consideration.

As per the Eleventh and the Twelfth Schedules of the Constitution, the water supply is now constitutional responsibility of the Panchayats and also of the Municipalities. Therefore, partnership in planning in water supply need to be worked out between the three constitutional partners namely, lines departments of the State Government, the tiers of the Panchayats and the Municipalities. Further, convergence among the water supply schemes of the programme partners need to be settled during the course of planning process. In this context Rajiv Gandhi Drinking Water Mission on Rural Drinking Water through NRDWP and the Central Government's flagship programme on Rural Water Supply, namely, Accelerated Rural Water Supply Programme (ARWSP) need to be taken into consideration. While planning for rural water supply, ARWSP coverage norms of 40 lpcd of drinking water for human beings; 30 lpcd of additional water for cattle in areas under the DDP; One hand pump or stand post for every 250 persons; and availability of water source within 1.6 kms in plains and 100 metres elevation in hilly areas have to be adhered to. For water quality control, ARWSP Sub-Mission on Water Quality may be appropriately made use of. For urban water supply, efforts need to be made to plan dedicated schemes under JNNURM, UIDSSMT and Centrally Sponsored Accelerated Urban Water Supply Programme (AUWSP) as much as possible. In the context of spread of sanitary pollution in the urban areas, the need for quality control planning of drinking water has increased tremendously. It has to be planned for the expansion of water quality testing laboratories in the urban areas network preferably, on PPP mode, with cost sharing basis.

Under the National Urban Sanitation Policy launched in December 2008, the main goal is to transform urban India into community driven totally sanitized healthy and liveable cities and towns. The vision of the policy is that all Indian cities and towns become totally sanitised, healthy and liveable and ensure and sustain good public health and environmental outcomes for all their citizens with a special focus on hygienic and affordable sanitation facilities for the urban poor and women. Awareness

Generation and Behavioural Change; Open Defecation Free Cities; Integrated City Wide Sanitation; Sanitary and Safe Disposal; and Proper Operation and Maintenance of all Sanitary Installations are components of the policy. The above national policy has to be kept in the upfront during State planning on sanitation.

In regard to Sanitation programme, the focus area on State planning is on rural sanitation programme because of its low coverage. For that end, the Total Sanitation Campaign (TSC) programme needs to be outreached extensively. The TSC programme can also be used for school sanitation and Anganwadi centres. For urban sanitation again, efforts need to be made to plan dedicated schemes under JNNURM and UIDSSMT. Finally, as per the Eleventh and the Twelfth Schedules of the Constitution, sanitation is also the constitutional responsibility of the Panchayats and also of the Municipalities. In planning sanitation under State Plan, this fact may also be taken into consideration for focusing on role of line department in given areas *vis-à-vis* those of the Panchayats and Municipalities.

8. Housing

Right to property is a fundamental right guaranteed by the Constitution of India. It is thus left to the individuals to build up their own property including their housing. The basic objective of housing under the State plan is, however, to increase the construction of more affordable and low-rent housing to different categories of citizens and the speeding up of slum demolition. Similarly, in rural areas, it has the objective to assist BPL categories of citizens to build up their own rural homes with State assistance and to move into their permanent houses.

Thc planning for Housing in any State normally revolves around rural housing, urban housing and police housing. There are dedicated central schemes for rural housing and urban housing which the State government usually relies on. Additionally, the different State governments also design their own schemes which have also taken into consideration while planning for housing. The police housing is taken up to take care of rental housing needs associated with their nature of jobs and of its transferable character.

9. Urban Development (Including State Capital Project and Slum Area Development)

Urban planning is a technical and administrative process for the controlled use of urban land and designed urban environment so that the development of urban areas takes place in ordered pattern. It concerns itself with research and analysis, strategic thinking, urban design, public consultations, policy recommendations, implementation and management. In the planning process, the vision plays the most crucial input in the planning decision. Such vision may be Metropolitan city specific, other city specific, district town specific or for any satellite town specific. Urban development takes place through serious programme efforts of multiple players—both in the government sector and outside. The scope of public-private partnership is most widespread in this area. After the Seventy-fourth Amendment, depending on the nature of devolution, the role of the Municipalities has also increased considerably. All the districts do now have Urban Plans. During the course of Urban Planning at the State level it has to take into consideration inputs from those decentralized urban plans also. Further, under Article 243ZE of the Constitution of India, the Metropolitan Planning Committee has also been empowered with planning function and to prepare the draft Metropolitan development plan. Such draft Metropolitan development plan has to be appropriately taken into consideration during the process of urban planning for the State. In a way, there has to have linkages, synergies and convergence between the Urban Plan for the State Annual Plan and the decentralized urban plans. Without any horizontal and vertical linkage and connectivity, the Urban Plan of the State would lose its wholesome character. In the State urban plan only those programmes are included which are by its nature State specific and not essentially district sector intervention. The onus of implementing the schemes lies with the Line Departments of the government. It is, however, another matter if the municipalities become executing agencies on behalf of Line Departments of the State.

The generic nature of broad items that are taken up for planning includes Infrastructure, Land Use and Environment Development, Social and Livelihood Development, Municipal Institutional Strengthening, Livelihood and Poverty Alleviation, Local Economic Development, Health Care Services Delivery Improvement and Primary Education Development Plan. On each of these items there are State schemes, Central Government schemes and other institutional schemes which have to be mapped up and taken for planning decision for appropriate intervention. For intervention through relevant schemes, Urban Infrastructure and Development Schemes for Small and Medium Towns (UIDSSMT), Improvement of Housing and Slum Development Project (IHSDPS), (JSRY), Jawaharlal Nehru National Urban Renewal Mission (JNNURM) are important.

10. Information and Publicity

The area of planning for the Information and Publicity relates to dissemination of the plans and programmes taken up by the Line Departments in the State. Apart from ensuring transparency in the planning and implementation process, it has the additional objective to generate awareness on socially relevant subject to create right kind of environment. The creation of information network, its upgradation and also setting up mechanism for interactions between the government and the civil society are items for State Planning. Dedicated portal could be the other option in this regard.

11. Development of SCs, STs and OBCs

From inclusive angle, the development of the Scheduled Castes and the Scheduled Tribes and OBCs is a priority item of State planning. The outreach of the benefits of the plan schemes is closely linked with the spread of human development of the social groups. The development for the SC, ST and OBCs has been designed under three counts: (a) by intervention of planned schemes by the nodal department of SC/ST/OBC; (b) by intervention of planned schemes of other line departments through SCSP and TSP; and (c) by other special programmes of the Central Government/Planning Commission. The planning in respect of each component may be discussed separately:

(a) By Intervention of Planned Schemes by the Nodal Department of SC/ST/OBC

Just like defined subject of any Line Department, the nodal department of SC/ST/OBC is also empowered to plan for its subject area, namely the welfare of SC, ST and OBC. Therefore, the major planning for the SC/ST/OBCs has to take place in this area with back-up funding support from the resources of the State plan. In drawing up plan for the schemes, it is required to have complete data on development deficit and human development deficit in the upfront for realistic planning. The spatial data from the NRDMS would be helpful to plan for uncovered or under-covered areas. Normally, infrastructural deficiency and lack of educational opportunities are two areas for which appropriate plan has to be made. For infrastructural development, village connectivity—not covered under PMGSY—may be taken up. Similarly, construction of school building and other facilities—not covered under SSA or under any programme of the School Education Department—may also be taken up. It may also be provided for construction of grain *gola* (godown, warehouse) or for ICDS buildings. Dedicated water supply schemes not covered under Public Health Department or dedicated schemes on irrigation may also be taken up here. For educational development, Book grants and Examination fees, Maintenance charges, Hostel charges, Post Matric scholarship, Vocational training programme, etc., may be taken up. In planning for the schemes, the deficit in development aspects of SC/ST or OBCs have to be kept in the upfront. The scheme specific financial provisioning and corresponding physical targets have also to be made.

(b) By Intervention of Planned Schemes of Other Line Departments through SCSP and TSP

The State Plan has to provide dedicated schemes for SC and ST under SCSP/TSP. These schemes are meant for dedicated programme intervention in that developmental functional area for the improvement of SC or ST, as the case may be. These are additive nature of intervention by the Line Departments to improve relative deficit in those areas. During the planning stage, the Line Departments have also to consult the nodal department of the welfare for SC and ST in the State in this regard and ensure that focused intervention does take place under SCSP and TSP and there does not take place any duplication of programme efforts with the programmes of the nodal department of the welfare for SC and ST. The financial outlay for each sector and corresponding physical targets have also to be settled.

(c) By Other Special Programmes of the Central Government/Planning Commission

The Ministry of Tribal Affairs provides Special Central Assistance to Tribal Sub-Plans (SCA to TSP) as additive to State Plan efforts for demand based employment-cum-income generation activities and the infrastructure incidental thereto, for Scheduled Tribes below the poverty line. Additionally, the Constitution of India required under Article 275(1) to meet the cost of schemes for the purpose of promoting the welfare of the Scheduled Tribes in the State or raising the level of administration of the Scheduled Areas therein to that of the administration of the rest of the areas of the State. The grants-in-aid so received are also to be taken into account for the available fund for TSP. Furthermore, the Integrated Action Plan (IAP) for 60 Selected Tribal and Backward Districts has been launched to take care of the critical development deficit of these areas. The IAP would be an additional central assistance (ACA), on 100 per cent grant basis for the concerned States.

Similarly, the Ministry of Social Justice and Empowerment (M/SJ&E) provides 100 per cent grant under the Central Sector Scheme of SCA to SCSP as an additive to SCSP to the States to fill the critical gaps and vital missing inputs in family oriented income generating schemes with supporting infrastructure development so as to make the schemes more effective.

Given the resource-back for the planning for SC and ST and the OBCs, the planning has to begin after mapping all available options and schemes, identified development deficit and also having interactions with all stakeholders including the DPCs and plan for bridging the gaps on development indicators between SC/ST/OBCs and the rest of the population by dedicated schemes in a time-bound manner.

12. Labour and Employment

Labour and Employment sub-sector addresses multi-dimensional socio-economic aspects affecting labour welfare, productivity, living standards of labour force and social security. Additionally, it also considers rehabilitation of Bonded Labour and prevention of Child Labour. For raising the living standards of the work force and achieving higher productivity, skill upgradation through suitable training is also to be planned. Manpower development is also required to provide adequate labour force of appropriate skills. Employment generation in all the productive sectors is one of the basic objectives. Efforts are also to be made for providing the environment for self-employment both in urban and rural areas. Adequate attention has also to be given to prevention of undesirable practices such as child labour, bonded labour, and also on aspects such as ensuring workers' safety and social security.

13. Social Security and Social Welfare

Social Welfare provides a minimal level of well-being and social support to identified socially disadvantaged section of citizens without the stigma of charity. Depending on the nature of disadvantages and the categories, the planning for dedicated services is to be made. Insofar as National

Social Assistance Programme and Annapurna is concerned, it has to decide on number of persons found eligible under two components of National Social Assistance Programme, namely, Indira Gandhi National Old Age Pension Scheme (IGNOAPS) and National Family Benefit Scheme (NFBS), and also under Annapurna Scheme. Since the pension amount under Indira Gandhi National Old Age is flexible, it has to work on the State Government's optional share, if any, over pension component of Rs. 200 per month per beneficiary from the Central Government.Only the State Government's share would come under the State Plan.

The National Family Benefit Scheme is a fully funded central assisted scheme in the form of lump sum family benefit of Rs. 10,000 for households below the poverty line on the death of the primary breadwinner in the bereaved family on certain exigencies. This programme, though a part of the sectoral programme of the State Government, does not directly come under State Plan as no resources of State Plan are attached to it. Similarly, Annapurna Scheme which provides10 kg of foodgrains per month to senior citizens, though eligible, remained uncovered under the NOAPS. The cost of the programme does not come under the resources of the State Plan and so it is also not shown as an item of the State Plan.

From inclusive angle, the physically and mentally challenged persons belong to priority area of planning and programme intervention. It has to plan for prosthetic aids of different forms for physically challenged persons, arrange scholarship and hostel support for formal education, setting up/modernisation of composite homes for hearing handicapped (Deaf and Dumb), and visually handicapped (Blind), arrange disability specific vocational training, arranging institutional linkages for credit and marketing outlets, and also disability pension for old age. The planning for mentally challenged persons has to be more elaborate requiring special medical and personal care associated with it at every stage of their living.

Social welfare planning also takes care of awareness building against drug habits, for setting up counselling centres and also for rehabilitation of drug addicts to come out of it.

14. (i) Empowerment of Women

The National policy on the Empowerment of Women 2001 is the overarching policy environment under which the planning initiative at the State level has to take place. It encompasses, among other things, creating an environment through positive economic and social policies for full development of women to enable them to realize their full potential, equal access to participation and decision making of women in social, political and economic life of the nation, equal access to women to health care, quality education at all levels, career and vocational guidance, employment, equal remuneration, occupational health and safety, social security and public office, etc., mainstreaming a gender perspective in the development process and building and strengthening partnerships with civil society, particularly women's organizations.

Empowerment of Women and Development of Children has emerged as an important planning issue at all levels of planning connected as it is with inclusiveness, empowerment and the MDG. However, no structured Gender Plan as such has come into being either at the national level or at the State level except under the State Annual Plan where it is required to submit Women Component in Annexure VIIIA (financial) and VIIIB (physical) to the Planning Commission. Capturing such components does not automatically lend itself to a creditable Gender Plan. In any case, in tune with the basic framework of national policy and for inclusive development, the planning for the women has to address comprehensively in the areas of livelihood, education, health and social sector areas after interactive discussions with the line departments and the women organisations. Incidentally, the Ministry of Finance, Government of India has already given circular to put in place Gender Budgeting under respective Central Ministries. It is expected that the State governments shall also follow suit the central initiative of Gender Budgeting. The Gender Budgeting will be meaningful when a well-baked Gender Plan is structured. Well conceived Gender Plan and Gender Budgeting would also help in realising MDG 3 (Promote gender equality and empower women) and MDG 5 (Improve maternal health) and also meet development deficit in the gender area considerably.

(ii) Welfare and Development of Children

The welfare of Children is the most important area for inclusive development. Integrated Child Development Service Scheme (ICDS) is the flagship programme and its six components (namely, supplementary nutrition, immunization, health check-up, referral services, non-formal pre-school education, and nutrition and health education) are designed to build up the foundation of nutrition, health and mental preparedness of the children to enter formal educational world of tomorrow. ICDS is now covered both in the rural and also in the urban areas and it would be imperative to plan for its six components severally or collectively to ensure that there does not exist unresolved issues for programme implementation. Further, institutional care and protection for disadvantaged children, Street children, prevention and control of juvenile social maladjustment are some other areas that need to be appropriately planned for.

(iii) Nutrition

Nutrition planning is a typical case for cross sectoral planning the essence of which is to improve the nutritional status of the citizens on a lifecycle approach. It has to address nutrition needs for pregnant mother for healthy baby, breast feeding for meeting wholesome nutrition needs of the child at least up to six months, locally available and culturally sanctioned food for the infant and the child, growth monitoring, supplementary nutrition, nutrition counselling, nutrition clinic, nutrition needs for the adolescents, nutrition education and its practices, nutrition of the aged, etc. For the supply side, planning has to work on with JSY, ICDS, MDM, RCH, NRHM, TPDS, Annapurna scheme, Antyodaya Anna Yojona, etc. In other words, based on scheme mapping and tied up resources it has to plan for several components of nutrition and also address them for different geographical locations including those underserved and unserved areas. The basic approach of Nutrition planning has, however, to be addressed to the deficient areas as revealed in NFHS survey for the particular State (currently NFHS-III) and make specific planning to improve the position through a set of programme interventions. Particular attention has to be given on under-weight, severely under-weight, stunting, severely stunting, wasting and severely stunting children. From inclusive angle, SC and ST families require priority consideration as malnutrition is consistently much higher in SC and ST families.

15. Programmes for Minority

The relative backwardness of the minorities in any State in terms of education, livelihood opportunities and other indices of social development, in keeping with the findings of the Sachar Committee Report, has to be taken up for appropriate planning intervention. Further, the State Annual Plan needs also to take into consideration of the Prime Minister's New 15-Point Programme for the Welfare of Minorities. While planning for the minorities the location of minority concentration areas has to be given due priorities. The Prime Minister's New 15-Point Programme is likely to be at the centrality of planning with the following:

(1) Integrated Child Development Services (ICDS) Scheme by providing services through Anganwadi Centres; (2) Sarva Shiksha Abhiyan; (3) Kasturba Gandhi Balika Vidyalaya; (4) Swarnjayanti Gram Swarojgar Yojana (SGSY); (5) Swarnjayanti Shahari Rojgar Yojana (SJSRY); (6) Upgradation of existing Industrial Training Institutes (ITIs) into Centres of Excellence; (7) Bank Credit under Priority Sector Lending; (8) Indira Awaas Yojana (IAY); (9) Integrated Housing and Slum Development Programme (IHSDP); and Jawaharlal Nehru National Urban Renewal Mission (JNNURM).

Further, the schemes of the Ministry of Minority Affairs for educational empowerment of minority communities are also to be taken up for planning. Gender-divide in the minority sector needs also to be bridged at this stage.

To sum up for designing the sectoral planning for each of the components of Social Services sector, it is required to have the complete list of all centrally sponsored schemes, central sector schemes, institutional schemes of the funding institutes and State schemes along with its location and outlay. Further, current status of implementation of the departmental schemes, projected requirement of fund and its utilising potentialities, etc., are needed to plan for details of the schemes (including location, etc.) *vis-à-vis* the larger vision of the sector with scheme-specific proposed outlay with due consideration of convergence wherever possible. The requirement of counterpart fund from the State Plan outlay for centrally sponsored schemes may also be worked out at this stage. Another area that is not adequately given importance is the quantification of physical targets. Scheme specific past achievement of targets and proposed targets for the next plan is very important. These have to be worked out with extreme care and application of mind. There has to exist prudent justification on quantum of investment and its output. Further, some of the social sector schemes under the State Plan are also subject areas of the Eleventh and Twelfth Schedules. In absence of any formal devolution on components of social sector services, it has to be seen that no duplication of planning efforts takes place on the same subject areas with those of the Panchayats and the Municipalities, and that convergence of programmes among them might be attempted wherever possible and desirable.

Additionally, at this stage of planning, inclusive factors have to be addressed and plugged in the proposed programmes/schemes itself. Accordingly, it has to be planned for TSP and SCSP and required percentage of plan outlay has to be booked for them. The proposed financial outlay along with its physical targets has to be worked out for defined schemes. In this matter, the nodal department on SC/ST in the State may be appropriately consulted. Further, for inclusive consideration and also on requirement of Women Component in the Social service sector, dedicated schemes have to be worked out. It need not be a mechanical exercise but a serious exercise on planning to ensure how the gender divide in the Social Service sector can be bridged by adopting women centric schemes. Proposed Financial Outlays along with target of its physical output has also to be settled. These have to be presented then in the Annexure designed by the Planning Commission.

XI. Sectoral Planning for General Services

The infrastructural development of jails is an important area in this sector. The ever increasing delinquent population of State has been posing commensurate demand for additional space for convicts and under trials in the jails. With the coming in of new generational approach to look upon jails as correctional homes, the need for upgradation and renovation of jails has increased considerably. New state of art of modern welfare programmes has now to be set up along with vocational training and rehabilitation programme for the inmates. While requirement of additional infrastructural support cannot be taken up simultaneously everywhere all at a time because of resource constraint, the planning has to concentrate on priorities after assessing relative merits of all proposals for inclusion and then settle for prioritisation based on objective criteria. Fund for jail infrastructure improvement is receivable from tied and untied sources from the awards of the Finance Commission, centrally sponsored programme and the State plan fund. At the end of the exercise, scheme-specific outlay linked with sources of fund has to be provided. The proposed outlay must be such as could be spent within the financial year.

The minor heads of development of Public Works relate to construction of government buildings across the State. It also includes expansion of infrastructural facilities for court buildings to facilitate proper justice delivery system. Because of the ever increasing demand for construction and renovation, it has to take decision on priorities based on possible fund availability, on urgency of State governance, on consideration of tied fund and also on the necessity to complete incomplete schemes. It has to assess also the number of schemes that can be taken up given the load bearing capabilities of the executing department, possible completion schedule of the pending schemes and the like. Planning includes also assessing and provisioning of counterpart fund for CSS programmes.

The importance of Administrative training both at induction level and also at the in-service level has gone up requiring expansion of such facilities with state of art of modern technology. Periodical upgradation and improvement both in respect of infrastructural facilities and course content is required to be made with resources under State Plan.

In designing the sectoral planning for the General Services, the availability of centrally sponsored schemes, central sector schemes and State schemes, etc., have all to be mapped, assess the current status of implementation, projected requirement of fund and its utilising potentialities and then settle the details of the schemes (including location etc.) *vis-à-vis* the vision of the sector with proposed outlay with due consideration of convergence wherever possible. The requirement of counterpart fund from the State Plan outlay, if required, for centrally sponsored schemes may also be worked out at this stage. Another area that is needed adequate importance is the quantification of physical targets. Scheme specific past achievement of targets and proposed targets for the next plan is very important. These have to be worked out with extreme care and application of mind. There has to exist prudent justification on quantum of investment and its output.

Additionally, at this stage of planning inclusive factors have to be addressed and plugged in the proposed programmes/schemes itself. Accordingly, it has to be planned for TSP and SCSP components and required percentage of plan outlay at the State level has to be booked for them. The proposed financial outlay for each scheme along with its physical targets have to be worked out. In this matter, the nodal department on SC/ST in the State may be appropriately consulted. Further, for inclusive consideration and also on requirement of Women Component in the General Services sector, dedicated schemes have to be worked out. It need not be a mechanical exercise but a serious exercise on planning to ensure how the gender divide in the General Services sector can be bridged by adopting women centric schemes. Proposed Financial Outlays along with target of its physical output has also to be settled. These have to be presented then in the Annexure designed by the Planning Commission.

8

Flagship Programmes

Flagship Programmes are a set of important socio-economic programmes of the Central Government having enough far-reaching potentialities to effect multi-sectoral base of the country. These programmes are intended to contribute significantly to bring about envisaged economic and social sector transformation in the country. The essence of these programmes in the context of the State Planning is that dedicated schemes under them have inherent strength to address unmet development needs in the related sector and could normally be the lead or even supportive intervention initiative to meet the mighty challenges under the State Plan. Adequate and comprehensive coverage have to be made to obtain maximum advantage of the Flagship Programmes. Incidentally, the States have not much to contribute on these programmes as the funding for these programmes are made by the Central Government. Among the various programmes being implemented in the country, eight programmes were initially short-listed as Flagship Programmes to give focused attention for its crucial role in the economy as below:

1. National Rural Employment Guarantee Scheme;
2. Sarva Siksha Abhiyan;
3. Mid-Day Meal Scheme;
4. Integrated Child Development Services (ICDS);
5. National Rural Health Mission (NRHM);
6. Jawaharlal Nehru National Urban Renewal Mission (JNNURM);
7. Total Sanitation Campaign (TSC); and
8. Bharat Nirman:
   (i) Rural Roads,

(ii) Rural Housing,
(iii) Rural Drinking Water Supply,
(iv) Irrigation,
(v) Rural Electrification,
(vi) Rural Telephony.

The number of such Flagship Programmes has increased from time to time with the launch of new programmes by the Central Government. The Press Information Bureau of the Government of India in its website mentions that sixteen Programmes are recognised by the Central Government as Flagship Programmes. However, the B.K. Chaturbedi Committee on its Report on Restructuring Centrally Sponsored Schemes has mentioned nine Flagship Programmes. In addition, the NRLM has also been proposed by the said Committee as Flagship programme in view of its financial outlay, broad scope and objectives. The Planning Commission at Box 1.1 in the Approach Paper of the Twelfth Plan has mentioned thirteen programmes as Flagship Programmes. Further, the Planning Commission has also mentioned seven major Flagship Programmes in rural areas at Para 6.8 in the said Approach Paper. Incidentally, the Planning Commission has mentioned fifteen Flagship Programmes for monitoring under State Plan at Annexure-IX in the draft Annual State Plan for 2012-13.

In view of the fact that there are no definite picture about the name and number of Flagship Programmes, it would be appropriate to place them separately under four parts:

- Part A (as mentioned at Box 1.1 in the Approach Paper of the Twelfth Plan);
- Part B (as mentioned at para 6.8 of the Approach Paper of the Twelfth Plan);
- Part C (as mentioned by the Planning Commission at Annexure-IX for the draft Annual State Plan), 2012-13; and
- Part D (additional programmes as mentioned by the Press Information Bureau of the Government of India).

Since these Flagship Programmes are very important for appropriate address during State Planning, a summary position of all of them is indicated below for planning guidance:

PART-A

(As mentioned at Box 1.1 in the Approach Paper of the Twelfth Plan)

1. National Rural Employment Guarantee Programme

The National Rural Employment Guarantee Act (NREGA), notified on September 7, 2005, is to enhance livelihood security in rural areas by providing at least 100 days of guaranteed wage employment in a financial year to every household whose adult members volunteer to do unskilled manual work. The NAREGA strives to achieve the following goals:

(a) Strong social safety net for the vulnerable groups by providing a fall-back employment source, when other employment alternatives are scarce or inadequate.

(b) Growth engine for sustainable development of an agricultural economy. Through the process of providing employment on works that address causes of chronic poverty such as drought, deforestation and soil erosion, the Act seeks to strengthen the natural resource base of rural livelihood and create durable assets in rural areas. Effectively implemented, NREGA has the potential to transform the geography of poverty.

(c) Empowerment of rural poor through the processes of a rights-based Law.

(d) New ways of doing business, as a model of governance reform anchored on the principles of transparency and grass root democracy.

Thus, NREGA fosters conditions for inclusive growth ranging from basic wage security and recharging rural economy to a transformative empowerment process of democracy. The Act was notified in 200 districts in the first phase with effect from February 2006 and then extended to additional 130 districts in the financial year 2007-08. The remaining districts have been notified under the NREGA with effect from April 1, 2008. Thus, NREGA covers the entire country with the exception of districts that have a hundred per cent urban population. The Act has since been renamed as Mahatma Gandhi National Rural Employment Guarantee Act (MGNREGA).

Salient Features of the NREGA

(i) Adult members of a rural household, willing to do unskilled manual work, may apply for registration in writing or orally to the local Gram Panchayat.

(ii) The Gram Panchayat after due verification will issue a Job Card. The Job Card will bear the photograph of all adult members of the household willing to work under NREGA and is free of cost.

(iii) The Job Card should be issued within 15 days of application.

(iv) A Job Card holder may submit a written application for employment to the Gram Panchayat, stating the time and duration for which work is sought. The minimum days of employment have to be at least fourteen.

(v) The Gram Panchayat will issue a dated receipt of the written application for employment, against which the guarantee of providing employment within 15 days operates.

(vi) Employment will be given within 15 days of application for work, if it is not then daily unemployment allowance as per the Act, has to be paid liability of payment of unemployment allowance is of the States.

(vii) Work should ordinarily be provided within 5 km radius of the village. In case work is provided beyond 5 km, extra wages of 10 per cent are payable to meet additional transportation and living expenses.

(viii) Wages are to be paid according to the Minimum Wages Act 1948 for agricultural labourers in the State, unless the Centre notifies a wage rate which will not be less than Rs. 60 per day. Equal wages will be provided to both men and women.

(ix) Wages are to be paid according to piece rate or daily rate. Disbursement of wages has to be done on weekly basis and not beyond a fortnight in any case.

(x) At least one-third beneficiaries shall be women who have registered and requested work under the scheme.

(xi) Work site facilities such as crèche, drinking water, shade have to be provided.

(xii) The shelf of projects for a village will be recommended by the Gram Sabha and approved by the Zilla Panchayat.

(xiii) At least 50 per cent of works will be allotted to Gram Panchayats for execution.

(xiv) Permissible works predominantly include water and soil conservation, afforestation and land development works.
(xv) A 60 : 40 wage and material ratio has to be maintained. No contractors and machinery is allowed.
(xvi) The Central Government bears the 100 per cent wage cost of unskilled manual labour and 75 per cent of the material cost including the wages of skilled and semi-skilled workers.
(xvii) Social Audit has to be done by the Gram Sabha.
(xviii) Grievance redressal mechanisms have to be put in place for ensuring a responsive implementation process.
(xix) All accounts and records relating to the Scheme should be available for public scrutiny.

Under Section 4 of the Act, the Scheme to be formulated by the State Government will conform to the legally non-negotiable parameters laid down in Schedules I and II of the Act. In addition, the Schemes will conform to the operational parameters delineated in the Guidelines. The Scheme so formulated will be called the National Rural Employment Guarantee Scheme (NREGS), followed by the name of the State. The national level name and logo is mandatory. This logo will be used for all IEC materials and activities.

The Scheme will be implemented as a Centrally Sponsored Scheme on a cost-sharing basis between the Centre and the States as determined by the Act.

2. Indira Awaas Yojana (IAY)

Indira Awaas Yojana seeks to provide financial assistance to the rural poor living Below the Poverty Line (BPL) for construction of a house. BPL rural households of Scheduled Castes, Scheduled Tribes, non-Scheduled Castes and non-Scheduled Tribes, Ex-servicemen of the armed and paramilitary forces killed in action, physically and mentally challenged persons, freed bonded labourers and Minorities are eligible to get assistance under Indira Awaas Yojana.

The financial assistance provided for new construction under IAY is Rs. 35,000 per unit for the plain areas and Rs. 38,500 for the hilly/difficult areas. The assistance for upgradation of unserviceable kutcha house to pucca/semi-pucca house is Rs. 15,000 for all areas. The assistance for credit-cum-subsidy scheme is also Rs. 12,500 per unit. Maximum of 20 per cent of IAY allocation can be utilized for upgradation and/or credit-cum-subsidy scheme. Further, provision has been made to extend lower interest rates for construction of IAY houses in rural areas.

Selection of beneficiaries is based on the permanent IAY waitlists wherever these have been prepared or from the BPL list 2002 with the poorest being selected on priority. On the basis of allocations made and targets fixed, District Panchayat/Zilla Panchayat/District Rural Development Agencies (DRDAs) decide the number of houses to be constructed/upgraded Panchayat-wise under IAY, during a particular financial year. The benefits of the Scheme have since been extended to the families of ex-servicemen of the armed forces and paramilitary forces killed in action. Besides, 3 per cent of the houses are reserved for the physically and mentally challenged persons of the rural BPL families. Funds are also been earmarked for coverage of minorities.

Funding of IAY is shared between the Centre and the State in the ratio of 75 : 25; in case of UTs the entire fund of IAY is provided by the Centre to the District Rural Development Agencies (DRDAs) which release funds to beneficiaries through Gram Panchayat.

3. National Social Assistance Programme (NSAP)

National Social Assistance Programme, which came into effect from 15th August, 1995, comprises of Indira Gandhi National Old Age Pension Scheme (IGNOAPS), National Family Benefit Scheme (NFBS) and Annapurna Scheme.

(a) Indira Gandhi National Old Age Pension Scheme (IGNOAPS)

The eligibility criteria under Indira Gandhi National Old Age Pension Scheme is that the age of the applicant (male or female) should be 65 years or above and that the applicant should be belonging to a household living below the poverty line according to the criteria prescribed by the Government of India.

The IGNOAPS is different from the earlier National Old Age Pension Scheme (NOAPS) in that under NOAPS, old age pension were granted to a person who is 65 years old or higher and who is destitute in the sense of having little or no means of regular income. Pension under IGNOAPS is now granted to a person who is 65 years or above and belongs to a household below the poverty line instead of only to destitute. The National Old Age Pension Scheme has also been renamed as Indira Gandhi National Old Age Pension Scheme (IGNOPS) and formally launched on

19th November, 2007. All the persons, including women, who are 65 years of age in a BPL family, are eligible to get old age pension.

The pension amount under Indira Gandhi National Old Age is rather flexible. However, the Central Government's contribution of pension under the Indira Gandhi National Old Age Pension Scheme (IGNOAPS) is Rs. 200 per month per beneficiary and the State Governments may contribute over and above to this amount. At present old age beneficiaries are getting anywhere between Rs. 200 to Rs. 1,000 depending on the State Contribution. As per the Government of India's decision, pension has to be credited in bank account/post office account of the beneficiary wherever feasible.

(b) National Family Benefit Scheme

Under National Family Benefit Scheme, Central Assistance is given in the form of lump sum family benefit for households below the poverty line on the death of the primary breadwinner in the bereaved family on the following conditions:

- The primary breadwinner shall be a member whose earnings contribute substantially to the household income.
- The death of such primary breadwinner occurs while he or she is more than 18 years and less than 65 years of age.
- The bereaved family qualifies as one below the poverty line according to the criteria prescribed by the Government of India.

The amount of benefit is Rs. 10,000 in case of death of primary breadwinner due to natural or accidental causes. The family benefit is paid to such surviving member of the household of the deceased who, after local enquiry is determined to be the head of the household.

(c) Annapurna Scheme

Annapurna Scheme introduced on 1st April, 2000 aimed at providing food security to meet the requirement of those senior citizens who, though eligible, have remained uncovered under the NOAPS. Under the Annapurna Scheme, 10 kgs of foodgrains per month are provided free of cost to the beneficiary.

4. Pradhan Mantri Gram Sadak Yojana (PMGSY)

Pradhan Mantri Gram Sadak Yojana launched in December 2000 is a centrally sponsored programme aimed at providing connectivity to target habitations through construction of good all-weather roads. This programme is a special central intervention as part of a poverty reduction strategy. Though rural roads are a State subject, the Central Government is providing 100 per cent financial assistance for construction and upgradation of Rural Roads.

The Primary objective of PMGSY is to provide connectivity to unconnected habitations in rural areas by good all-weather roads. Habitations with a population of 1,000 and above shall be eligible in the first phase, and those with a population of 500-1000 shall be eligible in the second phase. In respect of the Hill States, the objective is to connect habitations with a population of 250 and above.

The population, as recorded in the Census 2001, shall be the basis for determining the population size of the habitation. The population of all habitations within a radius of 500 metres (1.5 km of path distance in case of hills) may be clubbed together for the purpose of determining the population size. This cluster approach would enable provision of connectivity to a larger number of habitations, particularly in the Hill/ Mountainous areas. The eligible Unconnected Habitations are to be connected to nearby habitations already connected by an All-weather road or to another existing All-weather road so that services (educational, health, marketing facilities, etc.), which are not available in the unconnected habitation, become available to the residents.

All-weather road in this context means one which is negotiable in all seasons of the year. This implies that road-bed is drained effectively but this does not necessarily imply that it should be paved surface with black-topping or cement concrete. A gravel road can also be an all-weather road. Minor bridges on rivers/streams crossing the alignment of the road may also be taken up under the programme. In case the span of CD work exceeds 25m, *pro rata* cost beyond 25 m is required to be provided by the State Government. Incidentally, Rural Roads is a State subject and it is the responsibility of State Government/District Panchayat to ensure availability of land for construction of road works under the programme. If land is acquired for the purpose of construction of roads under PMGSY, the State Government is required to pay compensation. The routine maintenance of road works for a period of 5 years after completion of work is to be made by the contractor. Programme guidelines envisage transfer of road works for maintenance to Panchayati Raj Institutions after 5 years upon completion of the road work. The targets set under rural roads component of Bharat Nirman are being achieved through construction and upgradation of rural roads under Pradhan Mantri Gram Sadak Yojana.

5. National Rural Health Mission (NRHM)

National Rural Health Mission (NRHM) seeks to provide effective health care to the rural population, especially the disadvantaged groups including women and children, by improving access, enabling community ownership and demand for services, strengthening public health systems for efficient service delivery, enhancing equity and accountability and promoting decentralization. The NRHM covers the entire country, with special focus on 18 States where the challenge of strengthening poor public health systems and thereby improving key health indicators is the greatest. The States of Uttar Pradesh, Uttaranchal, Madhya Pradesh, Chhattisgarh, Bihar, Jharkhand, Orissa, Rajasthan, Himachal Pradesh, Jammu and Kashmir, Assam, Arunachal Pradesh, Manipur, Meghalaya, Nagaland, Mizoram, Sikkim and Tripura are priority States under NRHM.

The NRHM is basically a strategy for integrating ongoing vertical programmes of Health and Family Welfare and addressing issues related to the determinants of Health like Sanitation, Nutrition and Safe Drinking Water. NRHM subsumes key national programmes, namely, the Reproductive and Child Health II Project (RCH II), the National Disease Control Programmes (NDCP) and the Integrated Disease Surveillance Project (IDSP).

The core strategies of NRHM include, decentralized village and district level health planning and management, appointment of Accredited Social Health Activist (ASHA) to facilitate access to health services, strengthening the public health service delivery infrastructure, particularly at village, primary and secondary levels, mainstreaming AYUSH, improved management capacity to organize health systems and services in public health, emphasizing evidence based planning and implementation through improved capacity and infrastructure, promoting the non-profit sector to increase social participation and community empowerment, promoting healthy behaviours and improving intersectoral convergence.

The supplementary strategies of NRHM include regulation of the private sector to improve equity and reduce out of pocket expenses, foster public-private partnerships to meet national public health goals, reorienting medical education, introduction of effective risk pooling mechanisms and social insurance to raise the health security of the poor and taking full advantage of local health traditions.

6. Integrated Child Development Services (ICDS)

Integrated Child Development Services, popularly known as ICDS, is one of the largest programmes of Government of India. It takes care of all-round developmental needs of children who are below six years of age, pregnant women, lactating mothers in the age group of 15-45 years, through the Anganwadi Centres. A package of six services is provided under the ICDS. These are: supplementary nutrition, immunization, health check-up, referral services, non-formal pre-school education, and nutrition and health education. These services are provided in the Anganwadi which means a courtyard, that is, a play centre. It is located within a village or a slum. It is the focal point for delivery of all services provided under ICDS. An Anganwadi worker provides all these services in the Anganwadi Centre. She is an honorary worker selected from the village. She is assisted by a Helper in carrying out her day-to-day activities. The Helper also is selected by the villagers.

The Anganwadi Centre is open on all the six days in a week. It functions for four hours in a day in the morning. The timings may differ from State to State.

If any child is below three years of age, s/he will get supplementary nutrition and proper infant and young child feeding advice. The growth of a child is also regularly monitored at the Anganwadi Centre. In addition, the Anganwadi Centre will take the responsibility of checking up her/his health and also ensure that the child is immunized against six killer diseases like Tuberculosis (TB), Diptheria, Perthussis (whooping cough), Tetanus, Measles and Poliomyelitis by the Auxiliary Nurse Midwife (ANM). In case, any child is between 3-6 years, apart from the above services, s/he will be imparted preschool education also.

Pre-school education implies holistic development of children that ensures their overall physical, cognitive, language, social and emotional development. It also provides stimulating play environment whereby they learn about their surroundings and day-to-day interaction with others. A variety of play material like puppets, dolls, balls, wooden blocks, wet clay, flash card for story telling, puzzles, etc., are available for children in the Anganwadi Centre. Besides, charts of various kinds to identify colour, numbers, animals, vegetables, fruits, transport, etc., are also displayed in the Centres. Anganwadi workers keeps a regular check on the growth of the child by taking her/his weight on regular basis and plotting the same on the growth chart which is maintained separately for each child as per their age. Accordingly, their mothers are counselled so that their children develop in a healthy and robust manner.

A pregnant woman also receives services like health check-up, immunization against Tetanus Toxoid (TT), nutrition and health education and supplementary nutrition. A nursing woman can avail services like health check-up, nutrition and health education and supplementary nutrition. The adolescent girls receives services like nutrition and health education, iron and folic acid supplementation, deworming tablets, non-formal education, home based skill training and vocational training as well as supplementary nutrition. All women between the ages of 15 to 45 years are entitled to nutrition and health education only so that they can motivate others to lead a better quality of life.

7. Mid-Day Meal

The Mid-Day Meal is an important Flagship Programme to feed about 12 crore school children in over 12.65 lakh schools/EGS centres across the country. The programme started initially in three States, viz., Gujarat, Kerala and Tamil Nadu and the UT of Pondicherry in and around 1985 with their own resources for children studying at the primary stage on a universal basis. By 1990-91, twelve States started implementing the Mid-Day Meal programme with their own resources almost on a universal basis.

The National Programme of Nutritional Support to Primary Education (NP-NSPE) was launched as a Centrally Sponsored Scheme on 15th August, 1995 with a view to enhancing enrolment, retention and attendance and simultaneously improving nutritional levels among children initially in 2,408 blocks in the country. By the year 1997-98 the NP-NSPE was introduced in all blocks of the country. It was further extended in 2002 to cover not only children in classes I-V of Government, Government aided and local body schools, but also children studying in EGS and AIE centres. Central Assistance under the scheme consisted of free supply of foodgrains at the rate of 100 grams per child per school day, and subsidy for transportation of foodgrains up to a maximum of Rs. 50 per quintal.

In September 2004, the scheme was revised to provide cooked mid-day meal with 300 calories and 8-12 grams of protein to all children studying in classes I-V in Government and aided schools and EGS/AIE centres. In addition to free supply of foodgrains, the revised scheme provided Central Assistance for (a) Cooking cost at the rate of Re. 1 per child per school day, (b) Transport subsidy was raised from the earlier maximum of Rs. 50 per quintal to Rs. 100 per quintal for special category States, and Rs. 75 per quintal for other States, (c) Management, monitoring and evaluation costs at the rate of 2 per cent of the cost of foodgrains, transport subsidy and cooking assistance, and (d) Provision of mid-day meal during summer vacation in drought affected areas.

In July 2006, the scheme was further revised to provide assistance for cooking cost at the rate of (a) Rs. 1.80 per child/school day for States in the North Eastern Region, provided the NER States contribute Re. 0.20 per child/school day, and (b) Rs. 1.50 per child/school day for other States and UTs, provided that these States and UTs contribute Re. 0.50 per child/school day.

In October 2007, the scheme has been further revised to cover children in upper primary (classes VI to VIII) initially in 3,479 Educationally Backwards Blocks (EBBs). Around 1.7 crore upper primary children were included by this expansion of the scheme. From 2008-09, i.e., w.e.f. 1st April, 2008, the programme covers all children studying in Government, Local Body and Government-aided primary and upper primary schools and the EGS/AIE centres including *madarsa* and *maqtabs* supported under SSA of all areas across the country. The calorific value of a mid-day meal at upper primary stage has been fixed at a minimum of 700 calories and 20 grams of protein by providing 150 grams of food-grains (rice/wheat) per child/school day.

During the year 2009 the following changes have been made to improve the implementation of the scheme:

(a) Food norms have been revised to ensure balanced and nutritious diet to children of upper primary group by increasing the quantity of pulses from 25 to 30 grams, vegetables from 65 to 75 grams and by decreasing the quantity of oil and fat from 10 grams to 7.5 grams.

(b) Cooking cost (excluding the labour and administrative charges) has been revised from Rs. 1.68 to to Rs. 2.50 for primary and from Rs. 2.20 to Rs. 3.75 for upper primary children from 1-12-2009 to facilitate serving meal to eligible children in prescribed quantity and of good quality. The cooking cost for primary is Rs. 2.69 per child per day and Rs. 4.03 for upper primary children from 1-4-2010. The cooking cost is due to be revised by 7.5 per cent from 1-4-2011.

(c) The honorarium for cooks and helpers was paid from the labour and other administrative charges of Re. 0.40 per child per day provided under the cooking cost. In many cases the honorarium was so little that it became very difficult to engage manpower for cooking the meal. A separate component for Payment of Honorarium @ Rs. 1,000 per month per cook-cum-helper was introduced from 1-12-2009. Honorarium at the above prescribed rate is being paid to cook-cum-helper. Following norms for engagement of cook-cum-helper have been made:

(i) One cook-cum-helper for schools up to 25 students.

(ii) Two cooks-cum-helpers for schools with 26 to 100 students.

(iii) One additional cook-cum-helper for every addition of up to 100 students.

More than 26 lakhs cook-cum-helper at present are engaged by the State/UTs during 2010-11 for preparation and serving of Mid-Day Meal to Children in Elementary Classes.

(d) A common unit cost of construction of kitchen shed at Rs. 60,000 for the whole country was impractical and also inadequate. Now the cost of construction of kitchen-cum-store will be determined on the basis of plinth area norm and State Schedule of Rates. The Department of School Education and Literacy vide letter No. 1-1/2009-Desk (MDM) dated 31-12-2009 had prescribed 20 sq.mt. plinth area for schools having up to 100 children. For every additional up to 100 children additional 4 sq. mt plinth area will be added. States/UTs have the flexibility to modify the slab of 100 children depending upon the local condition.

(e) Due to difficult geographical terrain of the Special category States the transportation cost at Rs. 1.25 per quintal was not adequate to meet the actual cost of transportation of foodgrains from the FCI godowns to schools in these States. On the request of the North Eastern States the transportation assistance in the 11 Special Category States (Northern Eastern States, Himachal Pradesh, Jammu and Kashmir and Uttarakhand) have been made at par with the Public Distribution System (PDS) rates prevalent in these States with effect from 1-12-2009.

(f) The existing system of payment of cost of foodgrains to FCI from the Government of India is prone to delays and risk. Decentralization of payment of cost of foodgrains to the FCI at the district level from 1-4-2010 will allow officers at State and national levels to focus on detailed monitoring of the Scheme. Mid-Day Meal scheme is now serving primary and upper primary school children in the entire country.

The sharing of cost between the Government of India and the State governments varies from year to year.

8. Sarva Shiksha Abhiyan

Sarva Shiksha Abhiyan (SSA) is Government of India's Flagship Programme for achievement of Universalization of Elementary Education (UEE) in a time bound manner, as mandated by Eighty Sixth Amendment to the Constitution of India making free and compulsory Education to the children of 6-14 years age group, a Fundamental Right.

SSA is being implemented in partnership with State governments to cover the entire country and address the needs of 192 million children in 1.1 million habitations.

The programme seeks to open new schools in those habitations which do not have schooling facilities and strengthen existing school infrastructure through provision of additional class rooms, toilets, drinking water, maintenance grant and school improvement grants.

Existing schools with inadequate teacher strength are provided with additional teachers, while the capacity of existing teachers is being strengthened by extensive training, grants for developing teaching-learning materials and strengthening of the academic support structure at a cluster, block and district level.

SSA seeks to provide quality elementary education including life skills. SSA has a special focus on girl's education and children with special needs. SSA also seeks to provide computer education to bridge the digital divide.

9. Jawaharlal Nehru National Urban Renewal Mission (JNNURM)

The Mission

Mission Statement: The aim is to encourage reforms and fast track planned development of identified cities. Focus is to be on efficiency in urban infrastructure and service delivery mechanisms, community participation, and accountability of ULBs/Parastatal agencies towards citizens.

2. Objectives of the Mission

(1) The objectives of the JNNURM are to ensure that the following are achieved in the urban sector:

(a) Focused attention to integrated development of infrastructure services in cities covered under the Mission;.

(b) Establishment of linkages between asset-creation and asset-management through a slew of reforms for long-term project sustainability;.

(c) Ensuring adequate funds to meet the deficiencies in urban infrastructural services;.

(d) Planned development of identified cities including peri-urban areas, outgrowths and urban corridors leading to dispersed urbanisation;.

(e) Scale-up delivery of civic amenities and provision of utilities with emphasis on universal access to the urban poor;.

(f) Special focus on urban renewal programme for the old city areas to reduce congestion; and

(g) Provision of basic services to the urban poor including security of tenure at affordable prices, improved housing, water supply and sanitation, and ensuring delivery of other existing universal services of the government for education, health and social security.

3. Scope of the Mission

The Mission shall comprise two Sub-Missions, namely:

(1) *Sub-Mission for Urban Infrastructure and Governance:* This will be administered by the Ministry of Urban Development through the Sub-Mission Directorate for Urban Infrastructure and Governance. The main thrust of the Sub-Mission will be on infrastructure projects relating to water supply and sanitation, sewerage, solid waste management, road network, urban transport and redevelopment of old city areas with a view to upgrading infrastructure therein, shifting industrial and commercial establishments to conforming areas, etc.

(2) *Sub-Mission for Basic Services to the Urban Poor:* This will be administered by the Ministry of Urban Employment and Poverty Alleviation through the Sub-Mission Directorate for Basic Services to the Urban Poor. The main thrust of the Sub-Mission will be on integrated development of slums through projects for providing shelter, basic services and other related civic amenities with a view to providing utilities to the urban poor.

4. Strategy of the Mission

The objectives of the Mission shall be met through the adoption of the following strategy:

(1) *Preparing City Development Plan:* Every city will be expected to formulate a City Development Plan (CDP) indicating policies, programmes and strategies, and financing plans.

(2) *Preparing Projects:* The CDP would facilitate identification of projects. The Urban Local Bodies (ULBs)/parastatal agencies will be required to prepare Detailed Project Reports (DPRs) for undertaking projects in the identified spheres. It is essential that projects are planned in a manner that optimises the lifecycle cost of projects. The lifecycle cost of a project would cover the capital outlays and the attendant O&M costs to ensure that assets are in good working condition. A revolving fund would be created to meet the O&M requirements of assets created, over the planning horizon. In order to seek JNNURM assistance, projects would need to be developed in a manner that would ensure and demonstrate optimisation of the lifecycle costs over the planning horizon of the project.

(3) *Release and Leveraging of Funds:* It is expected that the JNNURM assistance would serve to catalyse the flow of investment into the urban infrastructure sector across the country. Funds from the Central and State Government will flow directly to the nodal agency designated by the State, as grants-in-aid. The funds for identified projects across cities would be disbursed to the ULB/Parastatal agency through the designated State Level Nodal Agency (SLNA) as soft loan or grant-cum-loan or grant. The SLNA/ULBs in turn would leverage additional resources from other sources.

(4) *Incorporating Private Sector Efficiencies:* In order to optimise the lifecycle costs over the planning horizon, private sector efficiencies can be inducted in development, management, implementation and financing of projects, through Public-Private Partnership (PPP) arrangements.

5. Duration of the Mission

The duration of the Mission would be seven years beginning from the year 2005-06. Evaluation of the experience of implementation of the Mission would be undertaken before the commencement of Eleventh Five Year Plan and if necessary, the programme calibrated suitably.

6. Expected Outcomes of the JNNURM

On completion of the Mission period, it is expected that ULBs and parastatal agencies will have achieved the following:

(1) Modern and transparent budgeting, accounting, financial management systems designed and adopted for all urban service and governance functions.
(2) City-wide framework for planning and governance will be established and become operational.
(3) All urban residents will be able to obtain access to a basic level of urban services.
(4) Financially self-sustaining agencies for urban governance and service delivery will be established, through reforms to major revenue instruments.
(5) Local services and governance will be conducted in a manner that is transparent and accountable to citizens.
(6) E-governance applications will be introduced in core functions of ULBs/Parastatal resulting in reduced cost and time of service delivery processes.

Financial Assistance under JNNURM

The Government of India has proposed substantial assistance through the JNNURM over the seven-year period. During this period, funds shall be provided for proposals that would meet the Mission's requirements. Under JNNURM financial assistance will be available to the ULBs and parastatal agencies which could deploy these funds for implementing the projects themselves or through the Special Purpose Vehicles (SPVs) that may be expected to be set up. Assistance under JNNURM is additional central assistance, which would be provided as grant (100 per cent central grant) to the implementing agencies. Further, assistance from JNNURM is expected to facilitate further investment in the urban sector. To this end, the implementing agencies are expected to leverage the sanctioned funds under JNNURM to attract greater private sector investments through PPP that enables sharing of risks between the private and public sector.

Areas of Assistance under JNNURM

(1) Assistance for Capacity Building, City Development Plan (CDP), Detailed Project Reports (DPRs), Community Participation, Information, Education and Communication (IEC)

The JNNURM will provide assistance for the above-stated components with a provision of 5 per cent of the total central assistance or the actual requirement, whichever is less. In addition, not more than 5 per cent of the Central grant or the actual requirement, whichever is less may be used for Administrative and Other Expenses (A&OE) by the States.

For capacity building, ULBs and parastatal agencies could engage consultants, in consultation with the SLNA, and seek reimbursement from the Ministry of Urban Development (MoUD) of the Ministry of Urban Employment and Poverty Alleviation (MoUEPA).

(2) Investment Support Component

Investment support will be provided to implementing agencies on a project-specific basis for eligible sectors and projects proposed to be undertaken in eligible cities subject to approval of the Central Sanctioning and Monitoring Committee (CSMC) of MoUD/MoUEPA. As part of the process for seeking investment support, each ULB seeking assistance from the JNNURM would be required to prepare a CDP that shall *inter alia* include strategy to implement reforms, city-level improvements and an investment plan to address the infrastructure needs in a sustainable manner. Assistance under investment support can be deployed in the following forms:

(a) *Enhancing Resource Availability:* The JNNURM assistance can be used to leverage additional resources available with the ULBs in addition to their existing resources and transfers from the State. These resources could be utilised for capital investment and O&M investments in a project.
(b) *Enhancing Commercial Viability of Projects*: In respect of projects, which are not commercially viable on a stand-alone basis, assistance under the JNNURM may be sought for enhancing project viability. This assistance could be in the nature of viability gap support to projects.

(c) *Ensuring Bankability of Projects:* Cash flows of infrastructure projects having long gestation periods are susceptible to variations in cash flows, rendering a project non-bankable. To enhance predictability of underlying cash-flows, credit enhancement mechanisms such as establishing liquidity support mechanisms, up-front debt-service reserve facility, deep discount bonds, contingent liability support and equity support are required in order to make the projects bankable. The JNNURM assistance could, therefore, be used for funding such support mechanisms.

10. Accelerated Irrigation Benefit Programme (AIBP) and Other Water Resources Programme

A large number of river valley projects, both multipurpose and irrigation have spilled over from Plan to Plan mainly on financial constraints being faced by the State governments. As a result, despite a huge investment on these projects, the country did not derive the desired benefits from around 171 Major, 259 Medium and 72 ERM ongoing Irrigation projects by the end of March 1997. This was a matter of grave concern and the AIBP was conceived by the Government of India in order to provide financial assistance to States to complete various ongoing projects to extend irrigation to more areas.

The eligibility criteria for inclusion of major/medium irrigation projects in AIBP are that only ongoing major/medium projects and Extension, Renovation and Modernisation projects having investment clearance of the Planning Commission and which could be completed in next 4 financial years and not receiving financial assistance from any other national or international agency, such as NABARD, etc., could be considered for inclusion in AIBP subject to fulfilment of other criteria prescribed in AIBP guidelines. A new project could be included in AIBP on completion of an ongoing project under AIBP in the State on 1 to 1 basis. However, projects included in PM package for agrarian distress districts, projects benefiting drought prone/tribal area and projects in States having irrigation development below national average could be included in AIBP in relaxation of 1 to 1 criteria.

A separate eligibility criteria has also been framed for inclusion of Surface Water Minor Irrigation schemes under AIBP. Surface Minor Irrigation (MI) schemes (both new as well as ongoing) of States of North-East, Hilly States (Himachal Pradesh, Sikkim, Jammu and Kashmir and

Uttaranchal) and drought prone Koraput, Bolangir and Kalahandi (KBK) districts of Orissa which are approved by State TAC/State Planning Department will be eligible for assistance under the programme provided that: (i) individual schemes are benefiting irrigation potential of at least 20 ha and group of schemes (within a radius of 5 km) benefiting total ultimate irrigation potential of at least 50 ha; (ii) proposed MI schemes have benefit cost ratio of more than 1; and (iii) the development cost of these schemes per ha. is less than Rs. 1.50 lakh.

For Non-Special category States, only those minor irrigation schemes with potential of more than 50 hectares benefiting tribal/drought prone areas could be included under AIBP. The schemes to be taken up are to be decided in consultation with Planning Commission.

Funding under AIBP was started as Central Loan Assistance (CLA). Initially 50 per cent of the project outlay was provided as CLA and the balance 50 per cent was to be met by State, i.e., on 1:1 basis. Subsequently Special Category States were provided CLA on 3:1 basis whereas non-Special Category States on 2:1 basis. Later, it was decided that 30 per cent of the CLA to non-Special Category States and 90 per cent for Special Category States be converted into grant. In March 2005 in order to accelerate the provision of irrigation to drought prone areas and tribal area, the project providing irrigation benefits to such area (in consultation with Planning Commission) were extended the same facility as allowable to the Special Category States. From April 2005, the Centre is providing only grant assistance to the projects under AIBP and rest of the finances are to be raised by States themselves either through Plan allocations or State resources or loans. AIBP guidelines were further modified in December 2006 to provide enhanced assistance at 90 per cent of the project cost as grant to Special Category States, Drought Prone Area Programme (DPAP) States/tribal areas/flood-prone areas and Koraput-Bolangir-Kalahandi (KBK) districts of Orissa.

11. Rajiv Gandhi Grameen Vidyutikaran Yojana (RGGVY)

Central Government launched "Rajiv Gandhi Grameen Vidyutikaran Yojana" on 4th April, 2005 for attaining the National Common Minimum Programme (NCMP) goal of providing access to electricity to all households in the country in five years. The scheme aims at electrification of over 1 lakh unelectrified villages and providing electricity connections to 2.34 crore rural households. The estimated cost of the scheme is approximately Rs. 51,000 crore.

Under the scheme, Central Government provides 90 per cent Capital subsidy for construction of Rural Electricity Distribution Backbone (REDB), Creation of Village Electrification Infrastructure (VEI), and Decentralised Distributed Generation (DDG). Below Poverty Line (BPL) households will be provided free electricity connections with 100 per cent capital subsidy amounting Rs. 2,200 per household in all rural habitations. APL (above poverty line) households will obtain connections according to procedure prescribed by State utilities.10 per cent of the project cost will be provided by Rural Electrification Corporation (REC) as soft loan. A village or hamlet with population of 100 or more is eligible for the scheme. All the BPL families are eligible for free connections under the scheme. In case of APL connection, applicant will have to make an application to the concerned Vidyut Karyalaya nearby State utility office. Households above poverty line will pay for their connections at the State prescribed connection charges and no subsidy will be available for this purpose. Access to electricity is also provided to school buildings/ dispensaries/Panchayat office under the scheme.

Under the scheme, State power utility prepares the Detailed Project Report in accordance with the RGGVY Guidelines. It is the responsibility of State power utility to include all the unelectrified villages and hamlets (above 100 population) in the DPR. The utility should also include already electrified villages, which need intensive electrification to provide access to electricity to all the rural households and to provide free connections to BPL families without electricity connection at present.

The RGGVY is funded by the Central Government and under the scheme, projects are financed with 90 per cent capital subsidy by the Central Government for provision of Rural Electricity Distribution Backbone (REDB), Creation of Village Electrification Infrastructure (VEI) and Decentralised Distributed Generation (DDG), wherever required. Electrification of unelectrified Below Poverty Line (BPL) households will be financed with 100 per cent capital subsidy amounting to Rs. 2,200 per household in all rural habitations. Households above poverty line will pay for their connections at State prescribed connection charges and no subsidy will be available for this purpose.

Based on recently awarded rural electrification projects, the Ministry of Power has formulated following cost norms for village electrification in various targeted areas:

1. Cost of electrification of unelectrified village:
   (a) In normal terrain . . . . . . Rs. 13 Lakh

(b) In hilly, tribal, desert areas . . . . . . Rs. 18 Lakh

2. Intensive electrification of already electrified village:
   (a) In normal terrain Rs. 4 Lakh
   (b) In hilly, tribal, desert areas Rs. 6 Lakh
3. Cost of electricity connection to BPL Household Rs. 0.022 Lakh

The State power utilities have the responsibility of implementing the work of rural electrification in their respective States. However, keeping in view the huge amount of work, Government of India has made the services of CPSUs available to the State utilities for implementing RGGVY scheme. States, interested in availing the services of CPSUs may enter into MoUs with the CPSU(s) for availing their services.

States are required to formulate their Rural Electrification Plans to achieve the goal of providing access to all households. The Rural Electrification Plan is to map the requirements in respect of rural electrification and detail the electrification delivery mechanism (grid or stand alone) planning for *inter alia*, the availability of sufficient power, provision of suitable transmission and sub-transmission network, electricity to remote villages, requirement and availability of funds from different sources, deployment of franchisee, determination of bulk supply tariff for franchisees, etc. The Plan may be linked to and integrated with district Development Plans as and when such plans become available. The plan should be intimated to the Appropriate Commission.

12. Rajiv Gandhi Drinking Water Mission (Rural Drinking Water)—NRDWP and Total Sanitation Campaign (TSC)

(a) National Rural Drinking Water Programme (NRDWP)

The Ministry of Drinking Water and Sanitation (MDWS) administers the National Rural Drinking Water Programme (NRDWP), through which the Central Government provides financial and technical support to supplement the efforts of States to provide adequate potable drinking water to the rural population. Rural drinking water supply is a State subject and has also been included in the Eleventh Schedule of the Constitution among the subjects that may be entrusted to Panchayats by the States.

The NRDWP has the following goals/objectives:

- To ensure provision of safe and adequate drinking water supply to all uncovered, partially covered and quality affected habitations in the rural areas of the country;

- To ensure that all schools and anganwadis have access to safe drinking water;
- To enable GPs/VWSCs to plan, manage, operate and maintain local water sources and water supply; to provide enabling support and environment for PRIs and local communities for this purpose;
- To enable rural communities to monitor and keep surveillance on their drinking water sources, water supply and initiate corrective action to have contaminants free water;
- To ensure equity—high priority in coverage/investment habitations with high SCs/STs and minority population;
- To promote participatory integrated water resources management with a view to ensure drinking water security—water availability, supply and consumption to be measured;
- To provide access to information through online reporting system with information in public domain to bring in transparency and informed decision-making;
- Ensuring household level drinking water security through water budgeting and preparation of village water security plans;
- Consciously move away from high cost treatment technologies for tackling arsenic and fluoride contamination to development of alternative sources in respect of arsenic and alternate sources/ dilution of aquifers through rainwater harvesting for tackling fluoride contamination; and
- To encourage handing over of management of Rural Drinking Water Schemes (RDWS) to the Panchayati Raj Institutions.

The NRDWP guidelines mandate that the PRIs and the local community be involved at all stages from planning, implementation, operation and maintenance and monitoring of drinking water supply schemes. This is because drinking water security is best managed at the local level where attention is given to conservation of water, equity in distribution and usage addressed and immediate action taken for necessary repairs so that regular supply is assured.

For the implementation of this the following structure is established.

(i) A *Water and Sanitation Support Organisation (WSSO)* in each State under the State Water and Sanitation Mission, to be staffed by consultants with expertise in IEC, HRD, Water Quality, Monitoring and Evaluation (M&E), Hydrogeology and Sanitation and Hygiene; and

(ii) The *District Water and Sanitation Mission (DWSM)* at district level with consultants having expertise in IEC, HRD, Monitoring and Evaluation, Hydrogeology Sanitation and Hygiene. This will strengthen the rural water supply department and also facilitate effective convergence with related departments and schemes such as SSA, NHRM, ICDS, BRGF, etc.; and

(*iii*) Establishment of *Block Resource Centre (BRC)* at the Block level under the administrative control and supervision of the Block Panchayat through an NGO, for community mobilization for formation/activation of Village Water and Sanitation Committees (VWSC) and enhanced IEC activities for awareness generation, technical support and capacity building for Gram Panchayats (GPs) to enable them to fulfil their role in sustainable water supply and sanitation; water quality monitoring and managerial aspects of operation and maintenance of the water supply systems. Each Block Resource Centre to be staffed with one to four grassroot level workers (depending on the population in the Block area).

Rural Water Supply in IAP District

NRDWP has now been made more flexible to ensure provision of Drinking Water and Sanitation under the Integrated Action Plan for tribal and backward districts across nine States. Unlike ARWSP, flexibility has now been brought under for the benefits of ST concentrated habitations and IAP areas in the following manner:

- The requirement of minimum population of 100 persons in a habitation to be considered for coverage with drinking water supply has been removed. Now habitations with less than 100 persons can and should also be covered under NRDWP.
  This will benefit tribal and small remote habitations in IAP districts.
- The norm that one hand pump be installed for every 250 persons at a distance of 1.6 km has also been removed, giving flexibility to States to install hand pumps based on need and convenience.
- For better coverage of ST concentrated habitations, funds under NRDWP have been earmarked and released for Tribal Sub-Plan in proportion to the ST population in each State. These are for utilisation only in ST concentrated habitations. States should

give priority for coverage of ST concentrated habitations and IAP districts.

(b) Total Sanitation Campaign

Government of India had launched Central Rural Sanitation Programme (CRSP) in the year 1986 with the objective of accelerating sanitation coverage in rural areas. CRSP was restructured and Total Sanitation Campaign (TSC) was launched in 1999 advocating a shift from high subsidy to a low subsidy regime, greater household involvement, demand responsiveness, and providing for the promotion of a range of toilet options to promote increased affordability. It also gives strong emphasis on Information, Education and Communication (IEC) and social marketing for demand generation for sanitation facilities, to set up a delivery system through Rural Sanitary Marts (RSMs) and Production Centres (PC) and a thrust on school sanitation. TSC is implemented in a campaign mode-taking district as a unit so that 100 per cent saturation in terms of households, Anganwadi and school toilets can be attained which would result in significant health benefits.

As per the Seventy Third Constitution Amendment Act 1992, sanitation is included in the Eleventh Schedule and is the responsibility of the Panchayats. At the district level, Zila Panchayat is empowered under TSC to implement the project. Similarly, at the Block and village levels, Panchayat Samiti and respective Gram Panchayats are involved in the implementation of TSC. Gram Panchayats have the pivotal role in the implementation of the Total Sanitation Campaign with VO/NGOs/to mobilize for the construction of toilets and also maintain the clean environment by way of safe disposal of wastes. They have the main responsibility in the O&M of the common facilities constructed. Panchayats can also contribute from their own resources for School and Anganwadi Sanitation. Panchayats may also open and operate the Production Centres/Rural Sanitary Marts.

NGOs have an important role in the implementation of TSC in the rural areas. They may be involved in IEC activities as well as in setting up PCs or RSMs. Their services are required to be utilized not only for bringing about awareness among the rural people for the need of rural sanitation but also ensuring that they actually make use of the sanitary latrines.

Under TSC, there is provision of part financing for construction of Individual Household Latrine (IHHL). There is no subsidy for superstructure. The incentive is limited and extended only to Below Poverty Line families as cash after the beneficiary completes the construction of toilet. The incentive is to be given as back ended incentive and shared between Government of India and State governments. There is no subsidy (incentive) for APL families, however, each APL family is to be motivated through IEC to take up IHHL construction. Currently, two models are funded whose unit costs are Rs. 1,500 and Rs. 2,000 respectively. The beneficiaries can spend additional amount for the construction of superstructure and for extra pit. Minimum of 25 per cent of funds for IHHL are marked for SC/ST community and 3 per cent of IHHL toilets are to be constructed for disabled persons.

Under TSC, the following facilities at school level can be provided:

- Toilets and urinals;
- Hand washing facilities;
- Water supply facilities;
- Healthy classrooms (lighting and ventilation) and playgrounds;
- Garbage pit and soakage pit; and
- Drainage system.

Incidentally, in TSC, only rural government schools are covered with water supply, toilet and hand washing facilities. However, private schools may be included in the training programme on health and hygiene education. The construction cost of single unit of school toilet has been kept at Rs. 20,000. Generally, one lavatory and three or four urinals may be sufficient for 100-150 students. For co-education school separate toilets for girls should be provided and there should be two toilets blocks in a school for boys and girls separately which are treated as two separate units and each unit is entitled to have a Central Subsidy up to Rs. 12,000 under TSC for a unit cost of Rs. 20,000.

Toilet without hand-washing facilities has no meaning and, therefore, hand-washing facilities must be provided simultaneously in each toilet block and the following arrangements have to be ensured for hand-washing:

- Wash basin or any other suitable arrangement for hand-washing
- Drums for water;
- Regular water supply;
- Buckets, mugs, soap and soap tray, brush, etc.; and
- Drainage system for washed water.

Village community complex can be set up in such villages where land for constructing individual household latrines is not available. Provision is made in TSC guidelines for construction of Anganwadi toilets in TSC districts. The funds will be shared in 60:30:10 ratio between Central Government, State Government and the community. The maximum unit cost prescribed is Rs. 5,000 for Anganwadi toilet.

Government of India also initiated an incentive scheme to add vigour to the TSC in June 2003, for fully sanitized and open defecation free Gram Panchayats, Blocks, and Districts called the 'Nirmal Gram Puraskar'. The incentive pattern is based on population criteria and it varies from Rs. 50,000 to Rs. 50 lakh.

13. Rashtriya Krishi Vikas Yojana (RKVY)

Concerned with the slow growth in the Agriculture and allied sectors during the Tenth Five Year Plan, the National Development Council (NDC) in its meeting held on 29th May, 2007 resolved to achieve 4 per cent annual growth in the agricultural sector during the Eleventh Plan and called upon the Central and State governments to evolve a strategy to rejuvenate agriculture special Additional Central Assistance Scheme (RKVY). In compliance of the same and in consultation with the Planning Commission, the Ministry of Agriculture prepared the guidelines for the RKVY scheme which are applicable to all the States and Union Territories that fulfil the eligibility conditions. The scheme has an envisaged outlay of Rs. 25,000 crore for the Eleventh Plan period in the form of Additional Central Assistance (ACA).

The main objectives of the scheme are:

(i) To incentivise the States so as to increase public investment in agriculture and allied sectors;
(ii) To provide flexibility and autonomy to States in the process of planning and executing agriculture and allied sector schemes;
(iii) To ensure the preparation of agriculture plans for the districts and the States based on agro-climatic conditions, availability of technology and natural resources;
(iv) To ensure that the local needs/crops/priorities are better reflected in the agricultural plans of the states;
(v) To achieve the goal of reducing the yield gaps in important crops, through focused interventions;
(vi) To maximize returns to the farmers in agriculture and allied sectors; and

(vii) To bring about quantifiable changes in the production and productivity of various components of Agriculture and allied sectors by addressing them in a holistic manner.

The RKVY is a State Plan Scheme. The eligibility for assistance under the scheme would depend upon the amount provided in State Plan Budgets for Agriculture and allied sectors, over and above the base line percentage expenditure incurred by the State governments on Agriculture and allied sectors. The list of allied sectors as indicated by the Planning Commission will be the basis for determining the sectoral expenditure, i.e., Crop Husbandry (including Horticulture), Animal Husbandry and Fisheries, Dairy Development, Agricultural Research and Education, Forestry and Wildlife, Plantation and Agricultural Marketing, Food Storage and Warehousing, Soil and Water Conservation, Agricultural Financial Institutions, other Agricultural Programmes and Cooperation. Each State will ensure that the baseline share of agriculture in its total State Plan expenditure (excluding the assistance under the RKVY) is at least maintained, and upon its doing so, it will be able to access the RKVY funds. The base line would be a moving average and the average of the previous three years will be taken into account for determining the eligibility under the RKVY, after excluding the funds already received. The RKVY funds would be provided to the States as 100 per cent grant by the Central Government. The States are required to prepare the Agriculture Plans for the districts and the State that comprehensively cover resources and indicate definite action plans. Since the RKVY is applicable to the entire State Plan for Agriculture and allied sectors, and seeks to encourage convergence with schemes like NREGS, SGSY and BRGF, the Planning Commission and the Ministry of Agriculture will together examine the States' overall Plan proposals for Agriculture and allied sectors as part of the Annual Plan approval exercise.

Once a State becomes eligible for the RKVY, the quantum of assistance and the process of subsequent allocation to the State will be in accordance with the parameters and the respective weights. There may arise a situation when a particular State becomes ineligible to avail of the funds under the RKVY in a subsequent year due to its lowered expenditure on Agriculture and allied sectors. If this were to happen, the States shall be required to commit their own resources for completing the sanctioned projects/schemes under the RKVY. Each State will prepare a comprehensive State Agricultural Plan (SAP) by integrating the District Plans. The State will have to, at the outset, indicate resources that can flow from the State to the district. The DAP will integrate multiple programmes that are in operation in the district concerned, include the resources and activities indicated by the State, combine the resources available from the other programmes and finalize the plan.

The preparation of the State Agricultural Plan could be a two-way process. In one method, the State nodal department (Agriculture Department) could obtain the draft DAPs from the districts in the first instance and examine if aspects of importance to the State are properly covered in the district plans or not. In the other method, the State Nodal Agency could communicate to the districts in the first instance, the State's priorities that ought to reflect in the respective district plans and the districts may incorporate these in their district plans.

Preface to Part B

The Approach Paper of the Twelfth Five Year Plan mentions at para 6.8 about 7 major Flagship Programmes in rural areas which include the following:

(1) Mahatma Gandhi National Rural Employment Guarantee Act (MGNREGA);
(2) National Rural Livelihood Mission (NRLM)
(3) *Indira Awaas Yojana* (IAY)
(4) National Rural Drinking Water Programme (NRDWP) and Total Sanitation Campaign (TSP)
(5) Integrated Watershed Development Programme (IWDP)
(6) *Pradhan Mantri Grameen Sadak Yojana* (PMGSY)
(7) Rural electrification, including separation of agricultural feeders and *Rajiv Gandhi Grameen Vidyutikaran Yojana* (RGGVY).

Except National Rural Livelihood Mission (NRLM) and Integrated Watershed Development Programme (IWDP), all other Flagship Programmes, as mentioned at Box 1.1 in the Approach Paper of the Twelfth Five Year Plan have been covered at Part-A. A brief outline on the two remaining Flagship Programmes, namely, National Rural Livelihood Mission (NRLM) and Integrated Watershed Development Programme (IWDP) is now indicated at Part B:

PART-B

B.K. Chaturbedi Committee on its Report on Restructuring Centrally

Sponsored Schemes has mentioned nine Flagship Programmes all of which have been included in the Approach Paper at Box 1.1. The said committee also recommended National Rural Livelihood Mission as Flagship Programme which, however, has been mentioned at para 6.8 of the Approach Paper of the Twelfth Plan. The salient features of the National Rural Livelihood Mission (NRLM) are described hereunder:

1. National Rural Livelihood Mission

As a part of national poverty reduction strategy, Swarnjayanti Gram Swarojgar Yojana (SGSY) has been restructured into National Livelihood Mission (NRLM) in 2010. The NRLM is the largest poverty reduction initiative, the largest programme for women, in the world with its goal of reaching nearly 70 million rural households in all rural districts of different States excluding the districts in *Delhi* and *Chandigarh*. However, the Governing Council of the Mission based on the latest available data is empowered to include or exclude the districts for the implementation of various components of the Mission. Government of India will invest substantial fund in terms of billion in NRLM over next seven years including expected allocation for Twelfth Five Year Plan. The objective of the Mission is to reduce poverty among rural BPL by promoting diversified and gainful self-employment and wage employment opportunities which would lead to an appreciable increase in income on sustainable basis. In the long run, it will ensure broad based inclusive growth and reduce disparities by spreading out the benefits from the islands of growth across the regions, sectors and communities.

The Mission has been designed to achieve the following 'Outputs' and 'Outcomes' by 2016-17 (Table 8.1).

The Rural Livelihoods Mission is proposed to have a three-tier interdependent structure. At the apex of the structure will be the National Rural Livelihoods Mission, under the Ministry of Rural Development, Government of India. At the State level, there will be an umbrella organization under the State Department of Rural Development/ Department which is responsible for implementing self-employment/rural livelihoods promotion programmes. The State Level Mission with dedicated professionals and domain experts under the State Department of Rural Department will be guided financially, technically and supported by the NRLM on need basis. The National and the State Mission will have a symbiotic relationship. They will have mutual access to the knowledge and services in the area of rural livelihoods.

Table 8.1: Output and Outcome Targets for the NRLM, 2016-17

(Rs. in lakh)

Sl. No.	*Output/ Outcome Indicator*	*Target for remaining period of 11th Plan*	*Tentative target for 12th Plan*	*Total target by 2016- 17*	*Number of BPL families*
I.	**Outputs***				
1.	Total number of new BPL SHGs to be formed	12.25	15.75**	28	280
2.	No. of SHGs to be provided Revolving Fund support	12.25	15.75	28	280
3.	No. of SHGs to be provided Capital Subsidy	5.25	10.75	16	160
4.	No. of SHGs to be provided Interest Subsidy	10	12	22	220
5.	No. of rural BPL youth to be provided Skill Development Training	15	60	75	75
II.	**Outcomes***				
1.	No. of SHGs to be entering at Micro enterprise level	5.25	10.75	16	160
2.	No. of rural BPL youth to be provided placement support	15	60	75	75

Note: Each SHG having on an average 10 members (one from each family).

* Subject to availability of resources and cooperation from other stakeholders.

The NRLM has been envisaged to perform the following functions:

(i) facilitate establishment of State level umbrella agencies by the State governments for providing institutional support for poverty elimination programmes;

(ii) support State level umbrella organizations in the design and implementation of pro-poor programmes;

(iii) provide professional, technical support and guidance to the State agencies by seeking out and disseminating pro-poor technologies and institutional innovations through research and development and forging linkages between the State agencies and the national centres of excellence;

(iv) liaise with other Missions/departments to explore areas for convergent action and facilitate such convergence to enhance the capabilities and facilitate access to other entitlements such as wage employment, food security, education, health, etc.;

(v) explore and facilitate partnerships between National/State Rural Livelihood Missions and public, private, NGO and Co-operative sector partners, for diversifying and sustaining the livelihoods of the poor;

(vi) undertake/commission studies to assess emerging self-employment/skill based employment opportunities and disseminate the information to the State agencies;

(vii) study best practices in self-employment/micro enterprise activities across the country and support their replication in other parts of the country through workshops, cross-learning visits and exchange programmes;

(viii) develop capacity building and training modules for functionaries of the peoples institutions as well as the State agencies and district units, and other stakeholders participating in the poverty elimination programmes;

(ix) facilitate analysis and dissemination of the impact of changing economic policies on the poor and play policy advocacy role;

(x) act as information warehouse on rural poverty statistics by accessing information from multiple sources;

(xi) identify shortcomings in programme design and implementation and facilitate debates/discussions thereof by experts for finding innovative and workable solutions and their dissemination to the State agencies;

(xii) promote institution of comprehensive monitoring and learning systems at the State agencies and district units, including web enabled MIS and community monitoring systems; and

(xiii) identify high quality institutions in livelihoods education and training and facilitate linkage of the State organizations with missions with such institutions for capacity building of professionals.

It is envisaged that the State governments will transit into the NRLM mode only in a phased manner. Till such time the States do not transit into NRLM mode, the SGSY activities will continue to be implemented as per current guidelines/norms and fund releases will be made to DRDAs as per existing procedures. Funds for implementing the Mission's programmes are proposed to be directly released separately to the State level agency and the DRDAs on the basis of the detailed district-wise annual action plans submitted by the State agencies and approved by the EC of the National Mission, but within the overall allocation indicated for each State on the basis of the poverty ratio. Funds will be released in two instalments based on the progress report and submission of utilization certificates by the district units under intimation to the State level agency. The State level agency will compile and consolidate expenditure details, physical progress and other details and submit to National Mission periodically. MoRD will release 75 per cent of the approved amount to the State Government/DRDA and the State Government will release the balance amount of 25 per cent. In respect of north-eastern States, J&K, Himachal Pradesh and Uttarakhand, the GoI and State share will be in the proportion of 90:10, respectively.

NRLM will have multi-pronged approach to strengthen livelihoods of the rural poor by promoting SHGs, improving existing occupations, providing skill development and placement and other activities thereof. The training and capacity building, deployment of multidisciplinary experts and other initiatives will enhance the credit worthiness of the rural poor. The services of craft persons, community resource persons etc., will be utilized as TOT for capacity building and training under NRLM. The periodic interaction of Mission with Public Sector Banks and other financial institutions to enhance the reach of rural poor to the unbanked areas will ensure their financial inclusion. Further, poors have multiple livelihoods and they need multi-pronged approach to strengthen it. The existing strategy of social mobilization of the poors, their organization into SHGs, training and capacity building, credit linkage for micro enterprise for self-employment will be continued to be one of the main components of NRLM. Emphasis will be on convergence with various schemes of Rural Development along with other Line Departments/Ministries to strengthen the existing occupations of the rural poors, ensure their participation as beneficiary of emerging opportunities as a result of various schemes for sustainable livelihood and also introducing newer technologies in their enterprises. The multidisciplinary domain experts at various levels will coordinate with all the stakeholders for benefiting the poor in risk mitigation, food security, training and capacity building, micro financing, infrastructure development and better marketing linkages for getting appropriate prices for their products. People owned and people centred organization by federating SHGs will act as facilitators for strengthening the SHGs and thereby benefiting the rural poor. In addition skill development and placement will be the subset of the redesigned programme for deploying the rural BPL poor in the sun-rising sectors of the economy. The Mission will make concerted efforts to train rural BPL to provide last tier implementation personnel as service providers, Lok Sevaks, etc., to local bodies to implement the programmes efficiently.

2. Integrated Watershed Development Programme (IWDP—Haryali)

Integrated Watershed Development Programme (IWDP—Haryali) was launched on 27th January, 2003 with the following objectives:

(i) Harvesting every drop of rainwater for purposes of irrigation, plantations including horticulture and floriculture, pasture development, fisheries, etc., to create sustainable sources of income for the village community as well as for drinking water supplies.

(ii) Ensuring overall development of rural areas through the Gram Panchayats and creating regular sources of income for the Panchayats from rainwater harvesting and management.

(iii) Employment generation, poverty alleviation, community empowerment and development of human and other economic resources of the rural areas.

(iv) Mitigating the adverse effects of extreme climatic conditions such as drought and desertification on crops, human and livestock population for the overall improvement of rural areas.

(v) Restoring ecological balance by harnessing, conserving and developing natural resources, i.e., land, water, vegetative cover especially plantations.

(vi) Encouraging village community towards sustained community action for the operation and maintenance of assets created and further development of the potential of the natural resources in the watershed.

(vii) Promoting use of simple, easy and affordable technological solutions and institutional arrangements that make use of, and build upon, local technical knowledge and available materials.

Criteria for Selection of Watersheds

(i) Watersheds where people's participation is assured through contribution of labour, cash, material, etc., for its development as well as for the operation and maintenance of the assets created;

(ii) Watershed areas having acute shortage of drinking water;

(iii) Watersheds having large population of Scheduled Castes/ Scheduled Tribes dependent on it;

(iv) Watershed having a preponderance of non-forest wastelands/ degraded lands;

(v) Watersheds having preponderance of common lands;

(vi) Watersheds where actual wages are significantly lower than the minimum wages;

(vii) Watershed which is contiguous to another watershed that has already been developed/treated; and

(viii) Watershed area may be of an average size of 500 hectares, preferably covering an entire village. However, if on actual survey, a watershed is found to have less or more area, the total area may be taken up for development as a project. In case a watershed covers two or more villages, it should be divided into village-wise sub-watersheds confined to the designated villages. Care should be taken to treat all the sub-watersheds simultaneously.

Activities for Watershed Development

(i) Development of small water harvesting structures such as low-cost farm ponds, nalla-bunds, check-dams, percolation tanks and other groundwater recharge measures;

(ii) Renovation and augmentation of water sources, desiltation of village tanks for drinking water/irrigation/fisheries development;

(iii) Fisheries development in village ponds/tanks, farm ponds etc;

(iv) Afforestation including Block plantations, agro-forestry and horticultural development, shelterbelt plantations, sand dune stabilization, etc.;

(v) Pasture development either by itself or in conjunction with plantations;

(vi) Land Development including *in situ* soil and moisture conservation measures like contour and graded bunds fortified by plantation, bench terracing in hilly terrain, nursery raising for fodder, timber, fuelwood, horticulture and non-timber forest product species;

(vii) Drainage line treatment with a combination of vegetative and engineering structures;

(viii) Repair, restoration and upgradation of existing common property assets and structures in the watershed to obtain optimum and sustained benefits from previous public investments;

(ix) Crop demonstrations for popularizing new crops/varieties or innovative management practices; and

(x) Promotion and propagation of non-conventional energy saving devices, energy conservation measures, bio fuel plantations, etc.

Transparency

(xi) Preparation of the Action Plan for the watershed by the Gram Panchayat in consultation with Self Help Groups/User Groups with the assistance of WDT members;

(xii) Approval of the Action Plan at the open meetings of the Gram Sabha;

(xiii) Display of approved Action Plan on a Notice Board at the Gram Panchayat Office, Village Community Hall and such other community buildings;

(xiv) Review of physical and financial progress of work during implementation phase through periodical meetings of the Gram Sabha; and

(xv) Payment to labourers directly and through cheques wherever possible.

Funding Pattern

The present cost norm is Rs. 6,000 per hectare. This amount shall be divided amongst the following project components subject to the percentage ceiling mentioned against each:

(i)	Watershed Treatment/Development Works/Activities	85%
(ii)	Community Mobilization and Training	5%
(iii)	Administrative Overheads	10%
	Total	**100%**

Savings, if any, in the administrative costs can be utilized for undertaking activities under the other two heads, viz., training and watershed works, but not *vice versa*. Purchase of vehicles, office equipment, furnitures etc., construction of buildings, and payment of salaries of government staff will not be permissible.

Incidentally, three other watershed programmes, viz., Integrated Wastelands Development Programme, Drought Prone Areas Programme, Desert Development Programme were earlier implemented separately. Since 1-4-2008, these programmes have been brought under a comprehensive programme named Integrated Watershed Management Programme (IWMP) to be implemented under Common Guidelines on Watershed Development, 2008.

PART-C

The Planning Commission has again designed a separate set of Flagship Programmes under Annexure-IX for 15 Flagship Programmes in the Guidelines for the Twelfth Plan and Annual Plan 2012-13 meant for the State Plan which may be noted below:

1. Mahatma Gandhi National Rural Employment Guarantee Act;
2. Indira Awaas Yojana;
3. National Rural Health Mission;
4. Sarva Shiksha Abhiyan;
5. Mid-Day Meal Scheme;
6. Jawahar Lal Nehru National Urban Renewal Mission;
7. Pradhan Mantri Gram Sadak Yojana;
8. National Social Assistance Programme;
9. Integrated Child Development Service Scheme;
10. National Rural Drinking Programme;
11. National Horticulture Mission;
12. Accelerated Irrigation Benefit Programme;
13. Rajiv Gandhi Grameen Vidyuitikaran Yojana;
14. Skill Development Mission; and
15. Total Sanitation Campaign.

Out of these fifteen Flagship Programmes, the summary position of all programmes, except the (11) National Horticulture Mission and the (14) Skill Development Mission have been discussed earlier. Now the two remaining programmes are discussed hereunder:

1. National Horticulture Mission

National Horticulture Mission (NHM) has been launched in the year 2005-06 to promote holistic growth of the horticulture sector covering fruits, vegetables, root and tuber crops, mushroom, spices, flowers, aromatic plants, cashew and cocoa for all the States and Union Territories of India except the North Eastern States, Himachal Pradesh, Jammu and Kashmir and Uttaranchal (for which a separate Technology Mission for integrated development of horticulture exists). Programmes for the development of coconut are, however, to be implemented by the Coconut Development Board (CDB), independent of the Mission. NHM is a Centrally sponsored scheme in which Government of India provided 100 per cent assistance to the State Missions during Tenth Plan. During the Eleventh Plan, the Government of India's assistance has been 85 per cent with 15 per cent contribution by the State Governments.

The main objectives of the Mission are:

(i) To provide holistic growth of the horticulture sector through an area based regionally differentiated strategies which include research, technology promotion, extension, post harvest management, processing and marketing, in consonance with comparative advantage of each State/region and its diverse agro-climatic feature;
(ii) To enhance horticulture production, improve nutritional security and income support to farm households;
(iii) To establish convergence and synergy among multiple on-going and planned programmes for horticulture development;
(iv) To promote, develop and disseminate technologies, through a seamless blend of traditional wisdom and modern scientific knowledge; and
(v) To create opportunities for employment generation for skilled and unskilled persons, especially unemployed youths.

The mission has been adopting the following strategies to achieve the above objectives:

(i) Ensure an end-to-end holistic approach covering production, post-harvest management, processing and marketing to assure appropriate returns to growers/producers;
(ii) Promote R&D technologies for production, post-harvest management and processing;
(iii) Enhance acreage, coverage, and productivity through:
    (a) Diversification, from traditional crops to plantations, orchards, vineyards, flower and vegetable gardens;

(b) Extension of appropriate technology to the farmers for high-tech horticulture cultivation and precision farming;

(iv) Assist setting up post-harvest facilities such as pack house, ripening chamber, cold storages, Controlled Atmosphere (CA) storages, etc., processing units for value addition and marketing infrastructure;

(v) Adopt a coordinated approach and promotion of partnership, convergence and synergy among R&D, processing and marketing agencies in public as well as private sectors, at the National, Regional, State and sub-State levels;

(vi) Where appropriate and feasible, promote National Dairy Development Board (NDDB) model of cooperatives to ensure support and adequate returns to farmers; and

(vii) Promote capacity-building and Human Resource Development at all levels.

The NHM required to prepare a State Horticulture Mission Document (SHMD) projecting a plan of action for the Five Year Plan periods which would be the basis for preparing Annual Action Plans (AAP). The AAP will be area based, on the basis of existing potential for horticulture development, available infrastructure for monitoring and implementation, available unspent balance out of previous release and capacity to absorb the funds. The Ministry of Agriculture is to communicate the tentative outlay for the year by April/May if not earlier to each State which in turn will indicate sector-wise/district-wise allocation. The agencies at the District level will prepare the Annual Action Plan (AAP) keeping in view their priority and potential and submit the plan to the State Horticulture Mission within the allocated sum. The States could engage TSG/ Consultancy services for preparing the SHMD and AAP. The State Horticulture Mission in turn has to prepare a consolidated proposal for the State as a whole and get it vetted by the State Executive Committee (SEC) before sending it to the National Executive Committee. The SHM may spend up to 5 per cent of the annual allocation for formulating the SHM and Annual Plans.

2. Skill Development Mission

The approach to Eleventh Five Year Plan has assessed that while India's young demographic profile has the country favourably placed in terms of manpower availability, talent supply shortages are emerging. This is extremely disconcerting especially for the knowledge services sector, which over the last few years has emerged as a significant growth engine which demonstrated gains in terms of exports, employment and very visibly in urban development across several cities in the country. Research has shown that so far, only a tenth of the global addressable market for these services has been tapped.

India is best positioned to take advantage of this opportunity with its early lead and strong fundamentals such as demographics, economics, and expertise. Yet the unsuitability of a large proportion of the talent pool in the country could lead to significant lost opportunities. The NASSCOM-McKinsey Report, 2005 Projections indicate that these will fall short by about 0.5 million suitable professionals by the end of the decade and in the absence of corrective action, this gap will continue to grow. However, if current trends are maintained, the IT and ITES sector will need an additional one million plus qualified people in the next 5 years.

If the country is to capitalize on the huge opportunity in this and other areas of knowledge services, a major thrust is needed at all levels of education and skill development. Accordingly Government has decided to set up a National Skill Development Mission under which 1,600 more ITIs and polytechnics, 10,000 vocational education schools and 50,000 skill development centres are planned proposed in Public Private Partnership mode in order to train 10 million/persons per annum.

The National Policy on Skill Development has been brought out by the Ministry of Labour and Employment considering the increasing proportion of working age group of 15-49 years providing the advantage of demographic dividend to the country. In order to harness the demographic dividend through appropriate skill development efforts, it has been targeted to impart skill in different employable areas to fifty crore people by the year 2022.

PART-D

(Additional Flagship Programmes as mentioned in the website of the Press Information Bureau of the Government of India)

1. Accelerated Rural Water Supply Programme (ARWSP)

Accelerated Rural Water Supply Programme (ARWSP) is the major water supply scheme of the government in the rural areas. The main components of ARWSP are—

(i) ARWSP (Natural Calamity),

(ii) ARWSP (DDP Areas),
(iii) ARWSP (Support activities/programme),
(iv) Sub-Mission on Water Quality, and
(v) ARWSP (Normal).

There is also stipulated norms for allocation of funds earmarked for the components of ARWSP namely,—

(i) ARWSP (Natural Calamity)—5 per cent,
(ii) ARWSP (DDP Areas)—5 per cent,
(iii) ARWSP (Support activities/programme)—2 per cent,
(iv) Sub-Mission on Water Quality—up to 20 per cent, and
(v) ARWSP (Normal)—Rest of the fund.

The coverage norms under ARWSP is as follows:

(i) 40 lpcd of drinking water for human beings;
(ii) 30 lpcd of additional water for cattle in areas under the DDP;
(iii) One hand pump or stand post for every 250 persons; and availability of water source within 1.6 km in plains and 100 metres elevation in hilly areas.

Under ARWSP, it intends to cover Habitations which have a safe drinking water source (either private or public) within 1.6 km in plains and 100 metres in hill areas. Incidentally the Habitations, where the capacity of the system ranges between 10 lpcd to 40 lpcd, are categorized as Partially Covered (PC) and those having less than 10 lpcd are categorized as Not Covered (NC).

The State/UTs are required to earmark and utilize at least 25 per cent of the ARWSP funds for drinking water supply to the SCs and a minimum of 10 per cent for the STs. Where the percentage of SC or ST population in a particular State is considerably high warranting earmarking/utilization of more than stipulated provisions, additional funds can be utilized. As a measure of flexibility, States may utilize at least 35 per cent of the ARWSP funds for the benefit of SCs/STs, particularly in those States where coverage of SC/ST population is less than the coverage of the general population.

2. Rashtriya Swasthaya Bima Yojana (RSBY)

Rashtriya Swasthaya Bima Yojana is a new health insurance scheme of the Central Government launched on October 1, 2007 for the Below

Poverty Line (BPL) families in the unorganized sector. The objective of RSBY is to provide the insurance cover to Below Poverty Line (BPL) households from major health shocks that involve hospitalization.

As per the guidelines, each State has to take up 20 per cent of the districts each year in the next five years. However, the Central Government would consider additional districts if slots become available on account of inability of other States in furnishing their proposals. Almost all the States in India have since started implementing the scheme and more than 388 districts have been covered as on date.

The majority of the financing, about 75 per cent, is provided by the Government of India (GoI), while the remainder is paid by the State Government. State governments have to engage in a competitive bidding process and select a public or private insurance company licensed to provide health insurance by the Insurance Regulatory Development Authority (IRDA). The insurer must agree to cover the benefit package prescribed by GoI through a cashless facility that in turn requires the use of smart cards which must be issued to all members. This requires that a sub-contract has to be arranged with a qualified smart card provider. The insurer must also agree to engage intermediaries with local presence such as NGOs, etc., in order to provide grass roots outreach and assist members in utilizing the services after enrolment. The insurer must also provide a list of empanelled hospitals that will participate in the cashless arrangement. These hospitals must meet certain basic minimum requirements (e.g., size and registration) and must agree to set up a special RSBY desk with smart card reader and trained staff. The list should include public and private hospitals.

BPL families are entitled to more than 700 in patient medical procedures with a cost of up to rupees 30,000 per annum for a nominal registration fee of 30 rupees. Pre-existing medical conditions are covered and there is no age limit. Coverage extends to the head of household, spouse and up to three dependents. The use of Smart Card has not only made the scheme truly cashless, it has also provided interoperability to facilitate use by migrant labour. Only for the first time, contribution of rupees 30 would be sought by way of Registration fee, from the BPL beneficiary with a view to inculcating a sense of ownership in them. Transportation cost of Rs. 100 per visit with an overall limit of Rs. 1,000 per annum is also admissible under the scheme. The registration fee of Rs. 30 would be collected from the beneficiary by the insurance company and adjusted against the payment of premium to be made to the insurance company by the State Government.

For a seamless flow of fund to the insurance companies, an independent legal entity, under the control of State Government, has to be designated as nodal agency. The fund flow will take place through this agency.

3. Programmes, Schemes and Initiatives for Minorities

The Prime Minister's New 15-Point Programme for the Welfare of Minorities was announced in June 2006. It envisages location of a certain proportion of development projects in minority concentration areas for ensuring that the benefits of the schemes included in the programme flow equitably to the minorities. It provides that, wherever possible, 15 per cent of targets and outlays under various schemes should be earmarked for the minorities.

Prime Minister's New 15-Point Programme which are considered amenable to earmarking included the following:

(1) Integrated Child Development Services (ICDS) Scheme by providing services through Anganwadi Centres;
(2) Sarva Shiksha Abhiyan;
(3) Kasturba Gandhi Balika Vidyalaya;
(4) Swarnjayanti Gram Swarojgar Yojana (SGSY);
(5) Swarn Jayanti Shahari Rojgar Yojana (SJSRY);
(6) Upgradation of existing Industrial Training Institutes (ITIs) into Centres of Excellence;
(7) Bank credit under priority sector lending.;
(8) Indira Awaas Yojana (IAY); and
(9) Integrated Housing and Slum Development Programme (IHSDP) and Jawaharlal Nehru National Urban Renewal Mission (JNNURM).

Additionally, Ministry for the Development of the Minority Communities took up the following schemes as well:

(i) Merit-cum-means scholarship for technical and professional courses at undergraduate and post-graduate levels;
(ii) Pre-matric scholarship;
(iii) Post-matric scholarship;
(iv) Coaching and allied scheme; and

(v) Multi-sectoral development programme for minority concentration districts.

Further, the schemes of the Ministry of Minority Affairs for educational empowerment of minority communities are as follows:

Three new scholarship schemes introduced under Centrally Sponsored Schemes and implemented through States/UT starting from class-I up to Ph.D. included the following:

(i) Merit-cum-means scholarship for technical and professional courses at under-graduate and post-graduate levels for students belonging to the minority communities;
(ii) Post-Matric scholarship from Class-XI up to Ph.D. including technical courses at XI and XII level recognized by NCVT; and
(iii) Pre-Matric scholarship from class-I to class X.

In all the scholarship schemes of the Ministry, 30 per cent of scholarships have been earmarked for girl students.

4. Telecommunication

Uncovered villages are to be provided with Village Public Telephone (VPT) facility under Bharat Nirman Programme to improve the telephone connectivity network in the country. 66,822 number of uncovered villages as per Census 1991 in the country excluding those villages having population less than 100, those lying in deep forests and those affected with insurgency are to be provided VPT facility under Bharat Nirman programme.

M/s. Bharat Sanchar Nigam Limited, a Government of India Undertaking, is providing VPTs in uncovered villages being a successful bidder as an outcome of the tendering process. Agreements were signed with M/s. BSNL in November 2004 to provide subsidy support for provision of VPTs in such 66,822 villages. Out of 66,822 VPTs, 14,183 remotely located villages are to be provided VPTs through Digital Satellite Phone Terminals (DSPTs) whereas the remaining VPTs are to be provided on other technologies including landline, Wireless in Local Loop (WLL), GSM, etc.

This is a central sector programme of the Government of India and there is no direct role with the State Planning.

5. Right to Information Act

The basic objective of the Right to Information Act is to empower the citizens, promote transparency and accountability in the working of the Government, contain corruption, and make our democracy work for the people in real sense. An informed citizenry will be better equipped to keep necessary vigil on the instruments of governance and make the government more accountable to the governed. The Act has created a practical regime through which the citizens of the country may have access to information under the control of public authorities. It includes records, documents, memos, e-mails, opinions, advices, press releases, circulars, orders, logbooks, contracts, reports, papers, samples, models, data material held in any electronic form. This right includes inspection of work, documents and records; taking notes, extracts or certified copies of documents or records; taking certified samples of material held by the public authority or held under the control of the public authority. Only such information can be had under the Act which already exists with the public authority. It also includes information relating to any private body which can be accessed by the public authority under any law for the time being in force.

A citizen has a right to obtain information in the form of diskettes, floppies, tapes, video cassettes or in any other electronic mode or through print-outs provided information is already stored in a computer or in any other device from which the information may be transferred to diskettes etc. The right to seek information from a public authority is, however, not absolute. Sections 8 and 9 of the Act enumerate the categories of information which are *ex A* citizen who desires to obtain any information under the Act, should make an application to the Central Public Information Officer (CPIO) of the concerned public authority in writing in English or Hindi or in the official language of the area in which the application is made. The applicant can send the application by post or through electronic means or can deliver it personally in the office of the public authority. The application can also be sent through a Central Assistant Public Information Officer appointed by the Department of Post at sub-divisional level or other sub-district level. The applicant, along with the application, should send a demand draft or a banker's cheque or an Indian Postal Order of Rs. 10 (Rupees ten), payable to the Accounts Officer of the public authority as fee prescribed for seeking information. The payment of fee can also be made by way of cash to the Accounts Officer of the public authority or to the Central Assistant Public

Information Officer against proper receipt. If the applicant belongs to Below Poverty Line (BPL) category, he is not required to pay any fee. However, he should submit a proof in support of his claim to belong to the Below Poverty Line. The application not accompanied by the prescribed fee of Rs. 10 or proof of the applicant's belonging to Below Poverty Line, as the case may be, shall not be a valid application under the Act and, therefore, does not entitle the applicant to get information. Information Officer shall render reasonable assistance to the persons seeking information. If a person is unable to make a request in writing, he may seek the help of the CPIO to write his application. Where a decision is taken to give access to a sensorily disabled person to any document, the Central Public Information Officer shall provide such assistance to enable access to information, including providing such assistance to the person as may be appropriate for the inspection. The addresses of some important websites which contain substantial information relevant to the right to information are as follows:

(i) Portal of the Government of India (http://indiaimage.nic.in)
(ii) Portal on the Right to Information (www.rti.gov.in)
(iii) Website of the Central Information Commission (http://cic.gov.in)

9

Important Mission Mode Programmes for the State Planning

Normal schemes of the Government—Central Sector Schemes, Centrally Sponsored Schemes or State Sector Schemes—are not usually equipped to address vision based high growth ended objectives of the economy spanning over a time period. The reaching of such futuristic goal requires robust approach and considerable resources to shape the growth vision and its spread in quantifiable format by a time line in all parts of the country. The Union Government takes up such nationally challenging tasks in the forum of Mission mode programme to address the mighty development deficit across the country with basketful of resources. A number of Mission mode programmes have been initiated by the Union Government in different sectors of the economy which have distinct linkage with State Planning. The backward and forward linkage of such Mission mode programmes calls for commensurate planning response during State planning. It also calls for revisiting the corresponding State sector schemes and may also press for appropriate programme convergence in some cases. The resources available for the Mission mode programmes would also be immensely helpful to address the sectoral planning of the State Plan. Some of such Mission mode programmes are discussed below to give appropriate consideration during State Planning:

I. National Horticulture Mission

National Horticulture Mission (NHM) has been launched in the year 2005-06 to promote holistic growth of the horticulture sector covering fruits, vegetables, root and tuber crops, mushroom, spices, flowers, aromatic plants, cashew and cocoa for all the States and Union Territories of India except the North Eastern States, Himachal Pradesh, Jammu and Kashmir and Uttaranchal (for which a separate Technology Mission for integrated development of horticulture exists). Programmes for the development of coconut are, however, to be implemented by the Coconut Development Board (CDB), independent of the Mission. NHM is a Centrally sponsored scheme in which Government of India provided 100 per cent assistance to the State Missions during Tenth Plan. During the Eleventh Plan, the Government of India's assistance has been 85 per cent with 15 per cent contribution by the State governments.

The main objectives of the Mission are:

(i) To provide holistic growth of the horticulture sector through an area based regionally differentiated strategies which include research, technology promotion, extension, post harvest management, processing and marketing, in consonance with comparative advantage of each State/region and its diverse agro-climatic feature;
(ii) To enhance horticulture production, improve nutritional security and income support to farm households;
(iii) To establish convergence and synergy among multiple ongoing and planned programmes for horticulture development;
(iv) To promote, develop and disseminate technologies, through a seamless blend of traditional wisdom and modern scientific knowledge; and
(v) To create opportunities for employment generation for skilled and unskilled persons, especially unemployed youth.

The mission has been adopting the following strategies to achieve the above objectives:

(i) Ensure an end-to-end holistic approach covering production, post-harvest management, processing and marketing to assure appropriate returns to growers/producers;
(ii) Promote R&D technologies for production, post-harvest management and processing;
(iii) Enhance acreage, coverage, and productivity through:
    (a) Diversification, from traditional crops to plantations, orchards, vineyards, flower and vegetable gardens;

(b) Extension of appropriate technology to the farmers for high-tech horticulture cultivation and precision farming;

(iv) Assist setting up post-harvest facilities such as pack house, ripening chamber, cold storages, Controlled Atmosphere (CA) storages, etc., processing units for value addition and marketing infrastructure;

(v) Adopt a coordinated approach and promotion of partnership, convergence and synergy among R&D, processing and marketing agencies in public as well as private sectors, at the National, Regional, State and sub-State levels;

(vi) Where appropriate and feasible, promote National Dairy Development Board (NDDB) model of cooperatives to ensure support and adequate returns to farmers; and

(vii) Promote capacity-building and Human Resource Development at all levels.

The NHM required to prepare a State Horticulture Mission Document (SHMD) projecting a plan of action for the Five Year Plan periods (e.g., Tenth Plan or Eleventh Plan) which would be the basis for preparing Annual Action Plans (AAP). The AAP will be area based, on the basis of existing potential for horticulture development, available infrastructure for monitoring and implementation, available unspent balance out of previous release and capacity to absorb the funds. The Ministry of Agriculture is to communicate the tentative outlay for the year by April/May if not earlier to each State which in turn will indicate sector-wise/district-wise allocation. The agencies at the District level will prepare the Annual Action Plan (AAP) keeping in view their priority and potential and submit the plan to the State Horticulture Mission within the allocated sum. The States could engage TSG/Consultancy services for preparing the SHMD and AAP. The State Horticulture Mission in turn has to prepare a consolidated proposal for the State as a whole and get it vetted by the State Executive Committee (SEC) before sending it to the National Executive Committee. The SHM may spend up to 5 per cent of the annual allocation for formulating the SHM and Annual Plans.

II. National Bamboo Mission (NBM)

The National Bamboo Mission (NBM) is a Centrally sponsored scheme with 100 per cent Central assistance. The scheme commenced in 2006-07 and aims at holistic development of the bamboo sector in India. The thrust of the Mission is area-based regionally differentiated strategy for forest and non-forest areas. It includes bamboo plantation, treatment for productivity improvement, nurseries for supply of quality planting material and capacity building programme for farmers/entrepreneurs/field functionaries to raise quality bamboo plantations and in marketing of bamboo produce. The NBM has plans to extend the Mission to the development of handicraft and marketing of bamboo. The Mission intends to establish 195 bamboo bazaars and 10 retail outlets (showrooms) in different metropolitan cities to promote marketing of bamboo and its products.

III. National Food Security Mission

The National Development Council (NDC) in its 53rd meeting held on 29th May, 2007 adopted a resolution to launch a Food Security Mission comprising rice, wheat and pulses to increase the production of rice by 10 million tonnes, wheat by 8 million tonnes and pulses by 2 million tonnes by the end of the Eleventh Plan (2011-12). Accordingly, 'National Food Security Mission', has been launched from 2007-08 to operationalize the above as a centrally sponsored scheme to be funded by the Central Government. The objective is to increase production and productivity of wheat, rice and pulses on a sustainable basis so as to ensure food security of the country. The approach is to bridge the yield gap in respect of these crops through dissemination of improved technologies and farm management practices. It is envisaged to focus on districts which have high potential but relatively low level of productivity performance at present. The States are required to prepare programmes based on their agro-climatic situations and adopt innovative measures.

The National Food Security Mission will have three components: (i) National Food Security Mission—Rice (NFSM-Rice); (ii) National Food Security Mission—Wheat (NFSM-Wheat); and (iii) National Food Security Mission—Pulses (NFSM Pulses). The focused area of operation of NFSM—Rice, NFSM—Wheat and NFSM—Pulses has been selected in 133, 138 and 168 identified districts of different States respectively.

The objectives of this Mission are to increase production of rice, wheat and pulses through area expansion and productivity enhancement in a sustainable manner in the identified districts of the country; restoring soil fertility and productivity at the individual farm level; creation of employment opportunities; and enhancing farm level economy (i.e., farm profits) to restore confidence amongst the farmers. The strategies adopted to achieve the above objectives are the following:

(i) Implementation in a mission mode through active engagement of all the stakeholders at various levels;
(ii) Promotion and extension of improved technologies i.e., seed, Integrated Nutrient Management including micronutrients, soil amendments, IPM and resource conservation technologies along with capacity building of farmers;
(iii) Flow of fund would be closely monitored to ensure that interventions reach the target beneficiaries on time;
(iv) Various interventions proposed would be integrated with the district plan and targets for each identified district would be fixed; and
(v) Constant monitoring and concurrent evaluation for assessing the impact of the interventions for a result oriented approach by the implementing agencies.

The State Level Agency will have to play crucial role in ensuring desired outcome by way of the following:

(i) Prepare perspective and State Action Plan in consonance with the Mission's goals and objectives and in close co-ordination with State Agriculture Universities (SAUs) and ICAR Institutes;
(ii) Organize/conduct baseline survey and feasibility studies in the area of operation (district, sub-district or a group of districts) to determine the status of crop production, its potential and demand. Similar studies would also have to be undertaken for other components of the programmes;
(iii) Implementation of the Mission's programmes in the State through farmers societies, Non-Governmental Organizations (NGOs), growers' associations, self-help groups, State institutions and other similar entities;
(iv) Organize workshops, seminars and training programmes for farmers and other stakeholders at the State level with the help of State Agriculture Universities and ICAR Institutes in the district/State; and
(v) Funds would be directly received by it from the National Food Security Mission to execute the approved Action Plan for the State.

At the district level, the scheme will be implemented through the Agricultural Technology Management Agency (ATMA). The State Level

Agency will provide the required funds to the District Level Agency for execution of the programme at the district/Block level.

IV. National Mission for Empowerment of Women

The National Mission for Empowerment of Women has a mandate to achieve inter-sectoral convergence of all pro-women/women centric programmes across Ministries. It is an attempt by the Government to put women's concerns at the very heart of public policy and governance. The National Mission will strive to achieve social, economic and legal empowerment of women by identifying gaps in developmental goals and setting up of an appropriate institutional framework to overcome bottlenecks in the process of ensuring coordinated and effective service delivery to women at the grass roots level. The Mission will focus on:

1. Economic empowerment of women;
2. Progressive elimination of violence against women;
3. Social empowerment of women with particular emphasis on health and education;
4. Gender mainstreaming of programmes, policies, institutional arrangements and processes of participating Ministries, institutions and organizations; and
5. Awareness generation as well as advocacy activities to fuel the demand for benefits under various schemes and programmes at the grass roots level.

V. National Missions in the Context of Climatic Change

The Prime Minister's Advisory Council on Climate Change has outlined a National Action Plan for Climate Change (NAPCC). The Action Plan was released by the Prime Minister in June 2008 and consists of eight Missions

- National Solar Mission seeks to deploy 20,000 MW of solar electricity capacity in the country by 2020. The first phase (2010-12) is currently underway during which 1,000 MW are planned to be installed.
- National Mission for Enhanced Energy Efficiency creates new institutional mechanisms to enable the development and strengthening of energy efficiency markets. Various programmes

have been initiated, including the Perform, Achieve and Trade (PAT) mechanism to promote efficiency in large industries, and the Super-Efficient Equipment Programme (SEEP) to accelerate the introduction of deployment of super-efficient appliances.

- National Mission on Sustainable Habitat promotes the introduction of sustainable transport, energy-efficient buildings, and sustainable waste management in cities.
- National Water Mission promotes the integrated management of water resources and increase water use efficiency by 20 per cent.
- National Mission for Sustaining the Himalayan Ecosystem establishes an observational and monitoring network for the Himalayan environment so as to assess climate impacts on the Himalayan glacier and promote community-based management of these ecosystems.
- National Mission for a "Green India" seeks to afforest an additional 10 million hectares of forest lands, wastelands and community lands.
- National Mission for Sustainable Agriculture focuses on enhancing productivity and resilience of agriculture so as to reduce vulnerability to extremes of weather, long dry spells, flooding, and variable moisture availability.
- National Mission on Strategic Knowledge for Climate Change identifies challenges arising from climate change, promotes the development and diffusion of knowledge on responses to these challenges in the areas of health, demography, migration and livelihood of coastal communities.

VI. National Solar Mission

The National Solar Mission is a major initiative of the Government of India and State governments to promote ecologically sustainable growth while addressing India's energy security challenge. It will also constitute a major contribution by India to the global effort to meet the challenges of climate change.

The National Action Plan on Climate Change also points out: "India is a tropical country, where sunshine is available for longer hours per day and in great intensity. Solar energy, therefore, has great potential as future energy source. It also has the advantage of permitting the decentralized distribution of energy, thereby empowering people at the grass roots level".

Based on this vision a National Solar Mission is being launched under the brand name "Solar India".

Objectives and Targets

The objective of the National Solar Mission is to establish India as a global leader in solar energy, by creating the policy conditions for its diffusion across the country as quickly as possible.

The Mission will adopt a 3-phase approach, spanning the remaining period of the Eleventh Plan and first year of the Twelfth Plan (up to 2012-13) as Phase 1, the remaining years of the Twelfth Plan (2013-17) as Phase 2 and the Thirteenth Plan (2017-22) as Phase 3. At the end of each plan, and mid-term during the Twelfth and Thirteenth Plans, there will be an evaluation of progress, review of capacity and targets for subsequent phases, based on emerging cost and technology trends, both domestic and global. The aim would be to protect Government from subsidy exposure in case expected cost reduction does not materialize or is more rapid than expected.

The immediate aim of the Mission is to focus on setting up an enabling environment for solar technology penetration in the country both at a centralized and decentralized level. The first phase (up to 2013) will focus on capturing of the low hanging options in solar thermal; on promoting off-grid systems to serve populations without access to commercial energy and modest capacity addition in grid-based systems. In the second phase, after taking into account the experience of the initial years, capacity will be aggressively ramped up to create conditions for upscaled and competitive solar energy penetration in the country.

To achieve this, the Mission targets are:

- To create an enabling policy framework for the deployment of 20,000 MW of solar power by 2022.
- To ramp up capacity of grid-connected solar power generation to 1000 MW within three years—by 2013; an additional 3000 MW by 2017 through the mandatory use of the renewable purchase obligation by utilities backed with a preferential tariff. This capacity can be more than doubled—reaching 10,000 MW installed power by 2017 or more, based on the enhanced and enabled international finance and technology transfer. The ambitious target for 2022 of 20,000 MW or more, will be dependent on the 'learning' of the first two phases, which if

successful, could lead to conditions of grid-competitive solar power. The transition could be appropriately upscaled, based on availability of international finance and technology.

- To create favourable conditions for solar manufacturing capability, particularly solar thermal for indigenous production and market leadership.
- To promote programmes for off grid applications, reaching 1000 MW by 2017 and 2000 MW by 2022.
- To achieve 15 million sq. metres solar thermal collector area by 2017 and 20 million by 2022.
- To deploy 20 million solar lighting systems for rural areas by 2022.

Mission Strategy (Phase 1 and 2)

The first phase will announce the broad policy framework to achieve the objectives of the National Solar Mission by 2022. The policy announcement will create the necessary environment to attract industry and project developers to invest in research, domestic manufacturing and development of solar power generation and thus create the critical mass for a domestic solar industry. The Mission will work closely with State governments, Regulators, Power utilities and Local Self-Government bodies to ensure that the activities and policy framework being laid out can be implemented effectively.

10

Important National Schemes for the State Planning

The Union Government takes up a variety of schemes through various Ministries which may be broadly divided under central sector and centrally sponsored programmes. These schemes are initiated, proposed and formulated by the Central Ministries concerned, approved by the Planning Commission and financed largely by the Centre. The schemes are implemented by the States because they are in the sector of States' competency. These may fall under Flagship Programmes, Mission mode Programmes or under other important programme areas. Other important schemes, like those of Flagship Programmes and Mission mode Programmes, have implication for the State Plan and are important partners for sectoral planning. These schemes have tied up financial resources and shared responsibility to ensure envisaged outcome. It would be relevant for the State Planning authority to map them up sector-wise and then undertake sectoral planning with them under State Plan in conjunction with State Government schemes. Brief outlines of a select list of important Schemes are discussed below:

I. Macro Management

Macro Management of Agriculture Scheme (MMA) was formulated in 2000-01, to bring under one umbrella 27 centrally sponsored schemes relating to cooperatives, crop production programmes, watershed development programmes, horticulture, fertilizer, mechanization and seeds. The Scheme has been revised during 2008-09 to improve its functional efficacy in supplementing or complementing the efforts of the

States towards enhancement of agricultural production and productivity. The Revised MMA comprises 10 sub-schemes relating to crop production and natural resource management. Some of the salient features of the revised Scheme are:

- the practice of allocating funds to States/UTs on historical basis has been replaced by new allocation criteria based on gross cropped area and area under small and marginal holdings;
- assistance is provided to the States/UTs as 100 per cent grant;
- the subsidy structure has been rationalized to make the pattern of subsidy uniform under all the schemes implemented by the Department of Agriculture and Cooperation;
- the revised subsidy norms indicate the maximum permissible limit of assistance. States may either retain existing norms, or increase them to a reasonable level provided that the norms do not exceed the revised upper limits specified;
- two new components have been added, namely:
  (a) Pulses and oilseeds crop production programmes for areas not covered under the Integrated Scheme of Oilseeds, Pulses, Oil palm and Maize (ISOPOM);
  (b) Reclamation of Acidic Soil along with the existing component of Reclamation of Alkali Soil;
- the permissible ceiling for new initiatives has been increased from the existing 10 per cent to 20 per cent of the allocation;
- at least 33 per cent of the funds is required to be earmarked for small, marginal and women farmers; and
- active participation of all tiers of the Panchayati Raj Institutions (PRIs) would have to be ensured in the implementation of the Revised MMA including review, monitoring and evaluation at district/sub-district level.

II. National Food Security Mission (NFSM)

With a view to enhancing the production of rice, wheat and pulses by 10 million tonnes, 8 million tonnes and 2 million tonnes respectively by the end of the Eleventh Plan, the Centrally sponsored NFSM has been launched from the rabi 2007-08 season. The three major components of the Mission are NFSM-rice, NFSM-wheat and NFSM-pulses. The Mission aims to increase production through area expansion and productivity enhancement; restore soil fertility and productivity; create employment opportunities; and enhances the farm-level economy to restore confidence of farmers. The NFSM is presently being implemented in 312 identified districts of 17 States of the country.

III. ISOPOM

The Ministry of Agriculture has restructured oilseeds, pulses, oil palm and maize development programmes into one Centrally Sponsored Integrated Scheme of Oilseeds, Pulses, Oil Palm and Maize which is being implemented in 14 major States for oilseeds and pulses, 15 States for maize and 8 States for oil palm. About 75-80 per cent area of pulses is already in the NFSM-Pulses districts under 14 States.

The Oil Palm Development Programme under ISOPOM is being implemented in the States of Andhra Pradesh, Karnataka, Tamil Nadu, Gujarat, Goa, Orissa, Kerala, Tripura, Assam and Mizoram.

Under ISOPOM, the Maize Development Programme is being implemented in 15 States, namely Andhra Pradesh, Bihar, Chhattisgarh, Himachal Pradesh, Jammu and Kashmir, Gujarat, Karnataka, Madhya Pradesh, Maharashtra, Orissa, Punjab, Rajasthan, Tamil Nadu, Uttar Pradesh and West Bengal.

IV. Accelerated Power Development Reforms Programme (APDRP)

The supply chain for power consists of generation, transmission and distribution. While significant strides have been taken to introduce reforms in the generation leg, a lot is left to be done in the transmission and distribution legs. Massive Aggregate Transmission and Commercial (AT&C) losses have long crippled the financial viability of State Distribution Companies (SDCs). To address this problem, a targeted funding mechanism was introduced in 2003 in the form of the Accelerated Power Development Reforms Programme (APDRP). Its key objectives were to reduce AT&C losses, improve customer satisfaction as well as financial viability of the SDCs, adopt a systems approach and introduce greater transparency. Unfortunately, the benefits under the first APDRP were not linked to demonstrable performance and it failed glaringly to achieve its goals. In several cases, funds under the first APDRP were utilised without taking cognisance of the need to reduce AT&C losses. It was in this backdrop that the Restructured APDRP (R-APDRP) was conceived in September 2008.

Funding under R-APDRP is contingent upon actual, demonstrable performance in terms of sustained reduction of AT&C losses. R-APDRP seeks to commence with tackling the problem of unmetered supply and lack of proper data acquisition systems, followed by system upgradation and modernisation of equipment. Proposals under R-APDRP are considered in two phases. In the first phase, proposals for establishing reliable and automated systems for the sustained collection of accurate baseline data and IT applications for energy accounting/auditing and IT-based consumer service centres are considered for funding. In the second phase, proposals for strengthening/upgradation of power distribution are considered.

For proposals under the first phase, 100 per cent funds for approved projects will be provided through loans from the Central Government on terms decided by the Finance Ministry. The loan shall be converted into a grant upon the establishment of the required systems (as verified by an independent agency), and interest on the converted loan will be capitalised. But, no conversion to a grant will be made in case the proposal is not implemented within three years from the date of sanction. For proposals taken up under the second phase, conversion into grants will take place annually, based on the relevant AT&C loss figures as on March 31 of that year (duly verified by an independent agency appointed by the Power Ministry). Up to 50 per cent (90 per cent for special category States) of the loan shall be converted into a grant in five equal tranches on achieving 15 per cent AT&C loss. If the SDC fails to achieve or sustain the 15 per cent AT&C loss target in a particular year, that year's tranche of conversion of loan to grant will be reduced in proportion to the shortfall. The scheme also envisages incentives for SDC staff in towns where AT&C losses are brought below 15 per cent. The funding corpus will be Rs. 515.77 billion. Initially Rs. 500 billion will be provided as a loan from the Central Government or financial institutions, out of which an estimated Rs. 300 billion is expected to be converted into grants.

Eligibility Criteria for Funding

Funding is subject to the following eligibility criteria: (i) Constitute the State Electricity Regulatory Commission; (ii) Achieve the following targets of AT&C loss reduction: For SDCs having AT&C loss above 30 per cent, reduction by 3 per cent per year; and for utilities having AT&C loss below 30 per cent, reduction by 1.5 per cent per year.

Coverage

The Power Finance Corporation (PFC) has been appointed the nodal agency to run R-APDRP under the Power Ministry. It will cover urban areas with a population of more than 30,000 (10,000 in case of special category States).

V. Backward Region Grant Fund

The Backward Regions Grant Fund is designed to redress regional imbalances in development. The fund will provide financial resources for supplementing and converging existing developmental inflows into 250 identified districts, so as to:

1. Bridge critical gaps in local infrastructure and other development requirements that are not being adequately met through existing inflows;
2. Strengthen, to this end Panchayat and Municipality level governance with more appropriate capacity building, to facilitate participatory planning, decision making, implementation and monitoring, to reflect local felt needs;
3. Provide professional support to local bodies for planning, implementation and monitoring their plans; and
4. Improve the performance and delivery of critical functions assigned to Panchayats, and counter possible efficiency and equity losses on account of inadequate local capacity.

Integrated development will commence with each district undertaking a diagnostic study of its backwardness by enlisting professional planning support. This will be followed by preparing a well-conceived participatory district development perspective plan to address this backwardness during 2006-07 and the period of the Eleventh Five-Year. The Panchayats at the village, intermediate and district level, referred to in Part IX of the Constitution, will undertake planning and implementation of the programme, in keeping with the letter and spirit of Article 243G, while the Municipalities referred to in Part IX A will similarly plan and implement the programme in urban areas in conformity with the letter and spirit of Article 243W, read with Article 243ZD of the Constitution.

The Programme has two components namely, a district component covering 250 districts and Special plans for Bihar and the KBK districts of Orissa. Out of this allocation Rs. 1,250 crore had been provided in the Demand for Grants of the Ministry of Finance for the Special Plans dealt with by the Planning Commission. The remaining amount of Rs. 3,750 crore had been placed at the disposal of the Ministry of Panchayati Raj for the District Component, covering 250 districts. The allocation of Rs. 3,750 crore consisted of two funding windows (a) capacity building fund of Rs. 250 crore; and (b) development grants of Rs. 3,500 crore for the financial year 2006-07. This allocation was reduced to Rs. 1,925 crore at the Revised Estimates stage.

The existing Rashtriya Sam Vikas Yojana (RSVY) has been subsumed into the BRGF Programme. The erstwhile districts under RSVY will receive their full allocation of Rs. 45 crore per district as per norms of RSVY. Thereafter, they will shift to the BRGF mode of funding.

VI. Border Area Development Programme

The Border Area Development Programme (BADP) is part of the comprehensive approach to the Border Management with focus on socio-economic development of the border areas and to promote a sense of security amongst the people living there. The programme was started during the Seventh Plan with the objective of balanced development of sensitive border areas in the western region through adequate provision of infrastructural facilities. The programme has been subsequently extended to States bordering Bangladesh, Myanmar, China, Bhutan and Nepal and it now covers 358 border blocks of 94 districts of seventeen (17) States, which share international land border with neighbouring countries.

BADP is a 100 per cent centrally funded programme. The main objective of the programme is to meet the special developmental needs of the people living in remote and inaccessible areas situated near the International border. The schemes/works like construction/maintenance of roads, water supply, education, sports, filling gaps in infrastructure, security, organization of early childhood care and education centre, education for physically handicapped and backward sections, etc., are being undertaken under the BADP. Preference is given to the villages/ habitations which are closer to the border line.

The Border Area Development Programme (BADP) is implemented under the guidelines framed by the Planning Commission. The funds are allocated by the Planning Commission annually which are re-allocated to the Border States taking into consideration (i) Length of International

Border (km); (ii) Population of the border block; and (iii) Area of the border block (sq. km). Weightage of 15 per cent over and above the total allocation is also given to States having hilly/desert/kuchchh areas. The funds are additive to normal central assistance and are allocated for addressing the special problems faced by the people of the border areas. Schemes/works to be undertaken under BADP are finalized and approved by the State Level Screening Committee (SLSC) headed by the Chief Secretary of the concerned State and executed by the agencies of the State Government. Security related schemes can be taken up under BADP but the expenditure on such schemes should not exceed 10 per cent of the total allocation in a particular year. The funds under BADP are to be used for schemes in the identified border blocks only.

VII. Hill Areas Development Programme (HADP)

HADP has been initiated to deal with special problems faced by hilly areas arising out of their distinct geo-physical structure and concomitant socio-economic development. It has been in operation since the inception of the Fifth Five Year Plan and is being implemented for the integrated development of designated hill areas. The main objective of this programme is to ensure ecologically sustainable socio-economic development of hill areas, keeping in view the basic needs of the people of hill areas.

The Designated Hill Areas covered under HADP were identified in 1965 by a Committee of the National Development Council (NDC). These included twelve districts of Uttar Pradesh. However, consequent on the formation of Uttaranchal as a separate State, HADP is no longer in operation in the hill districts of erstwhile Uttar Pradesh. Presently, the designated Hill Areas covered under HADP include:

(a) Two hill districts of Assam-North Cachar and Karbi Anglong.
(b) Major part of Darjeeling district of West Bengal.
(c) Nilgiris district of Tamil Nadu.

The main objectives of the Programme will continue to be eco-preservation and eco-restoration. However, the needs of the people particularly their economic needs have to be met, if the eco-system has to be preserved. Therefore, ecology and economy of the area have to be developed.

The Special Central Assistance (SCA) provided for HADP is additive to normal State Plan funds and supplements the efforts of the State governments towards accelerating the development of hill areas. This SCA is not meant to be utilized for normal State Plan activities. The schemes under the HADP are to be properly dovetailed and integrated with the State Plan schemes. The schemes undertaken under both these Programmes also need to be conceived and designed to achieve the specific objectives of this programme and should not be merely conventional State Plan schemes.

The Special Central Assistance available for HADP is now divided amongst the designated hill areas under HADP in the ratio of 60:40. The SCA is distributed amongst the designated hill areas on the basis of area and population, giving equal weightage to both the factors.

The State Governments are required to prepare a separate sub-plan for the Hill Areas indicating the flow of funds from the State Plan and Special Central Assistance.

VIII. Integrated Action Plan (IAP)

The Integrated Action Plan (IAP) for 60 Selected Tribal and Backward Districts has been launched to take care of the critical development deficit of these areas. The scheme would be an Additional Central Assistance (ACA), on 100 per cent grant basis for the concerned States. For the financial year 2010-11, the IAP started with a block grant of Rs. 25 crore which has been raised at Rs. 30 crore per district during 2011-12. The funds are placed at the disposal of the district administration and are to be spent for urgent development works decided by a Committee headed by the District Collector and two other members namely, the Superintendent of Police of the District and the District Forest Officer.

The District-level Committee will have flexibility to spend the amount on development schemes of their choice based on the need of the district. The Committee will draw up a Plan consisting of concrete proposals for public infrastructure and services such as School Buildings, Anganwadi Centres, Primary Health Centres, Drinking Water Supply, Village Roads, Electric lights in public places such as PHCs and schools, etc. The schemes so selected will show results in the short term. The Development Commissioner/equivalent officer in charge of development in the State will be responsible for scrutiny of expenditure and monitoring of the IAP. Macro-level monitoring of the IAP will be carried out by the Committee headed by the Member-Secretary, Planning Commission.

The scheme needs to address the following components:

(a) During the year 2011-12, the block grant will be raised to 30 crore per district. The scheme will be reviewed for implementation in the Twelfth Plan at a later stage.

(b) The existing KBK plan under BRGF will continue as before with annual allocation of 130 crore for all eight districts put together. The eight KBK districts have also been included under the IAP and will get additional block grant of 25 crore per district in the current year and suitable additional amount under both State and District Components of IAP in the subsequent years.

(c) The scheme will focus on improvements in governance and specific preconditions will need to be complied with by the States before availing of the second tranche of the proposed additional financial assistance in 2011-12 under the State Component of the IAP. However, these conditionalities will not apply to the District Components of IAP.

(d) The scheme will focus on effective implementation of the Provisions of the Panchayats (Extension to the Scheduled Areas) Act 1996 (PESA) and the Scheduled Tribes and Other Traditional Forest Dwellers (Recognition of Forest Rights) Act 2006 (Forest Rights Act).

(e) A mechanism for procurement and marketing of MFPs, including issues of manpower requirement, capacity building and development of value chain specific to MFPs would be worked out by the Planning Commission, in consultation with the Ministry of Panchayati Raj and Ministry of Tribal Affairs. The administrative mechanism for enforcement of the minimum support price for MFP in accordance with the mechanism so work out will be the responsibility of the State Government concerned.

The District Component will be administered by the Ministry of Panchayati Raj and the State Component by the Planning Commission.

IX. Tribal Development Programmes

Planning Commission attaches utmost importance for tribal development on consideration of inclusive economic and social development. For broad-based programme efforts funds are provided from two segments:

(a) The State Plan resources; and

(b) The Central Grants, which are further segregated into:

(i) Special Central Assistance to Tribal Sub-Plans (SCA to TSP); and

(ii) Grants under Article 275(1) of the Constitution of India.

The State Plan for the Scheduled Tribes has been covered under TSP and has been discussed separately at Chapter 11. When the TSP under State Plan is budgeted under sub-code 796, the budgetary resources of the State government are ensured for implementation of TSP programmes in the State.

As to the Central Grants, a brief position is discussed below:

(i) Special Central Assistance to Tribal Sub-Plans (SCA to TSP)

Special Central Assistance to Tribal Sub-Plans (SCA to TSP) is provided by the Ministry of Tribal Affairs to the State Government. SCA is additive to State Plan efforts for tribal development and forms part of TSP strategy. Funds under this programme are released for demand based employment-cum-income generation activities and the infrastructure incidental thereto, for Scheduled Tribes below the poverty line, thereby raising their economic and social status, including that of the Particularly Vulnerable Tribal Groups.

Some Important Features of the SCA to TSP are:

- 70 per cent of the SCA to be used for primary schemes supporting family/Self-Help Groups (SHGs)/community-based employment and income generation in sectors such as Agriculture/ Horticulture, Land Reforms, Watershed Development, Animal Husbandry, Ecology and Environment, Development of Forests and Forest villages, etc., and 30 per cent for the development of infrastructure incidental thereto,
- Priority to the neglected Scheduled Tribes living in forest villages and synchronization of the programmes with Joint Forest Management (JFM).
- Preparation of long term area specific micro plans for ITDAs/ ITDPs.
- 30 per cent of beneficiaries are to be women.

(ii) Grants under Article 275(1) of the Constitution of India

Grants under Article 275(1) of the Constitution of India is provided from the Consolidated Fund of India each year to the State Governments for promoting the quality of life of the Scheduled Tribes and the infrastructural development deficit for the given areas. The guidelines for release and utilization of grants under Article 275 (1) as modified in January 2008 for the Eleventh Five Year Plan, are the following:

- Taking up of specific projects for creation and upgradation of critical infrastructure required to bring the tribal areas at par with the rest of the country.
- Identification of areas/sectors critical for enhancement of Human Development Index (HDI) and projects can be taken up for bridging gaps in critical infrastructure.
- People's participation in planning and implementation of schemes and projects with due regard to State Panchayat Acts and the PESA Acts 1996.
- Integrated and holistic approach for preparing micro plans for ITDP/MADA/Cluster through multidisciplinary teams.
- At least 30 per cent projects should be targeted to benefit women.
- 2 per cent of the grants to be used for Project Management, Training, MIS, Administrative expenses, Monitoring and Evaluation.
- Up to 10 per cent of the allocation to the State can be used for maintenance of the infrastructure.
- Generation of Community Welfare assets like schools, skilled teaching, nutritional support, drinking water, etc.
- Innovative grants strictly meant for innovative schemes—in terms of final output/outcome or methods of delivery.
- State to formulate and operate efficient monitoring of the programmes.
- Ministry of Tribal Welfare to do secondary level monitoring.

This scheme covers all 22 TSP States and 4 tribal majority States—Arunachal Pradesh, Meghalaya, Mizoram and Nagaland.

X. Accelerated Urban Water Supply Programme (AUWSP)

(i) Scheme

Centrally Sponsored Accelerated Urban Water Supply Programme

(AUWSP) for towns having population less than 20,000 (as per 1991 Census).

(ii) Rationale

Due to the low economic base and lower priority given by the State governments to provide water supply to smaller towns, these are oftern neglected during normal times and are worst hit during the periods of drought as was observerd in 1987. Therefore., there is a need to extend financial support to the State governments/Local Bodies for providing water supply facilities in the towns having population less than 20,000 (1991 Census). With this in view a Centrally Sponsored Accelerated Urban Water Supply Scheme has been included in the Eighth Five Year Plan and has been continued since then.

(iii) Objectives

(i) To provide safe and adequate water supply facilities to the entire population of the towns having population less than 20,000 (as per 1991 Census) in the country within a fixed time frame;
(ii) To improve the environment and the quality of life; and
(iii) For better socio-economic condition and more productivity to sustain the economy of the country.

(iv) Features of the Programme

(i) In general, the overall emphasis is being given on creating a better incentive environment in the sector. There is a need to emphasize on rationalisation of tariffs separation of budget of water supply and sanitation from the municipal budget; subsidies being extended for well identified target groups; water conservation, Operation and Maintenance (O&M) and distribution being given priority over new capital works; emphasis on leak detection and preventive maintenance rehabilitation of existing system.
(ii) The water supply sector has to be treated as public utility rather than a service and efforts have also to be made, to bring about greater private sector participation and investment in this sector.
(iii) The principle aim of the programme will be to improve the quality of life of the poor, specially the most vulnerable sections

of the population such as women, children and other deprived sections who do not have access to safe water.

(iv) The Urban Local/Bodies will be suitably strengthened and closely associated in the implementation of Accelerated Urban Water Supply Programme (AUWSP) with a view to realising the objective of providing water supply to the unserved population.

(v) Community participation will be made the cardinal principle underlying the whole programme. Community participation implies organising local communities nurtured by field level staff of Urban Local Bodies and NGOs.

(vi) A Plan of Action will be formulated for each of the schemes comprising of town or towns depending upon the situation assessed by the concerned Department of the State Government responding directly to the felt needs of the population in these towns.

(vii) Special emphasis will be placed on privatisation of implementation, operation and maintenance and cost recovery so as to make the scheme self-sustaining.

(viii) The emphasis would be on whole town approach.

(v) Programme Implementation Approach

The programme should be operationally integrated with the State Public Health Engineering Department/Water Supply and Sewerage Board and Urban Local Bodies for the provision of water supply facilities if found feasible. Involvement of Non Government Organisations (NGOs) should also be considered. Insofar as the operation and maintenance of assets created under the programme are concerned efforts should be made, to operate and maintain such scheme by the community itself once they are properly trained to take up such a task. Till then these should be maintained by the agency responsible for its implementation/urban local body. Preferably however, the community while building up its own expertise and training during execution so that on completion of each project the local community could be ready and able to maintain it

(vi) Criteria for Allocation amongst States

The following criteria would be applied to determine the share of each qualifying State for assistance under the scheme:

(a) 50 per cent weightage being given to the population of such towns;
(b) 35 per cent weightage being given to the incidence of poverty in a State/UT;
(c) 5 per cent weightage being given to the number of such towns in States/UTs;
(d) 10 per cent weightage being given in terms of population of such towns to the 'special requirements of State/UTs covered under DPAP, DDP. HADP and Special Category hilly States.

(vii) Committee for Selection of Towns/Schemes

For selection of towns/schemes under the programme the State Governments/UT Administrations shall constitute a State Level Selection Committee under the Chairmanship of Secretary to the State Government in charge of Urban Water Supply with the following Members:

(a) Chief Engineer PHED/Managing Director, Urban Water Supply Board;
(b) A representative of the State Irrigation Department;
(c) A representative of the State Finance Department;
(d) A representative of the State Planning Department
(e) A representative from CPHEEO, MOUD;
(f) Director Municipal Administration/Urban Local Bodies Member-Secretary.

(viii) Guidelines for Selection of Towns/Schemes

The selection of towns/schemes shall be done only through the State Level Committee constituted for this purpose after considering the detailed project reports prepared in respect of the individual towns as per the guidelines of this scheme. Special attention should bc given to ensure that the following stipulations are fulfilled in the detailed project report.

(i) The populations of the town should not be more than 20,000 as per 1991 Census. For this purpose, the documents published by the Registrar General of India or the Director of Census Operations of the State concerned shall be the basis.
(ii) 95 per cent dependability and reliability of the water source is established.

(iii) Provision for separate maintenance of accounts is made.

(iv) Provision for sustainable O&M mechanism is evolved and incorporated in the DPR.

(v) A sustainable tariff system is evolved and approved by the State Government is incorporated in the DPR.

(vi) Provision is made for 5 per cent contribution from the urban local bodies towards the project cost.

(vii) The commitment of the urban local body for all the stipulations including improvement in institutional and tariff mechanism, their preparedness for maintenance through suitable arrangements should by obtained and be included in the DPR. If any of these stipulations are not fulfilled and incorporated in the DPR, the scheme will not be eligible for inclusion in the programme.

(ix) Priorities for Towns with Special Problems

Priority is to be given to towns with special problems like:

(a) Very low per capita supply;
(b) Very distant or deep water source;
(c) Drought-prone areas;
(d) Excess salinity, fluoride, iron content in the water source;
(c) High incidence of water borne diseases.

For this purpose, the States may at the first instance prepare the list of towns having these special problems before preparation of the detailed project reports. Similarly, priority is to be given to rehabilitations and augmentation schemes rather than new schemes. On selection by the State Level Committee the DPRs of the selected towns along with the information in the prescribed format may be sent to the Ministry of UD.

Per Capita Unit Cost

The per capita Unit Cost should normally be limited to Rs. 1,000. However, this is not very rigid. In individual cases, the specific justification is required to be furnished in the DPR if the per capita cost is more.

(x) Pattern of Finance

The Accelerated Urban Water Supply Programme being a Centrally sponsored scheme will be funded on grant basis by the Central Government on 50 per cent and State Government on 50 per cent including 5 per cent beneficiary/town contribution. In case of Union Territories, 100 per cent financing is available from the Central Share.

(xi) Release of Funds

The estimated cost of the selected scheme is to be borne on 50:50 basis between the Centre and the States. Accordingly 25 per cent of the Central Share will be released to the State Government or the designated agency on selection of the scheme. The second instalment of the Central Share which will be 50 per cent of the eligible Central Share for the scheme will be released on:

- Release of the first instalment of the State Share;
- Completion of the ground work for execution of the scheme including award of contracts or placing of orders for supply of material, etc., wherever required and;
- Utilisation of at least 50 per cent of the amount released for the scheme (25 per cent of the Central share plus 25 per cent of the State share);
- Submission of Detailed project report and its approval in case the first instalment is released before receipt of DPR. The third and final instalment amounting to 25 per cent of the Central share will be released on:
  (a) Release of second instalment of State share (50%); and
  (b) Utilisation of 80 per cent of the total funds released for the scheme.

XI. Urban Poverty Alleviation Programmes

Urban Poverty Alleviation is a challenging task before the nation which calls for imaginative new approaches. The goal is to adequately feed, educate, house and employ the large and rapidly growing number of impoverished city dwellers. The urban population has increased by 36.19 per cent from about 160 million in 1981 to about 217 million in 1991 further aggravating the scenario of urban employment. The National Sample Survey 43rd round (1987-88) has estimated that there are about 40 million persons living below the poverty line in urban areas. However, according to Lakdawala Committee Report of March 1994 (set up by the

Planning Commission) about 86 million persons (40% in Urban India) as against total population of 217 million lived below the poverty line. Incidence of urban poor at 40 per cent is higher than both rural and all India incidence of poverty at 39 per cent.

The bulk of the urban poor are living in extremely deprived conditions with insufficient physical amenities like low-cost water supply, sanitation, sewerage, drainage, community centres and social services relating to health care, nutrition, pre-school and non-formal education. A significant portion of the urban poor belongs to Scheduled Castes, Scheduled Tribes and minorities. The need of the hour is to improve the skills of the urban poor and to assist them to set-up micro enterprises thereby providing them avenues for enhancement of their incomes. Another major area for assistance to this target group is provision of funds for housing or shelter upgradation. The Central Government has accorded a high priority to the substantial expansion of programmes meant for improving the quality of life of the urban poor.

The Department of Urban Employment and Poverty Alleviation is monitoring the implementation of four significant urban poverty alleviation programmes :

(i) The Nehru Rozgar Yojana;
(ii) The Urban Basic Services for the Poor;
(iii) The Environmental Improvement of Urban Slums, and
(iv) Prime Minister's Integrated Urban Poverty Eradication Programme. A brief account of these schemes is given in the following paragraphs.

Nehru Rozgar Yojana

In response to the challenge posed by urban poverty, the Nehru Rozgar Yojana was launched by the Ministry in October 1989. It was recast in March 1990 and accordingly the guidelines were suitably revised. The Yojana consists of three schemes:

(i) the Scheme of Urban Micro Enterprises (SUME),
(ii) the Scheme of Urban Wage Employment (SUWE), and
(iii) the Scheme of Housing and Shelter Upgradation (SHASU).

The entire expenditure on the Yojana is to be shared on a 60:40 basis between the Central Government and the State Government w.e.f. Eighth Plan.

The Scheme of Urban Micro Enterprises (SUME)

The Scheme of Urban Micro Enterprises (SUME) assists the urban poor in upgrading their skills and setting up self-employment ventures. At present, the criterion of urban poverty is an annual household income less than Rs. 11,850. A subsidy is provided towards setting up the micro enterprises up to 25 per cent of the project cost with a ceiling of Rs. 5,000 for SC/ST/Women beneficiaries and Rs. 4,000 for general beneficiaries. The remaining amount of the project cost is available from banks as a loan up to a maximum of Rs. 15,000 for SC/ST and Women beneficiaries and Rs. 12,000 for general category beneficiaries. This Scheme is applicable to all urban settlements.

The Scheme of Urban Wage Employment (SUWE)

The Scheme of Urban Wage Employment (SUWE) provides wage opportunities to the urban poor by utilising their labour for construction of socially and economically useful public assets in the jurisdiction of Urban Local Bodies. A material-labour ratio of 60:40 is to be maintained under the Scheme for various public works aggregating at the district level. The minimum wages prevalent in each urban area are to be paid to the unskilled labour. This scheme is applicable to all urban areas with a population below one lakh.

The Scheme of Housing and Shelter Upgradation (SHASU)

The Scheme of Housing and Shelter Upgradation (SHASU) seeks to provide assistance for Housing and Shelter upgradation to economically weaker sections of the urban population as well as to provide opportunities for wage employment and upgradation of construction skills. A loan up to a ceiling of Rs. 9,950 and a subsidy up to a ceiling of Rs. 1,000 is provided under this scheme to entitled beneficiaries for housing/shelter upgradation. In case of enhanced financial requirement beyond Rs. 10,950 an additional loan up to Rs. 19,500 can be taken from HUDCO under its scheme for EWS Housing. This scheme is applicable to urban settlements having a population up to twenty lakh. Requirements for institutional finance for the scheme are met by the Housing and Urban Development Corporation (HUDCO).

Thus, the Nehru Rozgar Yojana through activities aimed at skill upgradation, assistance for setting up micro enterprises, wage opportunity through construction of public assets and assistance for shelter upgradation seeks to usher in a brighter future for the urban poor in India.

Urban Basic Services for the Poor (UBSP)

The Urban Basic Servlce (UBS) Programme in India was initiated during the Seventh Five Year Plan period for urban poverty alleviation. Based on the experience of implementing the UBS Programme and the recommendations of the National Commission on Urbanisation, the Government revised it as Urban Basic Services for the Poor (UBSP) (1991) and integrated it with other urban poverty alleviation programme, namely, Environmental Improvement of Urban Slums (EIUS), Nehru Rozgar Yojana (NRY) and Low Cost Sanitation (LCS).

Objectives: The objective of UBSP is to create participatory community based structures through which community participate in identifying normative/felt needs, prioritize them and play a major role in planning, implementing, maintaining services and monitoring progress.

Salient Features: One of the important features is to provide social services and physical amenities through convergence of various ongoing schemes of Ministry of Urban Affairs and Employment and various specialist departments like Health, Family Welfare, Women and Child Development, Education, Welfare Labour, Small Scale Industry, Non-conventional Energy Resources and Science and Technology. Such a convergent approach will lead to optimum utilisation of scarce resources and help in successful implementation of various sectoral programmes thereby providing social services and physical amenities to the urban poor.

Target Group: The urban poor residing in low income Neighbourhoods are the target groups for provision of social services under the Scheme and physical amenities to be provided under the Environmental Improvement of Urban Slums (EIUS) Scheme. Urban poor residing contiguous to low income neighbourhood slums would also be able to avail of the social services provided under the Scheme. Special emphasis is given to women and child beneficiaries.

Environmental Improvement of Urban Slums

The scheme of Environmental Improvement of Urban Slums (EIUS) was formulated as a response to the growing problem of slums during the

Fifth Five Year Plan. The scheme was made an internal part of the Minimum Needs Programme (MNP) in 1974 and was transferred to the State Sector. The scheme aims at ameliorating the living conditions of urban slums dwellers and envisages provision of drinking water, drainage, community baths, community latrines, widening and paving of existing lanes, street lighting and other community facilities. The improvements are meant to be carried out in notified slums which are not likely to be cleared within the next 10-15 years.

Prime Minister's Integrated Urban Eradication Programme (PMI UDEP)

Recognising the seriousness and complexity of urban poverty problems, especially in the small towns where the situation is more grave due to lack of resources for planning their environment and development, the Prime Minister had announced on 15th August, 1994 an integrated scheme for eradication of poverty known as Prime Minister's Integrated Urban Poverty Eradication Programme (PMI UPEP), which seeks to address the problems of urban poverty with a multi-pronged and long term strategy. The new strategy is to put the community structures in the centre with direct participation and control by the very groups who are envisaged to benefit from this programme.

The foremost objective of the new programme is to attack several root causes of urban poverty simultaneously in an integrated manner with an appropriate and suitable plan strategy for covering the inputs available in other sectoral programmes of Central Governments, Ministries/Departments as well as Non Government Organisations by envisaging participatory implementation of the programme with the aim to eradicate urban poverty from the targeted areas by the turn of the century.

The specific objectives under the new programme are (i) effective achievement of social sector goals, (ii) community empowerment, (iii) convergence through sustainable support system, (iv) improvement of hygiene and sanitation, (v) employment generation and shelter upgradation, and (vi) environmental improvement. The programme will be implemented on whole town/project basis extending the coverage to all the targeted groups for having visible impact and facilitating overall development of the towns to be covered. While the target group of the programme is urban poor, specially women beneficiaries and beneficiaries belonging to Scheduled Castes and Scheduled Tribes will constitute special target groups among the urban poor.

XII. Panchayat Yuva Krida Aur Khel Abhiyan (PYKKA) Scheme

1. The Scheme of Panchayat Yuva Krida Aur Khel Abhiyan (PYKKA) was introduced during Eleventh Five Year Plan as a centrally sponsored scheme with the objective of providing basic sports infrastructure/facilities in all village panchayats and block panchayats of the country in a phased manner during Eleventh and Twelfth Five Year Plan periods and providing access to organized sports competitions at block, district, state and national level. The Scheme was approved by the Cabinet in Mach 2008. Thereafter, the Scheme was made operational from 2008-09.

2. The scheme is being implemented through the State Governments/ UTs from 2008-09 to develop playfields in 2.50 lakh village panchayats and 6,400 block panchayats in a phased manner over a period of 10 years with an annual coverage of 10 per cent (20% in the case of North Eastern States and districts at international border in the Special Category States). Each village panchayat and block panchayat is provided a one-time capital grant of Rs. 1 lakh and Rs. 5 lakh, respectively on 75: 25 sharing basis between Centre and State (10% in the case of North Eastern and Special Category States).

3. In addition, Rs. 10,000 and Rs. 12,000 are provided to each village panchayat and Rs. 20,000 and 24,000 to each block panchayat for five years which includes honorarium for '*kridashrees*' and procurement of sport kit.

4. In addition to the above, the following sports competitions are organized annually under the Scheme:

(i) Rural sports competitions at Block, District, State and National level;
(ii) Inter-school competitions at district, State and National level;
(iii) North-East Games at district, State and National level; and
(iv) Women championships at district, State and national level.

5. Funding pattern for infrastructure development and conduct of sports competitions under the scheme of PYKKA is as under:

Infrastructure Grant: Development of basic sports infrastructure in village/Block Panchayats:

S. No.	Component	Village Panchayat	Block Panchayat
1.	One-time Capital Grant for levelling of playfields, etc. (in the ratio of 75:25 between Centre and States; and 90:10 in the case of Special Category States/North- Eastern States).	Rs.1 lakh	Rs.5 lakh
2.	Annual Acquisition Grant for 5 years, for sports kit/ equipment. (100% central grant)	Rs.10,000	Rs.20,000
3.	Annual Operational Grant for 5 years, for maintenance expenses, including honorarium to kridashrees. (100% central grant)	Rs.12,000	Rs.24,000

Annual Competitions (100% central grant): Quantum of grant-in-aid for holding competitions at various levels is tabulated below:

Competitions Funding Pattern

PYKKA Rural Competitions

1. *Block Level Competitions*: Rs. 50,000 @ Rs. 10,000 per discipline for 5 disciplines +Rs. 45,000 prize money for the first-three winning village Panchayats.
2. *District Level Competitions*: Rs. 2 lakh @ Rs. 20,000 per discipline for 10 disciplines + Rs. 90,000 prize money for the first-three winning Block Panchayats.
3. *State Level Competitions*:
   (i) Rs. 10 lakh for the State @ Rs. 1 lakh per discipline for 10 disciplines;
   (ii) Rs. 5 lakh for UT @ Rs. 50,000 per discipline for 10 disciplines
   Note: 20% of total amount will be utilized for award of prizes.
4. *National Level Competitions*: Rs. 70 lakh (Rs. 3.50 lakh per discipline for 20 disciplines) to host State.
   Note: Rs. 50,000 out of Rs. 3.50 lakh per discipline is earmarked for award of prizes.

North East Games: These games are meant for encouraging/ promoting traditional and tribal sports. Funding norms for conduct of district, State and national level games, limited to NE States had been enhanced with effect from 3rd February, 2010.

Competitions Funding Pattern

North East Games

(i) District Level—Rs. 50,000
(ii) State Level—Rs. 6 lakh @ Rs. 75,000 per discipline for 8 disciplines.
(iii) National Level—Rs. 55.90 lakh.

Inter-School Sports Competitions and National Sports Festival for Women: These games have been brought under PYKKA scheme with the following enhanced funding norms:

Competitions Funding Pattern

Inter-School Competitions

(i) District Level—Rs. 1 lakh @ Rs. 10,000 per discipline for 10 disciplines.
(ii) State Level—Rs. 3 lakh @ Rs. 30,000 per discipline for 10 disciplines.
(iii) National Level—Rs. 35 lakh (@ Rs. 3.50 lakh per discipline for 10 disciplines) + cash award of Rs. 1 lakh and rolling trophy to the best performing school.

Competitions Funding Pattern

Women Competitions

(i) District level—Rs. 1.20 lakh @ Rs. 10,000 per discipline for 12 disciplines.
(ii) State Level—Rs. 6 lakh for State @ Rs. 50,000 per discipline for 12 disciplines; Rs. 3 lakh for UT @ Rs. 25,000 per discipline for 12 disciplines.
(iii) National Level—Rs. 42 lakh @ Rs. 3.50 lakh per discipline for 12 disciplines.

XIII. Urban Sports Infrastructure Scheme

1. The Government approved introduction of a central scheme titled

'Scheme of Assistance for the creation of Urban Sports Infrastructure' on pilot basis in 2010-11 with a view to addressing the entire 'sports eco-system' holistically, i.e., players' training and development, coaching and infrastructure. The Scheme envisages development of playfields by the State Governments through Playfield Associations, coach development programme through Central and State Governments, setting up of players Academies, where SAI centres will provide the nucleus of a hub and spoke model for such academies catering to premier sports in each State. The Scheme will focus on promoting and supporting a mechanism at national and State level to encourage, assist and preserve community playfields, incentivizing utilization of infrastructure already available in the State at all levels by filling up critical gaps, creating need-based infrastructure and creating capacity building among coaches, including community coaches.

2. Salient features of the Scheme are as under:

(i) Annual assistance @ Rs. 50 lakh to each State and Rs. 25 lakh to each Union Territory for a period of 2 years to set up and operate a State-Level Playing Field Association. The association must be modelled on the lines of the National Playing Fields Association of India (NPFAI). The annual assistance is to be utilized to further the objectives of the Association, including meeting establishment and administrative expenses, maintaining a comprehensive database of registered playing fields, providing legal assistance to endangered playing fields, conducting seminars/workshops, and providing assistance to support pilot projects at the State level.

(ii) At the national level, NPFAI will receive an annual grant of 2.5 crore per annum for carrying out similar activities, including supporting pilot projects for States to emulate. All projects assisted by NPFAI have to get them registered with NPFAI and enter into Memoranda of Understanding (MoUs) with it as community playing facility as per a model MoU.

(iii) The development of sports training infrastructure on partnership mode with State governments/local bodies/colleges/universities/sports control boards on the one hand, and SAI on the other. Under the scheme, the Ministry of Youth Affairs and Sports (MYAS) will provide assistance through SAI, or directly, for the creation of need-based sporting infrastructure in States/UTs, which will function as SAI extension centres, but the entire responsibility of maintenance of the infrastructure will be that of the State Government/UT/beneficiary entity.

(iv) With a view to maintaining focus on mother sports and popular sports, especially those in which the country has good medal prospects, the following types of sports infrastructure will get preference over others:

(a) Synthetic playing surface (for hockey, football and athletics);

(b) *Multipurpose indoor halls*: CPWD, State PWD, or any Central or State PSU can be engaged for construction of the projects. The CPWD/State PWD schedule of rates will be adopted for preparing the estimates. The grant as per approved estimates will be released to SAI directly for taking up the project on partnership mode;

(v) State Governments, Local Civic bodies, schools, colleges and universities under Central/State Governments, Sports Control Boards will be eligible to receive assistance for creation of sports infrastructure.

(vi) The applicants will be required to furnish information about ownership of land, present performance of the entity in sports promotion, discipline-wise infrastructure owned, managed and operated by it, impact of proposed sports infrastructure/additionality in terms of growth in participation, retention of existing participation level, identification and development of new talent, a business plan for establishing sustainability of the project, including meeting of operation and maintenance cost, details of existing partnerships, if any, management structure for sports development and operation of the existing and proposed facilities, delivery capability, broad plan, estimate and time schedule for execution, budgetary support from State Government, if any, free public access to informal play spaces, affordable pay and play schemes for other facilities, availability of coaching facilities, cross subsidizing model through PPP, linkages with local clubs, sports clubs and leagues, sports associations, business partnerships to enhance viability, etc.

(vii) No State shall get more than one project in a year. States that have properly utilized facilities created under the erstwhile sports infrastructure schemes will get preference. The grant for creation of sports infrastructure will be released to SAI.

(viii) States/UTs will be assisted to depute 20/10 coaches per year to undergo one month refresher course in National Institute of Sports, Patiala. The maximum admissible assistance per coach shall be Rs. 50,000 towards training, training materials and boarding and lodging. The travel expenses and other allowances will be the responsibility of the State/UT Government. The State Governments/UTs will obtain a Bond from the nominated coaches that they will not leave service till 2 years after receiving the training.

XIV. Rashtriya Madhyamik Shiksha Abhiyan (RMSA)

As per the announcement made by the Hon'ble Prime Minister in his Independence Day, 2007 speech, a Centrally Sponsored Scheme for Universalisation of Access to and Improvement of Quality of Education at Secondary Stage (SUCCESS){ also known as Rashtriya Madhyamik Shiksha Abhiyan (RMSA)} is to be implemented during Eleventh Five Year Plan period. The scheme envisages:

(i) provision of infrastructure and resources in the secondary education sector to create higher capacity in secondary schools in the country, and for improvement in quality of learning in the school;
(ii) provision for filling the missing gaps in the existing secondary schools system;
(iii) provision of extra support for education of girls, rural children and students belonging to SC/ST, minority and other weaker sections of the society; and
(iv) a holistic convergent framework for implementation of various schemes in secondary education.

Goal and Objectives

The goal of RMSA is to make secondary education of good quality available, accessible and affordable to all young students in the age group of 15-16 years (classes IX and X). The major target of the scheme is (1) Universal access of Secondary level education to all students in the age group of 15-16 years by 2015 by providing a secondary school within 5 kilometres of any habitation and a higher secondary school within 7 kilometres of any habitation; and (2) Universal retention by 2020.

Strategies for Implementation of RMSA

(i) To provide access of secondary school to students, the following has been proposed:

(a) Upgradation of upper primary schools through construction of classrooms laboratories, computer rooms, headmaster room, library rooms, separate toilets for girls and boys, appointment of additional teachers; and

(b) Strengthening of existing secondary schools through construction of classrooms, computer rooms, separate toilets for girls and boys, appointment of additional teachers, strengthening of laboratories, facilities and repair and renovation of existing school buildings.

(ii) To remove the disparity among the different social groups of people, the scheme envisages the special incentive for students belonging to SC/ST/minority/other weaker sections of the society.

(iii) To improve the quality, the RMSA scheme proposes for:

(a) Construction of science laboratories, libraries;

(b) In service training of teachers;

(c) Leadership training of school head;

(d) Curricular reforms;

(e) Science and Mathematics education;

(f) Computer aided education;

(g) Co-curricular activities; and

(h) Teaching learning aids.

Requirement of Funds

For the effective implementation of the scheme (RMSA), the requirement of funds has been projected as under:

(a) *During the Eleventh Plan:* An amount of Rs. 20868.35 crore as Non-recurring and Rs. 14698.26 crore as recurring totalling Rs. 35566.62 crore (Central Share) were assessed.

(b) *Total requirement by 2020:* The total cost works out to Rs. 90485.11 crore with Rs. 37119.03 crore as Non-recurring and Rs. 53366.08 crore as recurring.

11

Tribal Sub-Plan (TSP) and Scheduled Castes Sub-Plan (SCSP)

The welfare of the Scheduled Castes and the Scheduled Tribes has been an important area on planning and the Planning Commission has been addressing this issue for long under the State Plan. The Tribal Sub-Plan (TSP) as a planning strategy has been taken up since 1974 to ensure adequate flow of plan resources for the development of Scheduled Tribes while the Special Component Plan for Scheduled Castes (SCP) has been in force since 1979-80 to ensure proportionate flow of plan resources for the development of Scheduled Castes. The SCP has been renamed as Scheduled Castes Sub-Plan (SCSP) since 2006.

The broad criteria for categorisation of any schemes as SCSP or TSP are as follows:

(a) Only those schemes should be included under SCSP or TSP which ensure *direct benefits* to individuals or families belonging to Scheduled Castes or Scheduled Tribes;

(b) Outlay for *Area oriented schemes* directly benefiting Scheduled Castes or Scheduled Tribes hamlets/villages having more than 40 per cent Scheduled Castes or Scheduled Tribes population shall be included in SCSP or TSP, as the case may be.

The existing guidelines further require to :

(a) earmark funds under SCSP/TSP from the State Plan outlay, at least in proportion of percentage of SC and ST population as per census, 2001.

(b) place funds earmarked for SCSP under a separate Minor Head '789' and for TSP under Minor Head '796' below the functional major Head/Sub-Major Heads to ensure their non-divertibility to any other scheme.

Tribal Sub-Plan (TSP)

Historically, the Tribal Community remained cut-off from the mainstream development activities. With the launching of the First Five Year Plan in our country, the first serious efforts to initiate development programme for the tribal community took place in 1955 in the form of Special Multipurpose Development Blocks. However, dedicated programmes were needed exclusively for the tribal community and as a result the concept of Tribal Development Block having more than 50 per cent of tribal population came into being during the Second Five Year Plan. It was, thereafter, realised that the Tribal Development Blocks to be a focal point for the welfare of the Scheduled Tribes need to be integrated with overall planning efforts of the State. The concept of Tribal Sub-Plan (TSP) thus came up during the Fifth Five Year Plan which required that within the State Plan there need to have dedicated programmes for the Scheduled Tribes of the State for their economic and social development. Such dedicated programmes taken up under TSP also receives Special Central Assistance (SCA) from the Central Government along with Central sector programme support. Additionally, the Constitution of India required under Article 275(1) to meet the cost of schemes for the purpose of promoting the welfare of the Scheduled Tribes in the State or raising the level of administration of the Scheduled Areas therein to that of the administration of the rest of the areas of the State. The grants-in-aid so received are also taken into account for the available fund for TSP.

The Planning Commission has stipulated that required flow of outlay for TSP should correspond with the percentage of the ST population in the State. However, this turned out to be mechanical exercise and the Planning Commission during the terminal year of the Tenth Plan revised it to ensure that scheme-specific aggregate outlays on TSP are at least equal to percentage of ST population in the State. The overarching objective of the TSP is to ensure inclusiveness of the ST population in the planning process and improve their human development status.

The focus under TSP has always been to meet the development deficit in general, however, the variations on status of human development of ST *vis-à-vis* the average status of the citizens are also important issues for planning considerations. The TSP programmes are in the nature of additionality; the ongoing general programmes are to proceed as usual with one rider that there has not to take place any duplication efforts and that distinct visibility for each of the programmes has to be ensured. The scope of programme convergence, wherever feasible, may, however, be attempted upon.

In terms of priorities in the TSP, all types of education-primary, upper primary, secondary, higher secondary, higher education, vocational education, etc., occupy important place. The gender gap and factors responsible for low level of achievement are to addressed.

The format of presentation of TSP in the Annual Plan has been discussed in detail at Annexure VA and VB.

Special Central Assistance to Tribal Sub-Plans (SCA to TSP)

SCA to TSP is provided by the Ministry of Tribal Affairs to the State Government. SCA is additive to State Plan efforts for tribal development and forms part of TSP strategy. Funds under this programme are released for demand based employment-cum-income generation activities and the infrastructure incidental thereto, for Scheduled Tribes below the poverty line, thereby raising their economic and social status, including that of the Particularly Vulnerable Tribal Groups.

Some important features of the SCA to TSP are:

- 70 per cent of the SCA to be used for primary schemes supporting family/Self Help Groups (SHGs)/community-based employment and income generation in sectors such as Agriculture/ Horticulture, Land Reforms, Watershed Development, Animal Husbandry, Ecology and Environment, Development of Forests and Forest villages, etc., and 30 per cent for the development of infrastructure incidental thereto.
- Priority to the neglected Scheduled Tribes living in forest villages and synchronization of the programmes with Joint Forest Management (JFM).
- Preparation of long term area specific micro plans for ITDAs/ITDPs.
- 30 per cent of the beneficiaries are to be women.

Scheduled Caste Sub-Plan (SCSP)

The Scheduled Caste Sub-Plan (SCSP), introduced during the Sixth Plan and known earlier as Special Component Plan (SCP), is Sub-Plan of the Annual Plan and Five Year Plan targeting the SC population to channelise the flow of funds from the general sectors in the Plans of the States/ Union Territories for development of SCs specially those below the poverty line. The SCP envisaged to help the SC families through composite income generating/welfare schemes. The system has evolved a useful mechanism to draw funds and physical benefits in various sectors for improving the socio-economic and living conditions of the Scheduled Castes people.

The strategy of Scheduled Castes Sub-Plan (SCSP) since evolved in 1979 is aimed at:

(a) Economic development through beneficiary oriented programmes for raising their income and creating assets;
(b) Basti-oriented schemes for infrastructure development through provision of drinking water supply, link roads, house-sites, housing etc.; and
(c) Educational and Social development activities like establishment of primary schools, health centres, vocational centres, community halls, women work place, etc.

The strategy of Scheduled Castes Sub-Plan envisages channelising the flow of outlays and benefits from all the sectors of development in the Annual Plans of States/UTs at least in proportion to their population both in physical and financial terms.

The format of presentation of SCSP in the Annual Plan has been discussed in detail at Annexures VIA and VIB.

Special Central Assistance (SCA to SCSP)

The Ministry of Social Justice and Empowerment (M/SJ&E) provides 100 per cent grant under the Central Sector Scheme of SCA to SCSP as an additive to SCSP to the States/UTs to fill the critical gaps and vital missing inputs in family oriented income generating schemes with supporting infrastructure development so as to make the schemes more effective. The objective of the SCA is to provide additional support to Below Poverty Line (BPL) SC families to enhance their productivity and income. SCA could also be utilized for infrastructural development in the Blocks having 50 per cent or more of SC population. SCA is released to these States/UTs on the basis of the following criteria:

(i) SC Population of the States/UTs: 40 per cent;
(ii) Relative backwardness of the States/UTs:10 per cent;
(iii) Percentage of SC families in the States/UTs covered by Composite economic development programmes in the State Plan to enable them to cross the poverty line:25 per cent; and
(iv) Percentage of SCSP to the Annual Plan as compared to SC population percentage of the States/UTs: 25 per cent.

12

Formulation of Draft State Plan

Formulation of Annual Plan is an important annual event in the functioning of the State Government as it shapes the economic agenda for the next financial year which also facilitates plan budget of the State. It is formulated by an interactive team efforts in compliance of Line departments' constitutional responsibility under Rules of Business published under Article 166(3) of the Constitution on priorities of the State Plan along with overarching core objectives of the national Five Year Plan as approved by the National Development Council. Additionally, the Annual Plan of the State needs to give appropriate consideration on inclusive agenda including the Scheduled Castes Sub-Plan and Tribal Sub-Plan and the need to provide adequate back-up support for the Flagship Programmes. This apart, in the guidelines on Plan formulation, the Planning Commission also mentions about importance to keep adequate provision towards the counterpart fund for Centrally Sponsored schemes to ensure that the State is not deprived of Central share of resources provided for them. Further, the Annual Plan needs to address inclusive development issues, human development issues, deficit in these areas and the monitorable items for the Five Year Plan.

During the formulation of the State Plan, the planning process which connects the State Plan and the District Plans is required to be appropriately linked. District Plans are a kind of Sub-State Plans, though the aggregation of the District Plans does not add up the State Plan. The defined boundary of planning for the District Plan represented by its planning units in the forum of the tiers of Panchayats and the Municipalities is distinctly different. However, total plan initiatives in a given year for a State are aggregated efforts of all planning partners in the State. The Annual State Plan needs to capture them in the format, GNC I and GNC II, already set by the Planning Commission.

Planning Commission has been advocating the crucial role of the Civil Society including the Non Government Organisations in the planning and development efforts of the State in furtherance of the National Policy on the Voluntary Sector. In the Annexure VII of Annual Plan of the State, the partnership efforts of the Voluntary sector are also needed to be captured. During the formulation stage of the Annual Plan, the interactive dialogue and shared perception would be crucial for possible quality improvement and ownership of the State Plan by a bigger audience.

Credit Plan is an issue that is usually mentioned in connection with State Plan. Credit Plan is an important item of governance but that it has no independent space in the Annual Plan of the State. It is a kind of follow-up action for working out complementary role on the Annual Plan of the State. Further, Annual Credit Plan of the NABARD and the Credit Plan that emerged at the State Level Consultation Committee—constituted with representatives of the State Government, R.B.I, Lead Bank and other banks and financial institutions working in the State—falls in the domain of Plan of Actions. It has no one to one correspondence between the draft State Plan and the Credit Plan at that stage of credit planning. In view of different time lines of credit planning it is not even included as an item of plan resource (except RIDF) for deciding the size of the Annual Plan by the Deputy Chairman, Planning Commission and the Chief Minister of the State nor the Working Groups take up any issue on Credit Plan at the discussion stage on the Annual Plan of the State. Planning Commission is concerned with the budgetary and other institutional supports which are to be routed through the State Budget.

The resource back-up of the size of the Annual Plan of a State at the draft stage is an important issue. At the preparatory state of draft plan, the size of availability of the Central support remains undecided and unavailable. The Planning Commission's usual advice in this regard is to proceed, on an *ad hoc* basis, on the basis of 10 per cent enhancement over the Central Support given to the State for the current year. The Central Support for the Annual Plan of the State is firmed up and settled in the meeting held in between the Deputy Chairman of the Planning Commission and the Chief Minister of the State on the Annual Plan of State. The size of the State Plan so agreed between them becomes the size of the State Plan for the Annual Plan of the State. The scheme of financing the Annual Plan of the State is also finally settled there.

The time-frame for submission and approval of the State Plan is another connected issue. It is also designed by the Planning Commission and communicated to the State Government by the Deputy Chairman of the Planning Commission to the Chief Minister of the State. It is followed up by a letter from the senior official of the Planning Commission to the Chief Secretary of the State. This covers detailed time lines on transaction of business on Annual Plan of the State between the Planning Commission and the State Government. An example is given below:

- Official level Resource discussion—1st to 25th December, 2011;
- Last date for receipt of draft plan documentation—15th Jnuary, 2012 from States/UTs;
- Working Group discussions—15th January, 2012 onwards;
- Deputy Chairman-Chief Minister level discussion—February, 2012 onwards; and
- Issue of finalised sectoral outlays and scheme of financing—within 15 days of the above meeting.

It does not touch upon time lines for planning for any individual department, as it falls on the domain of the State Government or to any other partners including the State Planning Board. As mentioned earlier, Planning Commission does not have any direct relationship with the State Planning Board. It operates through the State Government being represented by its Planning Department and the Finance Department of the State.

The draft State Plan prepared by the State Government and submitted thereafter to the Planning Commission is the beginning point for further discussions in the Working Groups and at other levels in the Planning Commission. The draft State Plan has a designed structured format. It has two parts:

(a) Descriptive Part

The descriptive part in textual form begins with the presentation of the State Plan by heads of development. It cannot be presented in terms of proposed outlay by the departments of the State. Planning Commission designed the concept of the heads of development to capture developmental function underlined in any scheme or set of schemes. Such developmental functions are reference points for planning. In real terms, the purpose of planning is to improve current status of quality life of citizens and identified deficit of such development functions through a set of schemes. In other words, schemes are means to an end-the end of improving given developmental function. Depending on the nature of schemes those are grouped under a particular minor head, major head and under the concerned sector. In a situation where a particular department addresses more than one head of development, the said components of development function have to be positioned under corresponding minor head of development. Similarly, in situation where a minor head of development is addressed by more than one department, it is to be so posted under the relevant minor head in a separate paragraph with a heading of that department. In all cases, the textual presentation of plan proposals may begin with a sub-heading of the department. In case of more than one department under a particular minor head, such sub-heading may be sequentially numbered. The State Plan may as well include a summary situation on current status and proposed planning efforts to address the said development function.

The textual part of the Annual Plan document needs also to describe the logic on inclusion of the proposals under the Annual Plan and salient features of the scheme along with investment proposal. In case of continuing schemes, the highlights of past performances, current proposal and the possible time line for completion is also required to be mentioned. All such narrations have to be made, sector-wise and major and minor head of development-wise. Further, such narrations should also address all issues from human development angle as far as possible and also comprehensively cover TSP, SCSP, OBCs, Women and Children.

For a quality State Plan document, it will be relevant to include a chapter on Overview of the Draft Annual Plan capturing therein the achievements and shortcomings of the previous plan period and how the State economy is being intended to go forward overcoming those deficits in the proposed Annual Plan. Textual presentation on Externally Aided Projects, Flagship Programmes, Centrally Sponsored Schemes, Tribal Sub-Plan, Scheduled Caste Sub-Plan, Voluntary Sector and Women Component are also needed. A separate chapter each on Plan Finance and also on improving the current status of Human Development would be very relevant.

(b) Statistical Presentation

Planning Commission has designed 13 Tables for presentation of the State Plan in Annexure IX. The Annexures are meant to capture financial outlay and physical targets. In fact, all these annexures taken together constitutes the statistical image of the State Plan. The Annexures have been divided into the following categories:

1(a). *Proposed Outlays*—Major Heads/Minor Heads of Development—GN Statement-A.
1(b). *Proposed Outlays*—Major Heads/Minor Heads of Development: From State Budget, State PSE's and Local Bodies GN Statement-B.
1(c). *Proposed Outlays*: Major Heads/Minor Heads of Development For Rural and Urban Local Bodies—GN Statement-C.
2. *Proposed Outlays* for Ongoing and New Schemes—Annexure-I.
3. *Physical Targets and Achievements*—Annexure-II.
4. *Statement Regarding Externally Aided Projects*—Annexure-III.
5. *Centrally Sponsored Schemes*—Annexure-IV.
6. *Tribal Sub-Plan (TSP)*: Financial Outlays—Annexure-VA.
7. *Tribal Sub-Plan (TSP)*: Physical Targets and Achievements: Annexure-VB.
8. *Special Component Plan for Scheduled Castes* (SCSP-II)-Financial Outlays—Annexure VIA.
9. Special Component Plan For Scheduled Castes (SCSP-II)-Physical Targets and Achievements—Annexure-VIB.
10. *Financial Outlays/Expenditure for Voluntary Sector*—Annexure-VII.
11. *Women Component in the State Plan Programmes*: Financial Outlays—Annexure VIIIA.
12. *Women Component in the State Plan Programmes*: Physical Targets and Achievements—Annexure-VIIIB.
13. *Information related to Flagship Programmes*—Annexure-IX.

13

Approval Procedure of the State Annual Plan in the Planning Commission

(a) Working Group Discussions

The Planning Commission works out a general schedule for Annual Plan Exercise for the States of India. The Schedule is indicative in nature and the State specific Working Group discussions and Deputy Chairman-Chief Minister level discussion related schedule are settled thereafter. A schedule drawn by the Planning Commission for the Annual Plan Exercise is indicated below:

- Official Level Resource discussion—1st to 25th December, 2011.
- Last date for receipt of draft plan documentation—15th Jnuary, 2012 from States/UTs.
- Working Group discussions-15th January, 2012 onwards.
- Deputy Chairman-Chief Minister level discussion—February, 2012 onwards.
- Issue of finalised sectoral outlays and scheme of financing—Within 15 days of the above meeting.

After the State Government submits its Annual Plan to the Planning Commission, the Planning Commission organises meeting for Working Groups discussions with State Government officials in the Planning Commission. Usually, the secretaries of the department and its directors participate in the discussions. Historically, two modes of Working

Groups meetings in the Planning Commission are found to have been organised:

(a) In mode 1, the Working Groups discussions were held on the second day after the Deputy Chairman had held the meeting with the Chief Minister on the previous day;
(b) In mode 2, the Working Group discussions took place in advance before the Deputy Chairman and Chief Minister level of meeting was held.

Both the modes have its positional advantages. The advantage of mode 1 is that the Working Group discussions commence in the background of the Plan Outlay finally settled for the State Annual Plan. The financial proposals in the State Annual Plan, including some items hitherto missed out or not included or proposed with inadequate outlay, will then be possible to be discussed with ease and can be recommended within the parameter of the size of the Annual Plan. The advantage of mode 2 is that the sectoral projections as well as problems of different sectors could be examined on merit and the observations could be used as possible inputs to settle the size of the State Plan at the Deputy Chairman-Chief Minister level of meeting. Currently, mode 2 is being followed in the Planning Commission.

The Working Groups discussions in the Planning Commission are organised on selected but important developmental function areas. The designs of discussions format are structured accordingly. Some of the Advisers in the Planning Commission remain very often in charge of a number of development functions and the format of the Working Groups discussions reflects such allocations. Apart from the designated Adviser, senior officials in the Planning Commission and representative of the related nodal Ministry in the Government of India also participate. As earlier mentioned, from the State Government side, the secretary of the State dealing with the developmental function related to the said Working Group leads the team. If any Working Group covers items covering more than one department of the State Government, the team for the State also includes other representative(s) from the related department(s). However, the Secretary of the department representing major items leads the team.

A typical format of the Working Group formation is shown below:

Sl. No.	*Nodal Officer*	*Sector*	*Room No.*	*Time*
1.	Shri Lambor Rynjah, Principal Advisor	Agriculture & Allied services	207	2.30 pm onwards
2.	Dr. S.P. Seth, Principal Advisor	Power & Energy	239A	do
3.	Shri Amitabha Bhattacharyya, Senior Consultant	Education	264	do
4.	Shri B. N. Puri, Senior Consultant	Transport &Tourism	206	do
5.	Prof. S.N. Sethi, Senior Advisor	Health, Family Welfare, Nutrition	261	do
6.	Shri S. Kolba, Senior Advisor	Industry/V&SE	202	do
7.	Shri A.K. Mishra, Senior Advisor	Rural Development/Power	204	do
8.	Shri Yudhvir Uppal, Senior Advisor	Water Resources	246	do
9.	Sm. Firoza Mehrotra, Special Consultant	Women & Child Development	256	do
10.	Dr.(Sm) Indrani Chandra Shekharan, Advisor	Environment & Forest	234	do
11.	Shri G.B.Pande, Advisor	Social Justice & Empowerment	225	do
12.	Smt Nuin Jayaseelan, Advisor	LEM	215	do
13.	Dr. C. Muralikrishna Kumar, Advisor	Communication & Information	217	do
14.	Shri A.K. Verma, Advisor	Science &Technology	235	do
15.	Shri M.S.Agarwal,Advisor	Rural Water Supply & Sanitation(WR)	321	do
16.	Shri L.P. Sankar, Advisor	MLP, Panchayati Raj, District Planning, Special Area Programme, Housing & Urban Development	231	do
17.	Member (AM)	Wrap up meeting with the Chief Secretary	112	12 noon on 10.3.2010

The salient features of the Working Group discussions are that all of them commence their discussions at the same time on the appointed day.

Further, all the Working Group Advisors give their specific observations in the related Group meeting itself informally but they send their written suggestions to the Advisor in charge of the State immediately after the meeting is over. All the written suggestions are formally taken up at the Wrap up meeting taken by the Member of the Planning Commission in Charge of the State with the Chief Secretary of the State and his team of officials. After interactive discussions on suggestions in the Working Groups and responses of the State Government on them, the Member in Charge of the State in the Planning Commission wraps up the meeting with his final observations and the way forward for follow up actions.

(b) Meeting between the Deputy Chairman, Planning Commission and the Chief Minister of the State

The most important forum for the finalisation of the State Plan is the interactive session between the Deputy Chairman, Planning Commission; and the Chief Minister of the State. The date of the meeting is worked out by the official of the Planning Commission with the CM Secretariat and finalise the same. The team to be accompanied with the Chief Minister for the said discussions is also required to be communicated in advance to the Planning Commission. Before the said meeting of the Deputy Chairman, Planning Commission with the Chief Minister of the State, the Member-Secretary, Planning Commission also takes a preparatory meeting with the Chief Secretary and other officials of the team. The meeting takes stock of latest update on plan finance and also reviews priorities on the State plan initiatives *vis-à-vis* development deficit as assessed by the Planning Commission.

The meeting between the Deputy Chairman, Planning Commission and the Chief Minister of the State covers major issues on State Plan, its priorities, strengths and weakness of plan implementation, special problems, if any, proposed financial proposals in the Annual Plan, position of State finance to meet such obligations, additional central assistance requirement, etc. After interactive discussions, the size of the State Annual Plan and the scheme of its financing the Plan is mutually agreed and settled.

Planning Commission formally communicates the decision of the meeting held between the Deputy Chairman, Planning Commission and the Chief Minister of the State on the size of the Annual Plan of the State and the scheme of its financing together with the minutes of the meeting. The State Planning Department is required to rework the investment proposals as per heads of development, in GN statement, in pursuance of the decisions on Deputy Chairman-Chief Minister level of meeting for sectoral adjustments, on final size of the Annual Plan, as agreed. The Planning Commission communicates its approval to enable the State Government to budget for the same. The approved Plan from the Planning Commission becomes the Annual Plan of the year for the State and after its budgeting, it becomes the Budgeted Plan Estimate of the State.

Budgeted State Plan of the State

On receipt of approval of the Annual Plan from the Planning Commission, the Planning Department of the State is required to communicate scheme-wise approved outlay for the Annual Plan to the Plan Implementing departments and ask them to take action for budgeting the same. Earlier, the Plan Implementing departments prepared their draft plan proposals in terms of the heads of development with suggested plan outlay for each of such schemes. The Plan implementing departments are now required to mention approved plan outlay for such schemes in the format of head of accounts for the Budget Estimates while submitting the same to the Finance Department. The proposals when passed by the Legislature of the State in the Budget Session and subsequently approved by the Governor of the State happen to be the budgeted estimate for the year and eligible for release of fund from the budgeted account of the department and utilise them. In the event the Budgeted Plan Estimate does not agree with the Approved State Plan, the State Government is required to send an explanatory memorandum with adequate justification to the Planning Commission.

Revised Annual Plan

The State Government is authorised to revise their Annual Plan in consultation and approval of the Planning Commission. The financial condition of the State may move up or down based on resources behaviour in the State and may necessitate correction on the portfolio of plan finance availability. This apart, intervening new plan scheme may need to be taken up in the plan year itself or that based on ground realities, the scheme of inter-sectoral outlay requires to be adjusted. This may call for upward or downward adjustment of the size of the Plan. Since the plan assistance is organically linked with utilisation of approved outlay, revision of the approved outlay becomes inescapably necessary in such circumstances.

The proposal for such revision has to be communicated by the State Government to the Planning Commission by 31st December of the said financial year with revised scheme of financing for the proposed Revised Plan Outlay. On receipt of such proposal from the State Government and after due examination, the Planning Commission accords approval to the said Revised Plan of the year and communicates the same. Revised Outlay is also connected with plan assistance from the Planning Commission as it takes care of approved outlay and expenditure.

Revised Budgeted State Plan of the State

As earlier mentioned, the State Government is authorised to revise their Annual Plan in consultation and approval of the Planning Commission. Depending on the financial condition of the State, it may be necessary to effect correction and adjustments on the portfolio of plan finance availability. The proposal for revision has to be communicated by the Planning department of the State Government to the Planning Commission by 31st December of the said financial year along with scheme of financing for the Revised Plan Outlay. The Revised Plan Outlay, when approved by the Planning Commission, becomes the basis of Revised Budget Estimate. Since budget cannot be revised every now and then and requires formal sanction from the Legislature and the Governor of the State, the Finance Department informally follows the restriction on outer limits of Revised Budget Estimate during such intervening period till it is passed formally along with the Budget Estimate for the next year in the Budget Session itself.

14

Implementation

Implementation is the final destination for any scheme. By such implementation, the inherent objectives of a scheme are actualised. The actualisation of objectives also helps to achieve the outcome of the scheme. Actualisation or implementation process is very challenging as it is linked with procedures, capacity building, time lines, funding, accounting, monitoring etc.

In a Government system, there are standard laid down procedures for commencement of actual work. Preparation of Project Report/Scheme, its vetting, clearance from designated authority/Empowered Committee etc. take its own time and in the process consume a sizeable portion of prime time. The Expression of Interest, Tender, Quotations, Work Order, etc., are other areas that also take away a big chunk of work time for some big schemes. Time slippage and cost escalation restarts the whole process and affects original schedule of completion of works. Rainy season and weather factors also affect schedule of works. Besides, performances of some tasks are linked with quality enhancement of capacity building and unless this part of requisites is previously performed, it will encroach upon schedule of time lines. Another factor that delays the implementation proceedings is not giving due importance to prepare an Action Plan requiring check list for sequential actions.

The macro-image of the implementation in the government sector is not very encouraging. The focus of aggregate status of financial expenditure at the fag end of financial year is not at all inspiring. Such year-end expenditure satisfaction system does not always reflect quality of investment and to that extent some of such investments are infructuous in real sense. An illustration might be useful. Supply of agricultural inputs to the cultivators after the cropping season, but within financial year, might jack up plan expenditure but has little contributing value for effecting incremental agricultural production The culture of release of considerable fund in the first week of March in a financial year by some State Government is not also implementation friendly; it leads to improper use of fund and explain in a big way for compromise of quality in execution of the schemes. The March syndrome is the single biggest factor for poor quality of implementation of works.

The Government sector is hierarchy based with defined functions at a particular level. The exact functional role relating to implementation of any scheme or a project is not always defined creating escape routes from accountability. Needless to mention, total of activities at all levels of functionaries ensure proper implementation of a scheme or a project. An activity mapping cataloguing of actions and responsibilities for such functionaries is helpful for timely completion of related tasks.

Implementation of a programme is organically connected with delivery of services. The quality of delivery of services depends on quality of implementation. It is in this area that inclusive approach and human development consideration come in. The attributes of access, choice, capability and participation are to be factored in while implementing related programme.

For improving quality of implementation, programme monitoring experts brought in various instruments to see that programmes/schemes are on right course. Some of such instruments belong to the category of concurrent monitoring just from the take off of the programme/schemes. Here comes the instrument of Process Performance Index. The process part comprises to perform a set of formalities and conditionalites before the actual production starts and also thereafter. It consists of, among other things, organising different inputs at a defined point of implementing process. The compliance of such scheduled tasks in time and in sequential order is a way forward to achieve the time lines for completion of the project. Other instruments brought in are concerned with the quality of output after completion of the project/scheme. There are a good number of instruments to assess and evaluate the final output of any programme/scheme. Of them three instruments are usually mentioned, namely, performance audit, outcome audit and social audit. The performance audit is undertaken by the office of the Accountant General of the State to correlate objectives of the programme/scheme, the expenditure incurred and final output delivered as per the project time schedule and also of its quality. The outcome audit examines not merely the output of a project *per se*, it wants to assess the linkage of the output with the greater objective of commissioning the programme itself, e.g., whether the introduction of the RKVY has in fact boosted the growth process to achieve targeted growth of agricultural production in the State. The social audit is undertaken by the stakeholders of the programme/scheme located at or near the command area from beneficiaries perceptional point of view and whether it met all or to what extent the community's expectation from the programme or where it went wrong. The offshoot of the above discussion is that different instruments have to be put in place to ensure that implementation process reaches its desired destination point. The implementation process seldom acts at its own as auto-generating process to achieve programme objectives.

15

Co-ordination, Convergence and Monitoring of Schemes of the Line Departments

Co-ordination is the act of working together for a goal or effect. Co-ordination is also a platform in which mutual gains are reaped if participants make mutually consistent decisions. All irritating roadblocks standing or surfaced in the programme implementation area and having linkage with other related partners are also taken up in the co-ordination meet for resolution. Based on a spirit of accommodation, a number of formal and informal co-ordination forums have come into being in the government system for bilateral interactions or for multilateral sectoral decisions, both at the secretariat of the Government or at the level of district administration. The co-ordination set-up at the secretariat addresses policy related issues, as relevant or where there are scope to issue guidelines to facilitate productive co-ordination and harmonious relations down the lines in furthering the implementation process. From operational angle, however, the most important layer of co-ordination is those connected with actual execution of schemes or those connected with its immediate supervision. However, administrative culture obtaining in the field necessitates the requirement of a third party facilitator with independent image to preside over such co-ordination interactions. The institution of the District Magistrate has come to establish as an acceptable personality of co-ordination maker in most of the districts in the country. As a result, the District Magistrate/Collector assumes crucial role in co-ordination and is in fact the principal coordinator in the district and presides over a number of such co-ordination meetings designed for bilateral partners or for plural number of stakeholders. Some of such co-ordination meetings include DM's development co-ordination meeting, irrigation co-ordination meeting, disaster management co-ordination meeting, Sports co-ordination meeting, etc. The essence of this co-ordination committee meeting is to remove hurdles to facilitate operational linkages and connectivity that inherently exists between one programme and the other for better output. An illustration may be given. Boro paddy cultivation depends on assured and timely release of specified quantum of water. The Irrigation department has to release water accordingly. Unless the time sequence and the requisite quantum of water are made available, the Boro production will fail. The co-ordination efforts would make the action process easier.

The co-ordination role of the Secretariat is meant for next layer of interactions to settle policy-linked field issues with related partner departments. Normally, field issues which cannot be resolved at the local level come up at the Secretariat. Critical issues are also referred to the Secretariat which is linked with policy forum for higher administrative decision. For uninterrupted energy supply to the pump-sets during Boro cultivation, for example, the Agriculture department is required to meet its counterpart in the Power department to ensure power supply in the related network and settle the issue. Similarly, for ensuring timely credit during particular crop season, the Agriculture department is required to interact with the Cooperation department for outreach of credit and settle it. There are other partners connected with it as well. In view of time lines linked with the crop season and other cross connectivity issues, all the partners usually sit together in a spirit of accommodation and take required decision. Normally, the Chief Secretary or the Planning Secretary takes such meeting. In some cases, senior most secretary of the related partner departments presides over the meeting.

The high valued platform of co-ordination meeting requires to be structured with due care and caution. Only coordinating functionaries of the appropriate level of the related departments need to be invited for interactions, for being in a position to participate in the decision taking exercises with authority and also empowered to follow them up. The token presence by a proxy representative has only notional value.Such a meeting needs to be preceded by situational analysis of the related implementation areas, the identification of causal factors of hurdles and possible role of partner departments to remove the hurdles. Thus, an in-depth home exercise on what, when and how aspects is a necessary requisite for effecting productive co-ordination. Otherwise, such co-ordination meeting would turn out to be simply futile and a ritual exercise only. No positive and implementation friendly decision would come out of it. The sufficient condition for productive co-ordination is to publish an ATR (Action Taken Report) on decisions earlier taken in a previous co-ordination meeting.

Convergence

Another area linked with co-ordination is Convergence. As a matter of fact, co-ordination spirit is a necessary requirement for convergence. Convergence indeed is a bigger functional concept implicit in which exists a framework of programme connectivity, a shared goal and focused output at a possible incremental scale. The presence of a lead scheme is the essential prerequisite. The schemes for convergent partnership could be collaborative, supportive, connected, linked, associated or additive. The bonding of convergence might be triggered by synergy; it might as well be driven by forces of investment to meet unmet demand or on spatial planning consideration. Such partnership may take the form of dovetailing; it may as well take the form of tie-up accommodation or it may converge under one window. The convergent junction has to be a shared work-out node based on activity mapping and properly sequenced.

While Working on Convergence, the following Cardinal Principles are required to be kept in mind

- Convergence of the works programme has to be at a particular place or location;
- The lead scheme in question needs to have backward or forward linkage;
- Such convergence may take place simultaneously with compatible scheme or immediately thereafter;
- Such convergence needs to ensure value addition;
- For ensuring visibility and transparency from audit angle, partner schemes must be distinct and obviously different;
- The schemes so partnered should be compatible with each other. It should not work at cross purposes; and
- Normally, such schemes should belong to the same sector so as to relate them in one developmental function.

There is a crucial role of third party in facilitating such convergence. However, the institution of the Secretariat cannot be the forum for facilitating convergence. Such facilitating forum has to exist near the local areas of programme implementation. The third party facilitation could be the district coordinating officer, the district planning body or the concerned local body empowered to attend to such kind of works. The lower is the location of such body; the greater is the chance for it being an effective convergence maker. Such third party might be better placed to see through the possible convergence space in the work formats in an objective and bias-free assessment of compatibility and potentialities of schemes. Such forum can also assume the role of independent convergent monitor later to facilitate timely convergence.

Monitoring of State Plans

Monitoring is defined as a process of measuring, recording, collecting, processing and communicating information to assist project management in decision making. Monitoring is a functioning tool to understand the flow character of a scheme right from the time of its commencement. It generates not only flow of data but deciphers also its inner meaning of the process behaviour signalling thereby the irritating points that need to be resolved. In that mould, it acts as supervising the functioning process to a particular work plan at a given point of time.

There are four critical aspects for productive monitoring. Those could be listed as below:

(i) What is to be Monitored

Monitoring items should be pointed, relevant and critical. It could be process monitoring or it could be monitoring of outcome. While both forms of monitoring are important to realise programme objectives, the nature of monitoring and its formats would be different with reference to the defined objective of monitoring. Further, monitoring may be related to financial progress, popularly known as expenditure monitoring or it may be both monitoring of expenditure and linked output. The ideal form of monitoring needs to include both physical and financial progress. However, in the real world of monitoring in the government programmes, monitoring ultimately lapses into expenditure monitoring which explains why visibie and quantifiable outputs are not in place even after project money has been fully spent.

Monitoring could be of different types depending on specific objective in view, e.g., there could be monitoring of programme implementation from human development angle (access, choice, capability enlargement and participation) or there could be monitoring on inclusiveness. It is possible to monitor on gender focus of implementation or monitoring of expenditure with reference to time lines of season specific agriculture crop. Similarly, there could be monitoring on trends of expenditure on irrigation project during the dry season (working season) and during the rest of the season. It is also possible to take up intensive monitoring on bulk fund released during February-March of the financial year to guard against wasteful expenditure. Further, there could be monitoring on Flagship Programmes of the country as covered under 20-point programme or there could be input-output focused monitoring on some subject. As a matter of fact there could be any types of monitoring depending on the purpose and objective to improve the functioning system by application of the tool of monitoring. Linked with it comes the focused items that are to be monitored. For facilitating effective monitoring, items for monitoring need to be carefully identified and clear correspondence between the items for monitoring and objects of monitoring are to be firmly structured in the design. Monitoring in the government sector very often does not achieve the ends of monitoring for a variety of reasons including crowding of non-essential items in the monitoring design and thereby losing its focus.

Design of the monitoring format is very crucial. In designing monitoring format it has to be kept in mind that format for Monitoring Report and the agenda items for Monitoring Meeting may not be the same. It is possible that items for monitoring meeting are different. Normally those items are taken up in a monitoring meeting which need interactive discussion for resolution of problems. Critical issues persistently standing in the work programme only qualify to be the agenda item for appropriate resolution in a monitoring meeting.

(ii) Who is to Monitor

The primary responsibility of monitoring lies with the implementation functionary on the job. The monitoring job at this level is to look into different tasks as per activity mapping already worked out before the commencement of the works. In the hierarchical order, the next order of monitoring forum lies with the supervisory functionary located either at the horizontal level or at the vertical level or with both. An illustration will make it clear. Supply of agricultural inputs in time is the responsibility of District Agriculture Officer in a district. Monitoring of the said job can be done at horizontal level by the Collector/DPC just as it can be done by the Joint Director/Director of the Agriculture Directorate at the vertical level. Similarly, the Secretariat, the Ministry and the State Planning Board may undertake monitoring jobs as relevant at those levels. The focus of monitoring for each level tends to be different connected as it is with monitoring objective for those levels. In other words, the first requisite for qualifying as monitoring unit is that there has to exist organisational or functional link in between the monitoring unit and the implementing agency. Further, for productive monitoring, each of the units needs to have its own and distinct monitoring area.

An important requisite for productive monitoring is also that monitoring team members must be well conversant with the subject areas under monitoring review including its objects, details of the scheme and time lines of its completion, etc. The updated domain knowledge of team members only ensures meaningful interactions and useful decisions.

(iii) How is to Monitor Them

The implementing unit needs to fill in designed monitoring format as per time design and submit to its monitoring units. Normally, the descriptive version should not be encouraged for the sake of easier comprehension and its consolidation. Based on analysis of monitoring data, a status position is needed to be worked out. The monitoring status with observations, if any, may require then to be communicated to all concerned for appropriate action. In case of necessity, it could be followed up by field inspection as well. A monitoring meeting may also be taken up to sort out recurring problems which have been road-blocking the implementation schedule or any cross sectoral issue which poses as irritant for completion of the scheme in time with desired quality standard.

(iv) Monitoring of Action Taken Report

Monitoring is for ensuring right course of programme implementation and, therefore, it is not a one time affair. It is a continuous process till the scheme is completed. The prescriptions for correction based on a monitoring report, say MR-1, need to be comprehensively addressed before submitting monitoring report, say MR-2. Mere communication of findings without follow-up compliance report would make the entire exercise redundant. ATR is in fact the essence of monitoring.

Monitoring *per se* is not an end in itself. It is a means to ensure proper implementation of scheme by acting as an indivisible supervisor during the process of implementation. Moreover, it is not enough that monitoring technique should alone be applied: it is also required to be buttressed by the other technique known as concurrent evaluation. In fact monitoring and concurrent evaluation are two activities which go hand in hand. Adequate monitoring is a basic requisite for undertaking concurrent evaluation and it is impossible to evaluate a scheme unless it has been adequately monitored over time.

PART-B

16

Presentation of State Annual Plan

Plan and Planning are two different interrelated but complementary functions. Planning is the process of taking decision on settling priorities among possible alternatives in consultation with stakeholders. Plan is the document in which the prioritised planning decisions are so captured. In real world, the plan document itself is the central focus of all discussions and the process part does not come up very significantly either in its document or in the forum of academic discussion. The postulate of the process is taken for granted and assumed that fundamentals of consultations, etc., have been adhered to. The Plan document usually contains two parts: In the first part it embodies the economic logic for inclusion of the subject and the basis of its prioritisation after due analysis of historical account, the performance status of the immediate past and its projection for the future; in its second part it captures the related investment decisions.

Following this usual pattern, the Planning Commission of India has designed the formats for the State Plan in two parts: In Part I, the descriptive part of the State Plan, with such process as relevant, has to be presented as per heads of development. In Part II, the statistical part of the State Plan has to be indicated under a given set of Annexure, also designed by the Planning Commission. The Annexure are expected to reveal the character and focus of the State Plan. The Statistical Part of the State Plan document is very important as essential inputs for productive discussions in the Working Group discussions in the Planning Commission. All the Working Groups in the Planning Commission consider this Statistical part as benchmark to understand inherent logic of State priorities, volume of investment proposals for the next Annual Plan *vis-à-vis* its expenditure behaviour over time in the context of targets so set for the Annual Plans and Five Year Plan for the related programme. The representatives of the State Government need to convincingly respond at the Working Group discussions to the queries of the Planning Commission and also from the related officials from the nodal Ministry of the Central Government for the planning logic of priorities and justification for quantum of investment proposals. Since the Planning Commission sets up Working Group discussions in terms of subject groups as per heads of development—and not in terms of departments of the State Government—the clarity in understanding the heads of development-wise posting in plan document is also very important. Incidentally, in some heads of development, there is likely to have more than one department as programme partners. There is, however, no scope to break them up in between departments as it will lose the meaning and focus of heads of development designed by the Planning Commission. The moot point here is to fill up the Annexure correctly.

17

Statistical Presentation of State Plan

Planning Commission has updated usual format of State Plan presentation with reference to the Twelfth Plan and Annual Plan, 2012-13. The list of Statements/Tables for draft Annual State Plan, 2012-13 is indicated below:

1(a) Proposed Outlays—Major Heads/Minor Heads of Development GN Statement-A.
1(b) Proposed Outlays—Major Heads/Minor Heads of Development: From State Budget, State PSE's and Local Bodies GN Statement–B.
1(c) Proposed Outlays—Major Heads/Minor Heads of Development: For Rural and Urban Local Bodies GN Statement–C.
2. Proposed Outlays on Ongoing and New Schemes Annexure-I.
3. Physical Targets and Achievements Annexure-II.
4. Statement regarding Externally Aided Projects Annexure-III.
5. Centrally Sponsored Schemes Annexure-IV.
6. Tribal Sub-Plan (TSP): Financial Outlays Annexure—V-A.
7. Tribal Sub-Plan (TSP): Physical Targets and Achievements Annexure—V-B.
8. Special Component Plan for Scheduled Castes (SCSP-I) — Financial Outlays: Annexure VI-A.
9. Special Component Plan for Scheduled Castes (SCSP-II) — Physical Targets and Achievements, Annexure—VI-B.
10. Financial Outlays/Expenditure for Voluntary Sector, Annexure-VII.
11. Women Component in the State Plan Programmes—Financial Outlays, Annexure VIII-A.
12. Women Component in the State Plan Programmes—Physical Targets and Achievements, Annexure—VIII-B.

13. Information relating to Flagship Programmes—Annexure-IX.

1(a) Proposed Outlays—Major Heads/Minor Heads of Development—GN Statement-A

Planning Commission annually updates the formats of State Plan presentation with reference to the new plan year. This year it has been updated with reference to the Twelfth Plan and the Annual Plan 2012-13. The fundamentals of filling the annexure have been explained in details below so as not to have any confusion. The GN Statement-A is the most important annexure and in a sense it carries the summary of the character of the State Plan.

1(a) Draft Annual State Plan (2012-13) Proposed Outlays—Major Heads/Minor Heads Of Development— GN Statement-A

GN Statement-A

DRAFT ANNUAL STATE PLAN (2012-13)—PROPOSED OUTLAYS

(Rs. in lakhs)

Sl. No.	*Major Heads/Minor Heads of Development*	*Eleventh Plan 2007-12 Projected Outlay (at 2006-07 prices)*	*Eleventh Plan 2007-12- Anticipated Expenditure (at current prices)*	*Annual Plan 2010-11*	*Annual Plan— 2011-12*		*Twelfth Plan 2012-17 Tentative Projected Outlay (at 2011-12 prices)*	*Annual Plan 2012-13 Proposed Outlay*
				Actual Expenditure	*Approved Outlay*	*Anticipated Expenditure*		
0	1	2	3	4	5	6	7	8
I.	AGRICULTURE & ALLIED ACTIVITIES							
	1. Crop Husbandry							
	2. Horticulture							
	3. Soil and Water Conservation (including control of shifting cultivation)							
	4. Animal Husbandry							
	5. Dairy Development							
	6. Fisheries							
	7. Plantations							
	8. Food, Storage and Warehousing							
	9. Agricultural Research and Education							
	10. Agricultural Financial Institutions							

(Contd.)

GN STATEMENT-A (*Contd.*)

0	1	2	3	4	5	6	7	8
	11. Cooperation							
	12. Other Agricultural Programmes:							
	(a) Agiculture marketing							
	(b) Others (to be specified)							
	Total: (I) (1 to 12)							
	II. RURAL DEVELOPMENT							
	1. Special Programme for Rural Development:							
	(a) Integrated Watershed Management Programme (IWMP)							
	(b) DRDA Administration							
	(c) Others (To be specified)							
	Sub-Total (Special Programme for Rural Development)							
	2. Rural Employment							
	(a) MG National Rural Employment Act							
	(b) Swaranjayanti Gram Swarozgar Yojana (SGSY)/National Rural Livelihood Mission							
	(c) Others (To be specified)							
	Sub-Total (Rural Employment)							
	3. Land Reforms							
	4. Other Rural Development Programmes							
	(a) Community Development & Panchayats							
	(b) Other Programmes of Rural Development							
	Sub-Total (Other Rural Development)							
	TOTAL—II (1 to 4)							

(*Contd.*)

GN STATEMENT-A (*Contd.*)

0	1	2	3	4	5	6	7	8
III.	**SPECIAL AREAS PROGRAMMES**							
	(a) Hill Areas Development Programme							
	(b) Other Special Areas Programme							
	(i) Border Area Development Programme							
	(ii) Backward Region Grant Fund (Backward Districts/Special Plan/Integrated Action Plan)							
	(iii) Grants under proviso to article 275(1)							
	(iv) Special Central Assistance to Tribal Sub-Plan							
	(v) Others (to be specified)							
	Sub-Total (Other Special Programme)							
	TOTAL—III (a+b)							
IV.	**IRRIGATION & FLOOD CONTROL**							
	1. Major and Medium Irrigation							
	2. Minor Irrigation							
	3. Command Area Development							
	4. Flood Control (includes flood protection works)							
	TOTAL—IV (1 to 4)							
V.	**ENERGY**							
	1. Power							
	2. Non-conventional Sources of Energy							
	3. Integrated Rural Energy Programme							

(*Contd.*)

GN STATEMENT-A (*Contd.*)

0	1	2	3	4	5	6	7	8
TOTAL—V (1 to 3)								
VI. INDUSTRY & MINERALS								
1. Village and Small Enterprises								
(i) Small Scale Industries								
(ii) Handlooms/Powerlooms								
(iii) Handicrafts								
(iv) Sericulture/coir/wool								
(v) Food Processing Industries								
(vi) Others (to be specified)								
Sub-Total (VSE)								
2. Other Industries (Other than VSE)								
3. Minerals								
TOTAL—(VI) (1 to 3)								
VII. TRANSPORT								
1. Minor Ports								
2. Civil Aviation								
3. Roads and Bridges								
4. Road Transport								
5. Inland Water Transport								
6. Other Transport Services (to be specified)								
TOTAL—(VII) (1 to 6)								
VIII. SCIENCE, TECHNOLOGY & ENVIRONMENT								
1. Scientific Research								

(*Contd.*)

GN STATEMENT-A (*Contd.*)

0	1	2	3	4	5	6	7	8
	2. Information Technology & E-Governance							
	3. Ecology & Environment							
	4. Forestry & Wildlife							
	TOTAL—(VIII) (1 to 4)							
IX.	**GENERAL ECONOMIC SERVICES**							
	1. Secretariat Economic Services							
	2. Tourism							
	3. Census, Surveys & Statistics							
	4. Civil Supplies							
	5. Other General Economic Services:							
	(a) Weights & Measures							
	(b) District Planning / District Councils							
	(c) Others (to be specified)							
	Sub-Total (Other General Economic Services)							
	TOTAL—(IX) (1 to 5)							
X.	**SOCIAL SERVICES**							
	1. General Education							
	(a) Elementary Education							
	(b) Literacy/Adult Education							
	(c) Secondary Education							
	(d) Higher Education							
	Sub-Total (General Education) (a to d)							
	2. Technical Education							
	3. Sports							
	4. Youth Services							

(*Contd.*)

GN STATEMENT-A (*Contd.*)

0	1	2	3	4	5	6	7	8
5. Art & Culture								
6. Medical & Public Health								
(i) Primary Health Care								
(a) Rural								
(b) Urban								
(ii) Secondary Health Care								
(iii) Tertiary Health Care/Super Speciality Services								
(iv) Medical Education & Research								
(v) Training								
(vi) AYUSH								
(vii) E.S.I.								
(viii) Control of—								
(a) Communicable diseases (to be specified)								
(b) Non-communicable diseases (to be specified)								
(ix) National Rural Health Mission (Activities to be specified)								
(x) Other Programmes								
Sub-Total (Medical & Public Health)								
7. Water Supply & Sanitation								
(i) Rural Water Supply								
(ii) Rural Sanitation								
(iii) Urban Water Supply								
(iv) Urban Sanitation								
8. Housing (incl. Police Housing)								
(i) Rural Housing (Programmes to be specified)								

(*Contd.*)

GN STATEMENT-A (*Contd.*)

0	1	2	3	4	5	6	7	8
	(ii) Urban Housing (Programmes to be specified)							
	Sub-Total (Housing)							
	9. Urban Development (incl. State Capital Projects & slum Area Development)							
	10. Information & Publicity							
	11. Development of SCs, STs & OBCs							
	(i) Development of SCs							
	(ii) Development of STs							
	(iii) Development of OBCs							
	Sub-Total (SCs, STs & OBCs)							
	12. Labour & Employment							
	A. Labour Welfare							
	(i) Labour & Labour Welfare							
	(ii) Social Security for labour							
	(iii) Labour Education							
	(iv) Rehabilitation of Bonded Labour							
	(v) Child Labour							
	B. Employment Services							
	C. Craftsmen Training (I.T.I.s) and Apprenticeship Training							
	Sub-Total (Labour & Employment)							
	13. Social Security & Social Welfare							
	(i) Insurance Scheme for the Poor through GIC, etc.							
	(ii) National Social Assistance Programme & Annapurna							
	(iii) Welfare of handicapped (includes assistance for Voluntary Organisations)							

(*Contd.*)

GN STATEMENT-A (*Contd.*)

0	1	2	3	4	5	6	7	8
	(iv) Social Defence (includes Drug Addicts, Rehabilitation Programmes, HIV/AIDS, etc.							
	(v) Others (to be specified)							
	Sub-Total (Social Security & Social Welfare)							
	14. Empowerment of Women & Development of Children							
	(i) Empowerment of Women							
	(ii) Development of Children (Includes Integrated Child Development Services, etc.)							
	(iii) Nutrition							
	(iv) Other Services (to be specified)							
	Sub-Total (Empowerment of Women & Development of Children)							
	TOTAL—(X) (1 to 14)							
	XI. GENERAL SERVICES							
	1. Jails							
	2. Stationery & Printing							
	3. Public Works							
	4. Other Administrative Services:							
	(i) Training							
	(ii) Others (to be specified)							
	TOTAL-(XI) (1 to 4)							
	GRAND TOTAL							

Column 0 is already filled up in the format itself. Nothing is to be done here.

Column 1 has also been filled up in the format itself. Nothing is to be done here also.

Column 2 is meant for the Eleventh Five Year Plan Outlay against each minor head, under its major head of a given sector. This column is also a given figure in that at the beginning of the Eleventh Plan the Planning Commission approved the Eleventh Plan Outlay of the State Plan. Those figures are to be posted here.

Column 3 is the Eleventh Plan Anticipated Expenditure at current prices. Normally Planning Commission communicates year-wise inflator for conversion of earlier expenditure at current prices. Pending receipt of such inflator, the total of first four year's expenditure, as obtained from the office of Accountant General may be added with the anticipated expenditure for the year 2011-12 and then post the aggregate figure at column 3, major and minor head of development-wise.

Column 4 is to capture actual expenditure for 2010-11. During November end, actual verified expenditure figures for the Annual plan, 2010-11 are likely to have reached the departments of the State Government from the office of the Accountant General. Since all the schemes have dedicated account code, scheme-wise actual expenditures could be filled up by the concerned Line Department and then posted against concerned minor head. If for some reason, the actuals from the office of the Accountant General are not available, verified figures of drawal of fund might be obtained from the related Treasury, compare it with utilisation certificates and then post the figures, head of development-wise, in the corresponding entry. It may be indicated 'provisional' by the side of the Actual within bracket in case verified figures from the office of the Accountant General have not been posted.

Column 5 refers to Approved Outlay for the Annual Plan, 2011-12, head of development-wise. This column is to be filled in from the approved letter of the Planning Commission for the Annual Plan, 2011-12.

Column 6 is meant for Anticipated Expenditure for 2011-12. As to the anticipated expenditure, it is desirable to give realistic expenditure based on half yearly situation or third quarterly figures of financial achievement, as available, with realistic assessment for the remaining period of the Annual Plan. In this aspect, release of budgeted State fund to the implementing agencies for the relevant schemes may be given appropriate consideration. Anticipated achievements indicating full coverage do not really make any planning sense and hence need to post realistic figures only.

Column 7 is to indicate. Tentative outlay for the Twelfth Plan which the State Government has to work, major and minor head-wise at this stage based on the Approach of the Twelfth Plan, the State vision based on development deficit, human development deficit and other compulsions at the State level as perceived by the State Planning Board and the Plan implementing departments of the State.

Column 8 is meant for proposals of the State Plan for the Annual Plan, 2012-13 which will be taken up for discussion by the Working Groups in the Planning Commission and later by the Deputy Chairman and the Chief Minister of the State for finalisation of the State Plan.

1(b) Proposed Outlays—Major Heads/Minor Heads of Development: From State Budget, State PSEs and Local Bodies—GN Statement–B

The GN Statements-B are a kind of break-up statements of GN-A on components of plan resources namely, budgetary sources (Part-1), resources from Public Sector Enterprises (Part-II) and resources from Local Bodies (Part-III). In larger number of States, it is the budgetary resources (i.e., Part-I) that shape the size of the State Annual Plan and contribution from the remaining two sources are rather nil or insignificant. There are, however, some States where the resources of PSEs contribute significantly on plan finances to meet the commitment of plan. The Panchayats and the Municipalities do generate substantial amount of own resources which, after meeting its non-plan expenditure, are not able to meet any significant part of State Annual Plan expenditure. Besides, the Panchayats and the Municipalities are not expected to contribute any resources for items on State Plan which belong to Seventh Schedule. However, in case the amount of State Plan resources is available from Local Bodies as well, those are to be captured here (i.e., in Part-III). Incidentally, unlike PSEs, the resources from such large number of local bodies cannot be assessed in advance and generally this component of plan resources is not normally taken into consideration for the size of the Annual Plan of the State. However, all the three parts of the B-Statements have to be filled in based on validated figures for understanding the nature of plan finance in the State. In case there would be Nil resources from Part-II or Part-III, it has to be so mentioned there.

GN STATEMENT—B

GN STATEMENT-B (PART-I) : DRAFT ANNUAL STATE PLAN (2012-13)— PROPOSED OUTLAYS (FROM STATE BUDGET)

(Rs. in lakhs)

Sl. No.	*Major Heads/ Minor Heads of Development*	*Eleventh Plan 2007-12 Projected Outlay (at 2006-07 prices)*	*Eleventh Plan 2007-12- Anticipated Expenditure (at current prices)*	*Annual Plan 2010-11*	*Annual Plan-2011-12*		*Twelfth Plan 2012-17 Tentative Projected Outlay (at 2011-12 prices)*	*Annual Plan 2012-13 Proposed Outlay*
				Actual Expenditure	*Approved Outlay*	*Anticipated Expenditure*		
0	1	2	3	4	5	6	7	8

GN STATEMENT–B (PART–II)

DRAFT ANNUAL STATE PLAN (2012-13): PROPOSED OUTLAYS (FROM STATE PSE's)

(Rs. in lakhs)

Sl. No.	*Major Heads/ Minor Heads of Development*	*Eleventh Plan 2007-12 Projected Outlay (at 2006-07 prices)*	*Eleventh Plan 2007-12- Anticipated Expenditure (at current prices)*	*Annual Plan 2010-11*	*Annual Plan-2011-12*		*Twelfth Plan 2012-17 Tentative Projected Outlay (at 2011-12 prices)*	*Annual Plan 2012-13 Proposed Outlay*
				Actual Expenditure	*Approved Outlay*	*Anticipated Expenditure*		
0	1	2	3	4	5	6	7	8

GN STATEMENT–B (PART–III)

DRAFT ANNUAL STATE PLAN (2012-13): PROPOSED OUTLAYS (FROM LOCAL BODIES)

(Rs. in lakhs)

Sl. No.	Major Heads/ Minor Heads of Development	Eleventh Plan 2007-12 Projected Outlay (at 2006-07 prices)	Eleventh Plan 2007-12 Anticipated Expenditure (at current prices)	Annual Plan 2010-11	Annual Plan 2011-12		Twelfth Plan 2012-17 Tentative Projected Outlay (at 2011-12 prices)	Annual Plan 2012-13 Proposed Outlay
				Actual Expenditure	Approved Outlay	Anticipated Expenditure		
0	1	2	3	4	5	6	7	8

Note: Major / Minor Head total across Parts I, II, III of GN-Statement-B should tally with Col. 7 and 8 of GN-Statement-A.

@: Appropriate and Required Major / Minor Heads from GN Statement-A may please be used.

The Annexure GN-B-I, GN-B-II and GN-B-III have identical columns in the format. Those may be discussed together. As mentioned earlier, these B-I, B-II and B-III add up GN-A. Columns 0 and 1 are common and identical in respect of all the segments of GN-B-I, GN-B-II and GN-B-III. It is in respect of Columns 2 and 3, 4, 5, 6, 7 and 8 that the figures are bound to be different. Only those items from the specified sources-State Budget or PSEs or Local Bodies and falling under particular heads of development, would have to be posted there. It is to be noted that total of Major /Minor Head across Parts B-I B-II and B-III of GN-Statement B has to tally with columns 2, 3, 4, 5, 6, 7 and 8 of GN-Statement-A.

It is observed that it is somewhat difficult to fill in columns under GN Statement-B (both Part II and Part-III) as the Planning Commission never worked out projected Outlay for a State Plan based on resources from State Budget, PSE and Local Bodies separately. Planning Commission works out Projected Outlay for a State based on total resources, and not segmenting it resource-wise. Its Eleventh Plan components, actuals of an Annual Plan, Agreed Outlay, Anticipated Expenditure or Proposed Outlay are not possible to be filled in resource-wise. Similarly, it would not be possible to fill in Twelfth Plan related Outlay or for the Annual Plan, 2012-13. As a matter of fact, most of the State governments never fill in these Annexes as it would amount to an exercise of estimation only. This is an area for reforms in the Annex area of plan presentation.

It would be desirable that Planning Commission would give appropriate instructions how to fill in the format.

1(c). Proposed Outlays—Major Heads/Minor Heads of Development : For Rural and Urban Local Bodies—GN Statement–C

The GN Statement-C is an extension of GN Statement–B (Part-III) in that it wants to capture proposed outlays, not in terms of contribution of aggregates of the local bodies, but its break-up position-separately for the aggregate position of the Rural local bodies (Panchayats) and the Urban local bodies (Municipalities). However, GN Statement-C (Part-III) intends to capture the same information as that of GN Statement--B (Part-III) and that the Planning Commission may consider to omit GN Statement-C (Part-III) altogether. Pending such withdrawal, the same data of GN Statement—B (Part-III) need to be copied and pasted for GN Statement–C (Part-III). The GN Statement–C (Part-I, Part-II and Part-III) are as follows:

GN STATEMENT–C (PART–I)

DRAFT ANNUAL STATE PLAN (2012-13) : PROPOSED OUTLAYS (RURAL LOCAL BODIES)

(Rs. in lakhs)

Sl. No.	*Major Heads/Minor Heads of Development*	*Eleventh Plan 2007-12 Projected Outlay (at 2006-07 prices)*	*Eleventh Plan 2007-12 Anticipated Expenditure (at current prices)*	*Annual Plan 2010-11*	*Annual Plan-2011-12*		*Twelfth Plan 2012-17 Tentative Projected Outlay (at 2011-12 prices)*	*Annual Plan 2012-13 Proposed Outlay*
				Actual Expenditure	*Approved Outlay*	*Anticipated Expenditure*		
0	1	2	3	4	5	6	7	8

GN STATEMENT–C (PART–II)

DRAFT ANNUAL STATE PLAN (2012-13) : PROPOSED OUTLAYS (URBAN LOCAL BODIES)

(Rs. in Lakhs)

Sl. No.	*Major Heads/ Minor Heads of Development*	*Eleventh Plan 2007-12 Projected Outlay (at 2006-07 prices)*	*Eleventh Plan 2007-12 Anticipated Expenditure (at current prices)*	*Annual Plan 2010-11*	*Annual Plan-2011-12*		*Twelfth Plan 2012-17 Tentative Projected Outlay (at 2011-12 prices)*	*Annual Plan 2012-13 Proposed Outlay*
				Actual Expenditure	*Approved Outlay*	*Anticipated Expenditure*		
0	1	2	3	4	5	6	7	8

GN STATEMENT–C (PART–III)

DRAFT ANNUAL STATE PLAN (2012-13) : PROPOSED OUTLAYS (TOTAL OF RURAL LOCAL BODIES AND URBAN LOCAL BODIES)

(Rs. in lakhs)

Sl. No.	Major Heads/Minor Heads of Development	Eleventh Plan 2007-12 Projected Outlay (at 2006-07 prices)	Eleventh Plan 2007-12 Anticipated Expenditure (at current prices)	Annual Plan 2010-11	Annual Plan 2011-12		Twelfth Plan 2012-17 Tentative Projected Outlay (at 2011-12 prices)	Annual Plan 2012-13 Proposed Outlay
				Actual Expenditure	Approved Outlay	Anticipated Expenditure		
0	1	2	3	4	5	6	7	8

It is observed once again that it is somewhat difficult to fill in columns under GN Statement-C (both Part I and Part-II) as the Planning Commission never worked out projected Outlay for a State Plan based on resources from Local Bodies separately. Planning Commission works out Projected Outlay for a State based on total resources, and not segmenting it resource-wise. Its Eleventh Plan components, actuals of an Annual Plan, Agreed Outlay, Anticipated Expenditure or Proposed Outlay are not possible to be filled in resource-wise from Rural and Urban Local bodies. Similarly, it would not be possible to fill in Twelfth Plan related Outlay or for the Annual Plan, 2012-13 from resources from Rural and Urban Local bodies. As a matter of fact, most of the State governments never fill in these Annexes as it would amount to an exercise of estimation only. This is an area for reforms in the Annex area of plan presentation. Incidentally, resources from Rural and Urban Local bodies are meant for District Plan only. It would be desirable that Planning Commission would give appropriate instructions how to fill in the format.

2. Proposed Outlays on Ongoing and New Schemes—Annexure-I

The architecture of plan presentation primary revolves around GN Statement. It captures financial outlay by Major Heads/ Minor Heads of Development with reference to Five Year Plan and also over previous two consecutive annual plans to enable to relate with current plan outlay in a comparative format. The heads of development indicate the nature of development functions, major or minor. The essence of presentation by heads of development, as earlier discussed, is to understand the functional movement of the economy. However, the aggregate outlay at GN statement does not give any scheme-specific information, number of schemes taken up there and the position of its implementation status. In Annexure-I, scheme specific on ongoing and New Schemes of the Twelfth Plan are to be made available. Before discussing how the different columns under Annexure–I have to be filled in, it would be relevant to know the exact meaning of continuing and new schemes.

Continuing and New Schemes: After the conclusion of any Five Year Plan, the schemes taken up during the said plan period can be classified as Completed and Not-completed. The schemes so completed do no longer remain plan schemes and its maintenance is taken care of by the non-plan component of the State budget. The schemes not completed may be for different reasons. One reason could be that the scheme in question had to be abandoned. There would be no scope to carry it forward on to the next Five Year Plan unless the scheme in question is redesigned. With its redesignation, it would altogether be a new scheme for the next Five Year Plan.

For other category of incomplete schemes, it could be that the time period for execution of such schemes was really long to perforce automatic spill over on to the next Five Year Plan or that the scheme in question is itself of continuing nature, e.g., Sarba Sikshya Abhiyan as it is destined to continue for some more time linked, as it is, with the primary education foundation of our country. External Aided Projects are usually designed with a longer time frame and that it automatically moves on the next Five Year Plan period. It may also be that a scheme which could not be completed for one reason or the other and needed to be completed in next plan year period. Such schemes that spill over on to the new Five Year Plan are called continuing schemes. Needless to mention, New schemes are those which are taken up for the first time to meet challenges of the new Five Year Plan.

The presentation of schemes as continuing and new has other dimensions also. The ratio gives an idea of the unfinished task of the earlier plan period that needed to be stepped up for its completion. It is also an indicator of new emerging areas that have been prioritised for the State economy. The positive new scheme ratio would also confirm that the State is sensitive, proactive, positive and innovative to serve as platform for implementing the new vision and the new priorities of the national Five Year Plan. In a sense, it defines the dynamic character of the State plan.

Planning Commission, like previous occasion, issued guidelines for defining Ongoing and New schemes. Incidentally, it may be mentioned that Planning Commission has this time used Ongoing Schemes instead of Continuing Schemes. The guidelines are reproduced below:

I. Ongoing Schemes

(i) Mandated by Legislation

Outlays connected with all ongoing Plan programmes/projects/schemes such as MGNREGA which have been mandated by legislation and, therefore, need to be continued.

(ii) Social Security Transfers

Outlays connected with regular social security transfers such as old age and disability pensions, scholarships and other social insurance schemes.

(iii) Schemes/Projects for Completion

Outlays connected with all Plan programmes/projects/schemes in project mode and defined objectives which have been sanctioned in the Eleventh Plan or earlier, and which have not been completed as on 31-03-2012. These may fall into following categories:

(a) *Projects/Schemes due for completion in the Twelfth Plan or beyond as per the approvals*: These can be included as plan projects.
(b) *Projects/Schemes due for completion by the end of the Eleventh Plan in which less than 10 per cent of the approved outlay as on 31-3-2012 will be spent*: These projects should be separately identified for weeding out/shelving/dropping or converging/transferring to the private/joint sectors, or PPPs as the case may be. Projects initiated prior to the Eleventh and where less than 20 per cent of the approved outlay for the project has been spent, so far, may be similarly treated.
(c) *Projects/Schemes due for completion by the end of the Eleventh Plan in which more than 75 per cent of the work has been completed*: These projects are to be indicated separately for accelerated completion. The revised estimates of time and costs and the phasing out are also to be included.
(d) States and Ministries are.to review afresh such projects for the Twelfth Plan as per the guidelines applicable for any new proposal. These should not be included as ongoing projects.

(iv) Other Schemes with Same or Changed Mandate

Outlays connected with all other ongoing schemes which may be continued with same or changed mandate with the approval of Planning Commission.

II. New Schemes

Development programmes/projects/schemes on capital/revenue account that have been cleared for inclusion in the Twelfth Plan, in principle or otherwise, or for which an investment decision has been taken or is in the process of being taken by the concerned authority as per the applicable guidelines.

ANNEXURE–I

DRAFT ANNUAL STATE PLAN (2012-13)—PROPOSED OUTLAYS FOR STATE PLAN (SCHEME-WISE)

(Rs. in lakhs)

Sl. No.	*Major Head / Minor Head of Development (Scheme-wise)*	*Implementing Agency*	*Eleventh Plan (2007-12) Projected Outlay at 2006-07 prices*	*Eleventh Plan Anticipated Expenditure (at current prices)*	*Annual Plan (2010-11) Actual Expenditure*	*Annual Plan (2011-12)*		*Twelfth Five Year Plan Tentative Projected Outlay (at 2011-12 prices)*	*Annual Plan 2012-13 (Proposed Outlay)*
		State Government / Public Sector Enterprises / Local Bodies				*Approved Outlay*	*Anticipated Expenditure*		
0	1	2	3	4	5	6	7	8	9

I. Ongoing State Plan Schemes

(a) Mandated by Legislation

(i) ……….   (i)………   (iii)………

ANNEXURE–I (*Contd.*)

0	1	2	3	4	5	6	7	8	9

(b) Social Security Transfers

(i) .... (ii)......... (iii).........

(c) Schemes/Projects for completion

(i) .... (ii)......... (iii).........

(d) Other schemes with same or changed mandate

(i) .... (ii)......... (iii).........

II. New State Plan Schemes (i) .... (ii).........

FILE NAME: A-1

GUIDELINES FOR FILLING IN ANNEXURE-I

Annexure-I has 9 columns. It is the most informative format from planning angle and all the details regarding plan schemes are available. Column 0 has two segments: I and II. Under segment I, details of Ongoing Schemes are to be captured while under segment II details of new Schemes will be posted. Segment I is again subdivided under four sub-segments, namely, (a) Schemes mandated by legislation, (b) Schemes on Social Security Transfer, (c) Schemes/ Projects for completion, and (d) Other schemes with same or changed mandate. Under segment II, only New State Plan Schemes are to be indicated.

Column 0 will be a running serial. It will begin with 1 and end with last number of the scheme of the Annual Plan

Under Column I, corresponding to schemes mentioned under column 0, Major Head/Minor Head of Development are to be posted.

Column 2 indicates the name of Implementing Agency. Such implementing agency could be departments of the State Government, Public Sector Enterprises and Local Bodies. It has to be mentioned against schemes posted at column 0.

Column 3 has to be filled in with reference to Eleventh Plan Outlay for such schemes. Incidentally, it would be relevant to point out that not for all such schemes there were projections for Eleventh Plan outlay as some of the schemes happened to be included at a later stage of the Eleventh Plan. In the event no projections were made, it should be mentioned so. In the event such projections for the Eleventh Five Year Plan were really made, it should be so posted with reference to the official documents. In any case all these figures have to be reworked at 2006-7 prices with the help of deflator provided by the Planning Commission. Further, for new schemes of the Twelfth Plan, there cannot have any Eleventh Plan component and it should be indicated as Nil.

Column 4 refers to anticipated expenditure for such schemes for the Eleventh Plan Period. Normally Planning Commission communicates year-wise inflator for conversion of earlier expenditure at current prices. Pending receipt of such inflator, the total of first four year's expenditure, as obtained from the office of Accountant General may be added with the anticipated expenditure for the year 2011-12 and then post the aggregate figure at column 4.

Column 5 is to capture the Actual Expenditure for the Annual Plan, 2010-11. During November end, actual verified expenditure figures for the Annual plan, 2010-11 are likely to have reached the departments of the State Government from the office of the Accountant General. Since all the schemes have dedicated account code, scheme-wise actual expenditures could be filled up by the concerned Line Department and then posted against concerned minor head. If for some reason, the actuals from the office of the Accountant General are not available, verified figures of drawal of fund might be obtained from the related Treasury, compare it with utilisation certificates and then post the figures, head of development-wise, in the corresponding entry. It may be indicated 'provisional' by the side of the Actual within bracket in case verified figures from the office of the Accountant General have not been posted.

Column 6 refers to Approved Outlay for the Annual Plan, 2011-12, for all schemes, head of development-wise. This column is to be filled in from the approved letter of the Planning Commission for the Annual Plan, 2011-12. However, scheme-specific approved outlay is not mentioned in the approved outlay of the Planning Commission. The State planning department has to indicate scheme-specific component out of head of development-wise approved outlay of the Planning Commission and post it here.

Column 7 is meant for Anticipated Expenditure for 2011-12. As to the anticipated expenditure, it is desirable to give realistic expenditure based on half yearly situation or third quarterly figures of financial achievement, as available, with realistic assessment for the remaining period of the Annual Plan. In this aspect, release of budgeted State fund to the implementing agencies for the relevant schemes may be given appropriate consideration. Anticipated achievements indicating full coverage do not really make any planning sense and hence need to post realistic figures only.

Column 8 is to indicate Tentative outlay for the Twelfth Plan which the State Government has to work, scheme-wise under major and minor head of development-wise based on the Approach of the Twelfth Plan, the State vision based on development deficit, human development deficit and other compulsions at the State level as perceived by the State Planning Board and the Plan implementing departments, of the State, pending its finalisation by the Planning Commission.

Column 9 is meant for proposals of the State Plan for the Annual Plan, 2012-13 which will be taken up for discussion by the Working Groups in the Planning Commission and later by the Deputy Chairman and the Chief Minister of the State for finalisation of the State Plan.

3. Physical Targets and Achievements—Annexure-II

The essence of planning is realisation of certain objectives expressed in terms of achievement of outputs and outcomes. It is not related to mere expenditure of fund as there is no symbiotic relationship between expenditure and outputs. For the same reason, a statement of proper utilisation of fund is not enough. While utilisation certificate is important from audit point of view, it does not give any planning expression of its use. The planning objective has been to achieve something concrete results out of this investment. It seeks to find out results of utilisation of fund for the scheme in question. The return of investment can only be seen when it is objectively expressed in terms of quantifiable physical figures. The ends of planning are served if by utilising such fund targets set for schemes have been achieved.

Incidentally, outcomes are not set as targets since it is not directly measurable though it is the destination point for planning and implementation of schemes. The Planning Commission has, accordingly, adopted the usual practice to capture physical target and its achievement at Annexure-II for assessment of any scheme.

The format for Physical Targets and Achievements at Annexure-II has ten columns. It has been mentioned in the Note that cumulative and additional Targets and Achievements should be given for each item. Given the structure of Annexure–II, it would be somewhat difficult how to post such additional component. However, this may be shown by way of a dividing line where denominator would indicate additional targets and achievements. The Annexure-II is as follows:

ANNEXURE-II

DRAFT ANNUAL STATE PLAN (2012-13): PHYSICAL TARGETS AND ACHIEVEMENTS

Sl. No.	Item	Unit	Eleventh Five Year Plan-2007-12		Annual Plan-2011-12		Eleventh Plan 2007-12-Anticipated Achievement (col. 4+6)	Twelfth Five Year Plan 2012-17 (tentative) Target	Annual Plan 2012-13 (proposed) Target	Remarks
			Eleventh Plan Target	Annual Plans (2007-08 to 2010-11) Actual Achievement	Target	Anticipated Achievement				
0	1	2	3	4	5	6	7	8	9	10

Note: Cumulative as well as Additional Targets and Achievements should be given for each item.

At column 0, the consecutive serial number is to be indicated.

Column 1 is not very simple in that it is not a scheme specific column. It intends to capture important functional item of any minor head of developments of Annexure-I. Items under any minor head could be plural as well. An example may be given. For crop husbandry, the items could be rice, wheat or pulses. Such items could be separately posted for kharif or Boro production. Similarly, for minor irrigation, items could be dugwells, tanks, river-lift irrigation, etc. Annexure II is, in fact, the physical counterpart of Annexure I and the intention of this column 1 is to capture physical output of all programmes/schemes—also in a sequential order as in Annexure 1. Since the Planning Commission has not prepared and enumerated model list of items, it would have to be worked out by the State Planning departments after going through the salient features of all schemes. Needless to mention, model list would have facilitated uniform presentation to capture focused items and its commensurate unit, etc. For monitoring of outputs angle as well, items are important and have to be carefully prepared and correctly posted there. This would also help to understand the process of journey from output to outcome.

Column 2 is the measurement index for column 1. Since there is no uniform measuring rod, the unit of measurement is bound to be different. Depending on the nature of items, units may be numbered as thousand, lakh, million, crore, etc. It may be metre, square metre, acre, hectare, km, kg, tonnes, mt etc. It is even possible to add description, e.g., number. of beneficiaries and the like.

Column 3 indicates the Eleventh Five Year Plan target for the items of column 1 expressed in terms of unit at column 2. Normally, these figures remain static throughout the Five Year Plan period as it were settled with the approval of the Five Year Plan by the Planning Commission. However, in case any mid-term correction of plan targets take place it may undergo that change only.

Column 4 indicates the achievement figures for items for the first four years of the Eleventh Plan. At this point of time, actual verified figures of the office of the Accountant General have reached the departments of the State Government and have also been taken care of at Annexure I. Though there is no system of verifying the actual physical figures by the office of the Accountant General, the figures as obtained from the implementing agencies need to be appropriately validated by field visits, wherever required, with reference to the actuals as available from the office of the Accountant General.

Column 5 and Column 6 are the corresponding figures of targets and anticipated achievements of the Annual Plan, 2011-12. Regarding the achievements in the current year it is only possible to give half yearly figures or at most third quarterly figures of achievement at the time of preparing annual plan proposals for the next year. The period covering these achievements may be mentioned in the column itself. Anticipated achievements of full coverage do not really make any planning sense and hence need not be posted there.

Column 7 is meant for the anticipated figures of achievements for the Eleventh Five Year Plan. This has to be worked out by adding column 4+column 6 and then post it here.

Column 8 is to indicate Tentative target for the Twelfth Plan which the State Government has to work, major and minor head-wise as a counterpart of the financial proposal for the Twelfth Plan as indicated at GN-A at column 7 and Annexure-I at column 8.

Column 9 is meant for proposals of the State Plan for the Annual Plan, 2012-13 which is again counterpart physical target of GN-A at column 8 and Annexure-1 at column 9.

At remarks column, additional targets and achievements may be mentioned in terms of the Note under Annexure-II.

4. Statement Regarding Externally Aided Projects—Annexure–III

EAPs or Externally Aided Projects constitute quite often a considerable portion of the total plan outlay of the State. Earlier, outlays of such EAPs could be routed outside the State Plan. The system has since been revised and all EAPs are now required to be routed through the Planning Commission and would also form part of State plan resources. In order to have a definite picture on possible EAPs for the approaching Annual Plan, Planning Commission takes meeting before finalising resources for the Annual Plan with the nodal departments on EAP in the State, the Planning Department and the Finance Department of the State along with the nodal officer of the Ministry of Finance of the Central Government. Annexure III intends to capture details of EAPs in the following manner:

ANNEXURE–III

DRAFT ANNUAL STATE PLAN (2012-13): STATEMENT REGARDING EXTERNALLY AIDED PROJECTS

(Rs. in lakhs)

Sl. No.	Name, nature & location of the Project with Project Code and name of external funding agency	Date of sanction / date of commencement of work	Terminal date of disbursement of external aid: (a) Original (b) Revised	Estimated cost (a) Original (b) Revised (Latest)	Pattern of funding (a) State's share (b) Central Assistance (c) Other Sources (to be specified) (d) Total	Eleventh Plan (2007-12) Projected Outlay (at 2006-07 Prices) (a) State's share (b) Central Assistance (c) Other Sources (to be specified) (d) Total
0	1	2	3	4	5	6
1						
2						
3						
4						
5						
6						

(Contd.)

ANNEXURE–III *(Contd.)*

Sl. No.	*Name, nature & location of the Project with Project code and name of external funding agency*	*Cumulative Expenditure from (2007-08 to 2010-11) at current prices*	*Annual Plan 2011-12*		*Twelfth Plan 2012-17 Tentative Projected Outlay at (2011-12 Prices)*	*Annual Plan 2012-13 (proposed)*
			Outlay	*Anti. Expenditure*		
		(a) State's share *(b)* Central Assistance *(c)* Other Sources (to be specified) *(d)* Total	*(a)* State's share *(b)* Central Assistance *(c)* Other Sources (to be specified) *(d)* Total	*(a)* State's share *(b)* Central Assistance *(c)* Other Sources (to be specified) *(d)* Total	*(a)* State's share *(b)* Central Assistance *(c)* Other Sources (to be specified) *(d)* Total	*(a)* State's share *(b)* Central Assistance *(c)* Other Sources (to be specified) *(d)* Total
0	1	7	8	9	10	11
1						
2						
3						
4						
5						
6						
7						
8						
	Grand Total					

At column 0, the consecutive serial number is to be indicated.

Column 1 intends to capture name, nature and location of the project with project code and name of the external funding agency. The particulars need to be filled with reference to the sanctioned letter of the project for the sake of accuracy of the description.

Column 2 refers to date of sanction of the related scheme and date of commencement of work. Date of sanction has to be noted with reference to the date of sanction mentioned in the letter received by the concerned department. Date of commencement of work has to refer to day one of implementation of the project.

Column 3 mentions stipulation of terminal date of disbursement of external aid. It has to be filled in again from the original letter of sanction of the scheme and not from any other sources. Since EAP projects undergo changes based on external evaluation and also on consideration of time slippage, revision on terminal date of disbursement takes place in respect of some projects. The revised date for such disbursement may be filled in from such letter of communication.

Column 4 is about estimated cost of the project as originally mentioned in the sanctioned letter. In the case of long duration EAP schemes, inflation and currency valuation related fluctuations impact the cost factors as estimated earlier and require revision of its estimated cost for the sake of implementing the project. Such revision effected through fresh sanctioned letter would be the basis for filling the relevant entry.

Column 5 is meant for pattern for funding. Cost of EAPs is normally shared among the State Government, Central Government and the External funding agency. The name of the external agency has to be noted from the sanction letter itself along with share of the State Government, Central Government and the External funding agency. In case there is more than one funding agency, the contribution of the respective agency has to be mentioned. It has also to be indicated total of all funding partners.

Column 6 is to capture projected outlay for the Eleventh Plan period for such schemes and the related share of the State Government, Central Government and the External funding agency, etc. In case there is more than one funding agency, the contribution of the respective agency has to be mentioned. It has also to be indicated outlay of all funding partners. In this connection it is to be mentioned that Eleventh Plan Projected Outlay has to be indicated at 2006-07 prices. Normally Planning Commission communicates year-wise deflator for any conversion of Projected Outlay at 2006-07 prices. Since EAPS were sanctioned at different periods of the Eleventh Plan period, the correct estimate can only be done after receipt of such deflator. Pending receipt of such deflator, the total of outlay as falling under the Eleventh Plan need to be posted here individually for all and then post its total at column 6.

Column 7 is to capture the Cumulative Expenditure for the first four years (2007-08 to 2010-11) at current prices with inflator provided by the Planning Commission. Here again respective share of the State Government, Central Government and the External funding agency, etc., has to be posted. Normally in the State budget separate account code for each of the funding agencies is provided. During November end, actual verified expenditure figures for the Annual plan, 2010-11 are likely to have reached the departments of the State Government from the office of the Accountant General. Thus, based on verified figures, scheme-wise cumulative expenditures for the four years could be filled up. If for some reason, the actuals for 2010-11 are not available, from the office of the Accountant General, verified figures of drawal of fund might be obtained from the related Treasury, compare it with utilisation certificates and then add with the verified figures of the first three years and post the figures at column 7. It may be indicated 'provisional' by the side of the Actual within bracket in case verified figures from the office of the Accountant General have not been posted.

Column 8 refers to Approved Outlay for the Annual Plan, 2011-12, for the concerned scheme for all programme partners. This column is to be filled in from the approved letter of the Planning Commission for the Annual Plan, 2011-12 and also with reference to the attached document of the Scheme of financing of the Planning Commission for 2011-12.

Column 9 is meant for Anticipated Expenditure for 2011-12. As to the anticipated expenditure, it is desirable to give realistic expenditure based on half yearly situation or third quarterly figures of financial achievement, as available, with realistic assessment for the remaining period of the Annual Plan. In this aspect, release of budgeted State fund to the implementing agencies for the relevant schemes may be given appropriate consideration. Anticipated achievements indicating full coverage do not really make any planning sense and hence need to post realistic figures only.

Column 10 intends to capture Tentative Projected Outlay for all the EAP Schemes for the Twelfth Plan, at 2011-12 prices. In other words, all previously sanctioned EAP Schemes at different plan years of the

Eleventh Plan have now to be scaled up with the inflator to be indicated by the Planning Commission. Further, it would be desirable to renew the MOU with the external funding agency, Central Government and the State Government for the Revised Projected Outlay for the unexpired period of project time line for the Twelfth Five Year Plan.

Column 11 is meant for proposals of the State Plan for the EAP Schemes for the Annual Plan, 2012-13 which will be taken up for discussion by the Working Groups in the Planning Commission and later by the Deputy Chairman and the Chief Minister of the State for finalisation of the State Plan.

5. Centrally Sponsored Schemes—Annexure–IV

The genesis of the Centrally Sponsored Schemes (CSS) owes its origin to the core of federal system where the Constitution of India, under Seventh Schedule, has enumerated the Union List, the State List and the Concurrent List. While the Central Government and the concerned State Government would be acting on subjects as per the Union List or the State List, as the case may be, both of them are, however, entitled to work on areas covered under the Concurrent List. As a general rule, schemes falling under Concurrent List are taken up under Centrally Sponsored Schemes. It is worth remembering that except under the route of the Central Finance Commission's recommendation under Article 280, there is no other way but the CSS format when the Union Government may release fund to the State Governments. Usually, all CSSs are to be funded on a partnership format—the share of funding participation varies from scheme to scheme and also on the basis of overall agreement with the State governments. The ratio of Central share and the State share varies in the range of 90:10, 80:20, 75:25, 50:50 and the like. Only in the case of the National Family Planning Programme, the Central share is 100 per cent. Needless to mention, all CSS are to be implemented by the concerned State government. The fund is released by the concerned Ministry of the Central Government on a periodical basis and also on utilisation of fund released earlier.

The essence of CSS under Annual Plan exercises is two-fold: first, it is incumbent upon the concerned department of the State government to provide required counterpart fund for concerned CSS in the Annual Plan to enable the Ministry to release matching contribution periodically. Secondly, the State planning departments need to take as much advantage as possible from such CSS as the State resources may not be good enough to meet adequately fund need for the related development area.

The list of CSS is rather quite big covering almost all the sectors of the State plan. Such schemes may not be universally applicable for all the States in India; it may even be limited to select group of States based on the very nature of the region and the CSS, e.g., drought prone area, desert development programme, hill development programme and the like. The List of CSS encompasses almost all important heads of development falling under concurrent list.

The Planning Department of the State and the planning unit of the Line Departments have a lot of jobs for planning for CSS. Incidentally, the Planning Department of the States does not always maintain records chronologically of all original notifications on CSS, the agreed central and State share or amendments thereon from time to time by the concerned Ministry of the Central Government. As a result, it sometimes becomes difficult to cross check the correctness of Central share and State share in proposed outlay for any CSS by the Line Departments. For the same reason it is also not always possible to ensure whether the Line Departments of the State have at all made exercise on planning on available CSS in their departmental plan. An e-Guard file needs to be opened for this purpose.

Similarly, the Line Departments of the State are also required to maintain original notifications on CSS and its amendments issued from time to time by the related Ministry of the Central Government. Such departments are also required to make use of available opportunities of CSS and keep itself updated about the timely release of fund. In that pursuit, the Line Departments need also to utilise the available fund meant for CSS and send its utilisation report from time to time to the concerned Ministry of the Central Government and Finance and Planning departments of the State.

ANNEXURE-IV

DRAFT ANNUAL STATE PLAN (2012-13): CENTRALLY SPONSORED SCHEMES

(Rs. in lakh)

Sl. No.	Name of the Scheme	Pattern of Funding		Eleventh Plan 2007-12 projected outlay at 2006-07 prices		Annual Plan-2010-11 Actual Expenditure		Annual Plan-2011-12 Outlay		Annual Plan-2011-12 Anticipated Expenditure	
		Central Share	State Share	Central Share	State Share	Central Share	State Share	Central Share	State Share	Central Share	State Share
0	1	2	3	4	5	6	7	8	9	10	11

Eleventh Plan 2007-12 Anticipated Exp. at current prices		12th Plan Tentative Projected Outlay at 2011-12 Prices		Annual Plan (2012-13) Proposed		Remarks
Central Share	State Share	Central Share	State Share	Central Share	State Share	
12	13	14	15	16	17	18

Note: Scheme-wise details may be furnished.

At Column 0, the consecutive serial number is to be indicated.

Column 1 is meant for the name of the scheme. The individual plan implementing departments would mention the name of the schemes in the sequential order of the heads of development administered by them. However, since there is no departmental concept in the order of presentation and that departmental sequential order is not likely to fall in line with the overall order of heads of development, it will have to be reworked by the Planning department of the State for posting them in sequential order of heads of development in the draft State Plan document on Annexure-IV.

Columns 2 and 3 denote the pattern of funding respectively for Central share in column 2 and State share in column 3 and should be filled in with reference to published and updated circular of the concerned Ministry of the Central Government only.

Column 4 and Column 5 refer to Central share and State share for Projected Eleventh Plan outlay at 2006-07 prices for each of the schemes. Now the pattern of fund sharing even for a CSS varies from year to year. A glaring example is that of Central share for SSA which was reduced from 75 per cent to 66.33 per cent at a later point of time. Further, all the CSS schemes did not commence at a particular point of time and, therefore, there would be needed year-wise deflator from the Planning Commission for conversion of Projected Outlay at 2006-07 prices. Since CSS schemes were sanctioned at different periods of the Eleventh Plan period, the correct estimate can only be done after receipt of such deflator. Pending receipt of such deflator, the total of outlay falling under the Eleventh Plan need to be posted here individually for all the CSS schemes and then post it at columns 4 and 5 respectively

Incidentally, it would be worth mentioning that there does not exist any planning culture either at the related Ministry of the Central Government or at the concerned State Government to communicate Five Year Projected Outlay on CSS and also of its validation with the Five Year Plan Outlay of the State. This issue also never features in the Working Group discussions in the Planning Commission. There is in fact no scope for estimation for figures in the Five Year Plan. This is a big area of institutional reforms.

Columns 6 and 7 are to capture the Actual Expenditure for the year 2010-11 for the Central Share and State Share respectively.

During November end, actual verified expenditure figures for the Annual plan, 2010-11 are likely to have reached the departments of the State Government from the office of the Accountant General. Thus, based on verified figures, scheme-wise actual expenditures for the year, 2010-11 may be filled in. If for some reason the figures are not available from the office of the Accountant General, verified figures of drawal of fund might be obtained from the related Treasury, compare it with utilisation certificates and then fill in the respective columns 6 and 7. It may be indicated 'provisional' by the side of the Actual Expenditure within bracket in case verified figures from the office of the Accountant General have not been posted. Incidentally such figures already posted for such schemes at Annexure 1 need to be posted here.

Column 8 and Column 9 are for the Central share and State share for the Approved outlay for the year, 2011-12. As to the Central share, this has to be filled in with reference to communications received earlier from the counterpart nodal Ministries in the Central Government. In the event such communication has not been received, it has two options to fill up the Central share: (a) it may indicate such figure based on agreed Central share as quoted by the representative of the related nodal Ministry during Working Group discussions on Annual Plan in the Planning Commission; (b) in case no agreed discussion has taken place, it may be mentioned as Not Communicated or Not Available. It need not be kept blank.

Column 10 and Column 11 relate to corresponding expenditure figures of Central share and State share for the Annual Plan, 2011-12. As to the anticipated expenditure it is desirable to give realistic expenditure based on half yearly situation or third quarterly figures of achievement, as available, with realistic assessment for the remaining period of the annual plan. In this aspect, receipt of Central fund from the Central Government and release of budgeted State fund for the scheme in question may be given appropriate consideration. Anticipated achievements of full coverage do not really make any planning sense and hence need not be posted there.

Column 12 and Column 13 are meant for the Eleventh Plan, 2007-12 Anticipated Expenditure at current prices. Normally Planning Commission communicates year-wise inflator for conversion of earlier expenditure at current prices. Pending receipt of such inflator, the total of first four year's expenditure, as obtained from the office of Accountant General may be added with the anticipated expenditure for the year 2011-12 and then post the aggregate figure at columns 12 and 13 respectively for the Central Share and State Share.

Column 14 and column 15 refer to Tentative Projected Outlay for the Twelfth Plan at 2011-12 prices which the State Government has to work on CSS schemes proposed to be taken up during the Twelfth Plan based also on current ongoing CSS, its possible Central Share component and its corresponding State Share. Further, such CSS have to be based on the Approach of the Twelfth Plan, the State vision based on development deficit, human development deficit and other compulsions at the State level as perceived by the State Planning Board and the Plan implementing department of the State.

Column 16 and column 17 refer to the proposals of such CSS meant for the Annual Plan, 2012-13, with its possible Central Share and State Share component, based on such records as available. It will be taken up for discussion by the Working Groups in the Planning Commission and later by the Deputy Chairman and the Chief Minister of the State while finalising the State Plan.

Column 18 is intended to record any explanatory statement for any item.

6. Tribal Sub-Plan (TSP): Financial Outlays—Annexure V-A

Tribal Sub-Plan (TSP) is an essential component of any State plan. It is also an inclusive initiative under the State Plan. Normally, in almost all major sectors, Tribal Sub-Plan components can be found whose financial and physical positions are captured in Annexures V-A and V-B respectively.

ANNEXURE V-A

DRAFT STATE ANNUAL PLAN 2012-13—FINANCIAL OUTLAYS: PROPOSALS FOR TSP

(Rs. in lakhs)

Sl. No.	Major Head/ Sub-head/ Schemes	Eleventh Plan 2007-12 Projected Outlays (At 2006-07 Prices)		Annual Plan 2010-11	Annual Plan 2011-12				Eleventh Plan 2007-12	Twelfth Plan Tentative Projected Outlay (at 2011-12 Prices)		Annual Plan 2012-13 (Proposed)	
				Actual Expen-diture under TSP	Approved Outlay		Anticipated Expenditure		Anticipated Expenditure under TSP (at current prices)				
		Total Outlay	Of which flow to TSP		Total Out-lay	Of which flow to TSP	Total Out-lay	Of which flow to TSP		Total Out-lay	Of which flow to TSP	Total Outlay	Of which flow to TSP
0	1	2	3	4	5	6	7	8	9	10	11	12	13

At Column 0, the consecutive serial number is to be indicated.

Column 1 is meant for the name of the scheme along with its major and minor heads. (Incidentally, there is no concept of sub-head under major head as included in the Annexure-V-A. Every major head has a number of minor heads and, therefore, sub-head should be read as minor head). The individual plan implementing departments would mention the name of the schemes in the sequential order of the major heads/minor heads of development administered by them. However, since there is no departmental concept in the order of presentation and that departmental sequential order is not likely to fall in line with the overall order of heads of development, it has to be reworked by the Planning Department of the State for sequential order of heads of development in the draft State plan document on Annexure-V-A.

Columns 2 and 3 denote respectively for Total Outlay and the amount of fund falling under TSP for the entire Eleventh Plan, (2007-12) Projected Outlay at 2006-7 prices. Some States do not show in their plan document the name of the schemes but indicate aggregates under major and minor heads of development. Such presentations defeat the very purpose of knowing dedicated schemes having specific possible components for TSP. These have to be reworked with reference to the official records and scheme-specific outlay within major and minor heads as worked out. Incidentally, Total of Eleventh Plan outlay, major and minor head-wise, as shown here must agree with those approved earlier by the Planning Commission and also shown at Column 3 of Annexure-I.

Now regarding column 3, scheme specific flow of outlay for TSP has to be mentioned. Planning Commission wants to see whether the State Plan has adequately taken cognizance of sizable ST population in the State and provided commensurate outlay for its inclusion and the connected outreach. Therefore, the flow calculation has to be worked out as objectively as possible with reference to the possible location of schemes and the recorded ST population in the area as per the published figures of the Census of India. For some budgeted TSP schemes of course there are no problems as those will come under 100 per cent flow. Now the figures have to be shown with reference to 2006-7 prices. Normally Planning Commission communicates year-wise deflator for any conversion of Projected Outlay at 2006-07 prices. Therefore, the correct estimate can only be done after receipt of such deflator. Pending receipt of such deflator, the flow of outlay falling under the Eleventh Plan need to be posted here individually for all the schemes under the related major and minor head and then post its total at column 3.

Column 4 is meant for Actual Expenditure under TSP for the Annual Plan, 2010-11. Such expenditure need to be posted only for dedicated schemes having budget code of 796. Otherwise, the very purpose of this column would be defeated. Now, during November end, actual verified expenditure figures for the Annual Plan 2010-11 are likely to have reached the departments of the State Government from the office of the Accountant General. Based on verified figures for schemes having account code No. 796, actual expenditures for the year 2010-11 may be filled in. If for some reason the figures are not available from the office of the Accountant General, verified figures of drawal of fund might be obtained from the related Treasury, compare it with utilisation certificates and then fill in the column 4. It may be indicated 'provisional' by the side of the Actual Expenditure within bracket in case verified figures from the office of the Accountant General have not been posted. Incidentally the figures for such schemes have already been posted for such schemes at column 5 at Annexure 1.

Columns 5, 6, 7 and 8 refer respectively to 2011-12 Total Plan Outlay, its flow to TSP, anticipated plan expenditure and its TSP flow component for the schemes under major and minor heads of development. In filling the column 5, it would be appropriate to consult the Approved Outlay communicated to the State by the Planning Commission and the flow of such Outlay for TSP as approved and indicated in the letter of Planning Commission at column 6. Regarding anticipated expenditure in column 7 as against Total Outlay it is desirable to give realistic expenditure based on half yearly situation or third quarterly figures of financial achievement, as available, with realistic assessment for the remaining period of the annual plan. In this aspect, release of budgeted State fund for the schemes in question may be given appropriate consideration. Anticipated achievements of full coverage do not really make any planning sense and hence need to post realistic figure. For checklist, it has to be ensured that total of column 7 must agree with the total of column 6 of GN-A and of column 7 of Annexure-1. The column 8 can be filled in scheme-wise with reference to flow percentage of total anticipated expenditure as recorded in the previous column 7.

Column 9 is to capture anticipated expenditure of TSP for the entire Eleventh Plan at current prices. Normally Planning Commission communicates year-wise inflator for conversion of earlier expenditure at current prices. Pending receipt of such inflator, the total of first four year's expenditure, as obtained from the office of Accountant General may be added with the anticipated expenditure for the year 2011-12 and then post the aggregate figure at column 9.

Column 10 and column 11 refer to Tentative Projected Outlay for the Twelfth Plan at 2011-12 prices. The State has already addressed the matter, scheme-wise, at Annexure-I at column 8. The column 10 is to be filled in just by posting those figures of column 8 of Annexure-I for such schemes which have TSP components. Column 11 may be filled in with reference flow to TSP.

Column 11 may be filled in with reference to its TSP flow.

Column 12 and Column 13 are meant for the proposed Annual Plan outlay for 2012-13 and of its flow to TSP. The State has already addressed the matter, scheme-wise, at Annexure–1 at column 9. Column 12 can be filled in by posting figures of column 9 of Annexure-1 for such schemes which have TSP components.

Column 13 may be filled in with reference to its TSP flow.

At the end it will be desirable to calculate percentage for TSP *vis-à-vis* Total State Outlay by inserting a line.

7. Tribal Sub-Plan (TSP): Physical Targets and Achievements—Annexure V-B

Annexure VB is the physical description of proposals under TSP as shown at Annexure VA. Planning Commission intends to capture the physical character of schemes taken up for TSP only at Annexure V-B, and not its relation with the total physical targets and achievements of the State Plan as in Annexure V-A. In other words, the physical targets are TSP-specific to throw light on the extent of programme coverage and outreach. The physical targets set for the TSP in the Eleventh Five Year Plan and its related annual targets and performances for the immediate past year are to be indicated along with designed physical targets for the Twelfth Plan and also for the Annual Plan 2012-13.

ANNEXURE V-B

TRIBAL SUB-PLAN (TSP)
DRAFT ANNUAL STATE PLAN 2012-13 : PHYSICAL TARGETS AND ACHIEVEMENTS—PROPOSALS FOR TSP

Sl. No.	Major Head/ Sub-head/ Schemes	Unit	Eleventh Plan (2007-12)	Annual Plan-2010-11		Annual Plan-2011-12		Eleventh Plan (2007-12)	Twelfth Five Year Plan (Tentative)	Annual Plan 2012-13 (Proposed)
			Target	Target	Actual Achievement	Target	Anticipated Achievement	Anticipated Achievement	Target	Target
0	1	2	3	4	5	6	7	8	10	11

At column 0, the consecutive serial number is to be indicated.

Column 1 in Annexure V-A and V-B is identical. It has to be posted likewise.

Column 2 is the measurement index for column 1. Since there is no uniform measuring rod, the unit of measurement is bound to be different. Depending on the nature of items, units may be number-thousand, lakh, million, crore, etc. It may be metre, square metre, acre, hectare, km, kg, tonnes, mt, etc. It is even possible to add description, e.g., nnmber of beneficiaries and the like. The measuring units would, however, be the same as those adopted at Annexure-II.

Column 3 indicates the Eleventh Five Year Plan target on TSP for the schemes of column 1, to be expressed in terms of identical unit as at column 2. Normally, these figures remain static throughout the Five Year Plan period as it were settled at the time of approval of the Five Year Plan of the State. However, in case any mid-term correction of plan targets take place it may undergo that change only.

Column 4 indicates the Target and column 5 mentions about Achievement for the Annual Plan 2010-11. As to Target for Annual Plan of TSP for 2010-11, it has to be found out from the approved physical target of TSP from the Annual Plan for 2010-11. The column 5 of Annexure V-B is the physical counterpart of column 4 of Annexure V-A. There has to have symbiotic relationship between expenditure and output. Though there is no system of verifying the actual physical figures by the office of the Accountant General, the figures as obtained from the implementing agencies need to be appropriately validated by field visits, wherever required, with reference to the actual as mentioned at column 4 of Annexure V-A.

Column 6 and Column 7 are to capture the Targets and Achievements for TSP for the Annual Plan, 2011-12. As to Target for Annual Plan of TSP for 2011-12, it has to be found out from the approved physical target of TSP from the Annual Plan for 2011-12. The column 7 of Annexure V-B is the physical counterpart of column 8 of Annexure V-A. There has to have symbiotic relationship between expenditure and output. Though there is no system of verifying the actual physical figures by the office of the Accountant General, the figures as obtained from the implementing agencies need to be appropriately validated by field visits, wherever required, with reference to the actual as mentioned at column 8 of Annexure V-A. Further, regarding the achievements in 2011-12, it is only possible to give half yearly figures or at most third quarterly figures of achievement at the time of preparing annual plan proposals for the next year. The period covering these achievements may be mentioned in the column itself. Anticipated achievements of full coverage do not really make any planning sense and hence need not be posted there.

Column 8 is meant for the Anticipated Physical Achievement of TSP for the entire Eleventh Plan. This is the physical counterpart of column 9 of Annexure V-A. There has to have symbiotic relationship between expenditure and output. Though there is no system of verifying the actual physical figures by the office of the Accountant General, the related figures as mentioned earlier for the first three plan years (2007-8, 2008-9 and 2009-10) and duly validated, would now have to be added with the figures as noted in columns 5 and 7 of Annexure V-B for arriving Anticipated Physical Achievement of TSP for the entire Eleventh Plan for column 8.

(There is no number for any column 9 under Annexure V-B. Since it has been addressed by the Planning Commission, the number as given is taken for granted).

Column 10 of Annexure V-B is the tentative Physical Target for the Twelfth Plan. It is in fact physical counterpart of Column 11 of Annexure V-A. Similarly, Column 11 of Annexure V-B is the physical counterpart of Column 13 of Annexure V-A. These items have to be filled in with due caution. Units for physical outputs would be in same manner as were selected for Annexure-II.

8. Special Component Plan for Scheduled Castes (SCSP-I)—Financial Outlays: Annexure VI–A

Special Component Plan For Scheduled Castes (SCSP-I) is an essential component of any State plan. It is also an inclusive initiative under the State Plan. Normally, in Special Component Plan for Scheduled Castes (SCSP-I) almost all major sectors components can be found whose financial and physical positions are captured in Annexures VI-A and VI-B respectively.

ANNEXURE VI-A

DRAFT ANNUAL STATE PLAN 2012-13 : FINANCIAL OUTLAYS—PROPOSALS FOR SCSP

(Rs. in lakh)

Sl. No.	Major Head/ Sub-head/ Schemes	Eleventh Plan 2007-12 Projected Outlays (At 2006-07 Prices)		Annual Plan 2010-11	Annual Plan 2011-12				Eleventh Plan 2007-12	Twelfth Plan Tentative Projected Outlay (at 2011-12 Prices)		Annual Plan 2012-13 (Proposed)	
				Actual Expenditure Under SCSP	Approved Outlay		Anticipated Expenditure		Anticipated Expenditure under SCSP (at current prices)				
		Total Outlay	of which flow to SCSP		Total Outlay	of which flow to SCSP	Total Outlay	of which flow to SCSP		Total Outlay	of which flow to SCSP	Total Outlay	of which flow to SCSP
0	1	2	3	4	5	6	7	8	9	10	11	12	13

At Column 0, the consecutive serial number is to be indicated.

Column 1 is meant for the name of scheme along with its major and minor heads. (Incidentally, there is no concept of sub-head under major head as included in the Annexure VI A. Every major head has a number of minor heads and, therefore, sub-head should be read as minor head). The individual plan implementing departments would mention the name of the schemes in the sequential order of the major heads/minor heads of development administered by them. However, since there is no departmental concept in the order of presentation and that departmental sequential order is not likely to fall in line with the overall order of heads of development, it has to be reworked by the Planning department of the State for sequential order of heads of development in the draft State plan document on Annexure VI-A.

Columns 2 and 3 denote respectively for Total Outlay and the amount of fund falling under SCSP for the entire Eleventh plan, (2007-12) Projected Outlay at 2006-7 prices. Some States do not show in their plan document the name of the schemes but indicate aggregates under major and minor heads of development. Such presentations defeat the very purpose of knowing dedicated schemes having specific possible components for SCSP. These have to be reworked with reference to the official records and scheme-specific outlay within major and minor head as worked out. Incidentally Total of Eleventh Plan outlay, major and minor head-wise, as shown here must agree with those approved earlier by the Planning Commission and also shown at Column 3 of Annexure-1.

Now regarding column 3, scheme specific flow of outlay for SCSP has to be mentioned. Planning Commission wants to see whether the State Plan has adequately taken cognizance of sizable SC population in the State and provided commensurate outlay for its inclusion and the connected outreach. Therefore, the flow calculation has to be worked out as objectively as possible with reference to the possible location of schemes and the recorded SC population in the area as per the published figures of the Census of India. For some budgeted SCSP schemes of course there are no problems as those will come under 100 per cent flow. Now the figures have to be shown with reference to 2006-7 prices. Normally Planning Commission communicates year-wise deflator for any conversion of Projected Outlay at 2006-07 prices. Therefore, the correct estimate can only be done after receipt of such deflator. Pending receipt of such deflator, the flow of outlay falling under the Eleventh Plan need to be posted here individually for all the schemes under the related major and minor heads and then post its total at column 3.

Column 4 is meant for Actual Expenditure under SCSP for the Annual Plan 2010-11. Such expenditure need to be posted only for dedicated schemes having budget code of 789. Otherwise, the very purpose of this column would be defeated. Now, during November end, actual verified expenditure figures for the Annual plan 2010-11 are likely to have reached the departments of the State Government from the office of the Accountant General. Based on verified figures for schemes having account code No. 789, actual expenditures for the year 2010-11 may be filled in. If for some reason the figures are not available from the office of the Accountant General, verified figures of drawal of fund might be obtained from the related Treasury, compare it with utilisation certificates and then fill in the column 4. It may be indicated 'provisional' by the side of the Actual Expenditure within bracket in case verified figures from the office of the Accountant General have not been posted. Incidentally the figures for such schemes have already been posted for such schemes at column 5 at Annexure 1.

Columns 5, 6, 7 and 8 refer respectively to 2011-12 Total Plan Outlay, its flow to SCSP, anticipated plan expenditure and its SCSP flow component for the schemes under major and minor heads of development. In filling the column 5, it would be appropriate to consult the Approved Outlay communicated to the State by the Planning Commission and the flow of such Outlay for SCSP as approved and indicated in the letter of Planning Commission, at column 6. Regarding anticipated expenditure in column 7 as against Total Outlay it is desirable to give realistic expenditure based on half yearly situation or third quarterly figures of financial achievement, as available, with realistic assessment for the remaining period of the annual plan. In this aspect, release of budgeted State fund for the schemes in question may be given appropriate consideration. Anticipated achievements of full coverage do not really make any planning sense and hence need to post realistic figure. For checklist, it has to be ensured that total of column 7 must agree with the total of column 6 of GN-A and of column 7 of Annexure-1. The column 8 can be filled in scheme-wise with reference to flow percentage of total anticipated expenditure as recorded in the previous column 7.

Column 9 is to capture anticipated expenditure of SCSP for the entire Eleventh Plan at current prices. Normally Planning Commission communicates year-wise inflator for conversion of earlier expenditure at current prices. Pending receipt of such inflator, the total of first four year's expenditure, as obtained from the office of Accountant General may be added with the anticipated expenditure for the year 2011-12 and then post the aggregate figure at column 9.

Column 10 and column 11 refer to Tentative Projected Outlay for the Twelfth Plan at 2011-12 prices. The State has already addressed the matter, scheme-wise, at Annexure-1 at column 8. The column 10 of Annexure VI-A is to be filled in just by posting those figures of column 8 of Annexure-1 for which there are SCSP component.

Column 12 and Column 13 are meant respectively for the proposed Annual Plan outlay for 2012-13 and of its flow to SCSP. The State has already addressed the matter, scheme-wise, at Annexure-1 at column 9. Column 12 thus can be filled in by posting figures of column 9 of Annexure-1 for such schemes which have SCSP component. Its flow to SCSP has to be indicated as column 13. At the end it will be desirable to calculate percentage for SCSP *vis-à-vis* Total State Outlay by inserting a line.

9. Special Component Plan for Scheduled Castes (SCSP-II)—Physical Targets and Achievements—Annexure VI-B

Annexure VI-B is the physical description of proposals under SCSP as shown at Annexure VI-A. Planning Commission intends to capture the physical character of schemes taken up for SCSP only at Annexure VI-B, and not its relation with the total physical targets and achievements of the State Plan as in Annexure VI-A. In other words, the physical targets are SCSP-specific to throw light on the extent of programme coverage and outreach. The physical targets set for the SCSP in the Eleventh Five Year Plan and its related annual targets and performances for the immediate past year are to be indicated along with designed physical targets for the Twelfth Plan and also for the Annual Plan 2012-13.

ANNEXURE VI-B

SCHEDULED CASTE SUB-PLAN (SCSP) DRAFT ANNUAL STATE PLAN 2012-13 : PHYSICAL TARGETS AND ACHIEVEMENTS—PROPOSALS FOR SCSP

Sl. No.	Major Head/ Sub-head/ Schemes	Unit	Eleventh Plan (2007-12)	Annual Plan-2010-11		Annual Plan-2011-12		Eleventh Plan (2007-12)	Twelfth Five Year Plan (tentative)	Annual Plan 2012-13 (proposed)
			Target	Target	Actual Achievement	Target	Anticipated Achievement	Anticipated Achievement	Target	Target
0	1	2	3	4	5	6	7	8	10	11

At column 0, the consecutive serial number is to be indicated.

Column 1, in Annexure VI-A and VI-B, is identical. It has to be posted likewise.

Column 2 is the measurement index for column 1. Since there is no uniform measuring rod, the unit of measurement is bound to be different. Depending on the nature of items, units may be number—thousand, lakh, million, crore, etc. It may be metre, square metre, acre, hectare, km, kg, tonnes, mt, etc. It is even possible to add description, e.g., number of beneficiaries and the like. The measuring units would, however, be the same as those adopted at Annexure-II.

Column 3 indicates the Eleventh Five Year Plan target on SCSP for the schemes of column 1, to be expressed in terms of identical unit as at column 2. Normally, these figures remain static throughout the Five Year Plan period as it were settled at the time of approval of the Five Year Plan of the State. However, in case any mid-term correction of plan targets takes place it may undergo that change only.

Column 4 indicates the Target and column 5 mentions about Achievement for the Annual Plan 2010-11. As to Target for Annual Plan of SCSP for 2010-11, it has to be found out from the approved physical target of SCSP from the Annual Plan for 2010-11. The column 5 of Annexure VI-B is the physical counterpart of column 4 of Annexure VI-A. There has to have symbiotic relationship between expenditure and output. Though there is no system of verifying the actual physical figures by the office of the Accountant General, the figures as obtained from the implementing agencies need to be appropriately validated by field visits, wherever required, with reference to the actual as mentioned at column 4 of Annexure VI-A.

Column 6 and Column 7 are to capture the Targets and Achievements for SCSP for the Annual Plan 2011-12. As to Target for Annual Plan of SCSP for 2011-12, it has to be found out from the approved physical target of SCSP from the Annual Plan for 2011-12. The column 7 of Annexure VI-B is the physical counterpart of column 8 of Annexure VI-A. There has to have symbiotic relationship between expenditure and output. Though there is no system of verifying the actual physical figures by the office of the Accountant General, the figures as obtained from the implementing agencies need to be appropriately validated by field visits, wherever required, with reference to the actual as mentioned at column 8 of Annexure VI-A. Further, regarding the achievements in 2011-12, it is only possible to give half yearly figures or at most third quarterly figures of achievement at the time of preparing annual plan proposals for the next year. The period covering these achievements may be mentioned in the column itself. Anticipated achievements of full coverage do not really make any planning sense and hence need not be posted there.

Column 8 is meant for the Anticipated Physical Achievement of SCSP for the entire Eleventh Plan. This is the physical counterpart of column 9 of Annexure VI-A. There has to have symbiotic relationship between expenditure and output. Though there is no system of verifying the actual physical figures by the office of the Accountant General, the related figures as mentioned earlier for the first-three plan years (2007-8, 2008-9 and 2009-10) and duly validated, would now have to be added with the figures as noted in columns 5 and 7 of Annexure VI-B for arriving Anticipated Physical Achievement of SCSP for the entire Eleventh Plan for column 8.

(There is no number for any column 9 under Annexure V-B. Since it has been addressed by the Planning Commission, the number as given is taken for granted).

Column 10 of Annexure VI-B is the tentative Physical Target for the Twelfth Plan. It is in fact physical counterpart of Column 11 of Annexure VI-A. Similarly, Column 11 of Annexure VI-B is the physical counterpart of Column 13 of Annexure VI-A. These items have to be filled in with due caution. Units for physical outputs would be in same manner as were selected for Annexure-II.

10. Financial Outlays/Expenditure for Voluntary Sector—Annexure VII

The Voluntary sector is an active partner in the building up of new India with commitment-based programme initiatives in difficult areas. They are also programme partners and implement a number of schemes under State Plan. As a matter of fact under the National Policy on Voluntary Sector, the NGOs are also empowered to participate effectively in the planning and implementation process in the State. The purpose of this Annexure-VII is to capture programme coverage, its linked financial outlay and the extent of its expenditure by the Voluntary Sector out of resources under State Plan. In this format, there is nothing to capture own resources of the voluntary sector. Such resources of the Voluntary sector, if any, are not part of State resources meant for State Plan. Accordingly, those are not included in the format and here actual expenditure means utilisation of fund earlier released to them by the related department of the State.

ANNEXURE-VII

DRAFT ANNUAL STATE PLAN 2012-13 : PROPOSED OUTLAYS FINANCIAL OUTLAYS/ EXPENDITURE FOR VOLUNTARY SECTOR

(Rs. in lakh)

Sl. No.	Schemes	Eleventh Plan (2007-11) Projected Outlay (at 2006-07 Prices)	Annual Plan 2010-11	Annual Plan (2011-12)		Eleventh Plan (2007-12)	Twefith Five Year Plan Tentative Projected Outlay at 2011-12 Prices	Annual Plan 2012-13 (Proposed Outlay)
			Actual Expenditure	Approved Outlay	Anticipated Expenditure	Anticipated Expenditure (at current prices)		
0	1	2	3	5	6	7	8	9
1.								
2.								
3.								
4.								
5.								
6.								
7.								
8.								
	Total							

FILE NAME: A7

There are nine columns in the Annexure.

At Column 0, the consecutive serial number is to be indicated.

Column 1 is meant for the name of the scheme of the voluntary sector which has been entrusted for execution of a scheme with financial assistance from the individual plan implementing department. Though there is nothing to indicate otherwise in the format, it would be appropriate to mention the name of the schemes of the voluntary sector in the sequential order of the heads of development as followed in other Annexure. Since there is no departmental concept in the order of presentation and that departmental sequential order is not likely to fall in line with the overall order of heads of development, it would have to be reworked by the Planning department of the State in terms of sequential order of heads of development on Annexure-VII.

Column 2 refers to total of the Eleventh Plan Outlay at 2006-7 prices for the schemes of the Voluntary sector. Voluntary sector-wise approval of schemes under Five Year Plan normally does not take place. In case it exists there is no problem in filling it up. However, since the column is meant for projected outlay for the Eleventh Plan, the figures could be arrived at by adding five annual plan figures of the Eleventh Plan on voluntary sector as well. Further, it would be needed year-wise deflator from the Planning Commission for conversion of Projected Outlay at 2006-07 prices. It is also for other reason that some of the schemes have come into being at different periods of the Eleventh Plan period. These have to be worked out as objectively as possible with reference to records kept in the line departments. Pending receipt of such deflator, the outlay for schemes of the Voluntary sector falling under the Eleventh Plan need to be posted at column 2.

Column 3 is meant for Actual Expenditure for schemes under Voluntary sector for the Annual Plan 2010-11. Such expenditure need to be posted only for dedicated schemes having budget code of Grant-in-aid. Otherwise, it would be difficult to identify such schemes and the very purpose of this column would be defeated. However, it has also to be remembered that not all schemes having Grant–in-aid code belong to the Voluntary sector. Now, during November end, actual verified expenditure figures for the Annual Plan 2010-11 are likely to have reached the departments of the State Government from the office of the Accountant-General. Based on verified figures for schemes having Grant-in-aid account code, actual expenditures for the year 2010-11 may be filled in. If for some reason the figures are not available from the office of the Accountant General, verified figures of drawal of fund might be obtained from the related Treasury, compare it with utilisation certificates and then fill in the column 4. It may be indicated 'provisional' by the side of the Actual Expenditure within bracket in case verified figures from the office of the Accountant General have not been posted.

Column 5 refers to Approved Outlay for the Annual Plan 2011-12, for schemes of the Voluntary sector and column 6 intends to capture Anticipated Expenditure. This column is to be filled in from the approved letter of the Planning Commission and components of Voluntary sector as recorded in the State Annual Plan 2011-12.

Column 6 is meant for Anticipated Expenditure for 2011-12. As to the anticipated expenditure, it is desirable to give realistic expenditure based on half yearly situation or third quarterly figures of financial achievement, as available, with realistic assessment for the remaining period of the Annual Plan. In this aspect, release of budgeted State fund to the implementing agencies for the relevant schemes may be given appropriate consideration. Anticipated achievements indicating full coverage do not really make any planning sense and hence need to post realistic figures only.

Column 7 is to capture anticipated expenditure of the Voluntary Sector for the entire Eleventh Plan at current prices. Normally Planning Commission communicates year-wise inflator for conversion of earlier expenditure at current prices. Pending receipt of such inflator, the total of first four year's expenditure, as obtained from the office of Accountant General may be added with the anticipated expenditure for the year 2011-12 and then post the aggregate figure at column 7.

Column 8 is to indicate, scheme-wise, the Tentative Projected Outlay of the Voluntary sector for the Twelfth Plan which the State Government has to work out at this stage based on the Approach of the Twelfth Plan, the State vision based on possible role of Voluntary sector for meeting development deficit, human development deficit and other compulsions at the State level as perceived by the State Planning Board and the Plan-implementing departments of the State.

Column 9 is meant for, scheme-wise proposals of Voluntary sector for the State Annual Plan 2012-13 which will be taken up for discussion by the Working Groups in the Planning Commission and later by the Deputy Chairman and the Chief Minister of the State for finalisation of the State Plan.

11. Women Component in the State Plan Programmes—Financial Outlays—Annexure VIII-A

Inclusive development has been the core focus of the Eleventh Five Year Plan, the Twelfth Five Year Plan has also to further strengthen this move. Programme intervention on Gender areas necessitates inclusiveness to extend to hitherto underserved areas of social concern. In practical terms, it is reflected in the coverage of schemes. Such schemes may be women specific altogether, it may be primarily for the women group or it may be a common programme where women do participate as stakeholders. It is worthwhile to state that when such schemes are budgeted with gender account code, the schemes turn out to be gender inclusive altogether. Such women specific schemes would be really meaningful to ensure target specific outcome. It will also be relevant to track down the quality of its performances by appropriate monitoring.

Incidentally, the Ministry of Finance, Government of India has given circular to put in place Gender Budgeting under respective Central Ministries. In that context there would be paradigm shift from Women Component Plan to Gender Plan and then of Gender budgeting in the Central Government Sector. It is expected that the State governments shall also follow suit the central initiative of Gender Budgeting. The Annexure VIII-A is, however, designed to capture financial aspect of Women Component Plan.

ANNEXURE VIIIA

WOMEN COMPONENT (WC) IN THE STATE PLAN PROGRAMMES
DRAFT ANNUAL STATE PLAN 2012-13 : FINANCIAL OUTLAYS—PROPOSALS FOR WC

(Rs. in lakh)

Sl. No.	Major Head/ Sub-head	Schemes*	Eleventh Plan 2007-12 Projected Outlays (At 2006-07 Prices)		Annual Plan 2010-11	Annual Plan 2011-12				Eleventh Plan 2007-12	Twelfth Five Year Plan Tentative Projected Outlay at 2011-12 Prices		Annual Plan (2012-13) Proposed	
					Actual Expenditure under WC	Approved Outlay		Anticipated Expenditure		Anticipated Expenditure under WC				
			Total Outlay	of which flow to WC		Total Outlay	of which flow to WC	Total Outlay	of which flow to WC		Total Outlay	of which flow to WC	Total Outlay	of which flow to WC
0	1	2	3	4	5	6	7	8	9	10	11	12	13	14

* Scheme-wise details may be given.

At Column 0, the consecutive serial number is to be indicated.

Column 1 is meant for the major and minor heads. (Incidentally, there is no concept of sub-head under major head as included in the Annexure VIIIA. Every major head has a number of minor heads and, therefore, sub-head should be read as minor head).

Column 2 is to capture schemes which may be women specific altogether, primarily for the women group or a common programme where women do participate as stakeholders. The individual plan implementing departments would mention the name of the schemes in the sequential order of the heads of development administered by them. However, since there is no departmental concept in the order of presentation and that departmental sequential order is not likely to fall in line with the overall order of heads of development as in column 1, the schemes have to be rearranged by the Planning department of the State in the sequential order of heads of development in Annexure VIII-A.

Column 3 refers to Women component specific Scheme's Projected Outlay of the Eleventh Plan 2007-12, at 2006-07 prices with deflator wherever required. The Scheme-specific projected outlay of the Eleventh Plan has already been worked out at Annexure-1 at column 3. Now, out of such Scheme-specific projected outlay of the Eleventh Plan as worked out at Annexure-1 at column 3, only those schemes have to be captured at Column 3 of this Annexure VIII-A which have earlier been captured at column 2 also (i.e. schemes having Women component) and post its projected outlay for the Eleventh Plan.

Column 4 is to capture the projected flow to women component from any scheme's Total Outlay during the Eleventh Plan Outlay as recorded in previous column 3. Now, it would be appropriate to record in figure such projected flow and in bracket, its flow percentage. Further, in filling this column 4, for abundant caution, it would be appropriate to consult budgeted schemes for women either under dedicated code or otherwise. For dedicated women schemes, the percentage flow would be 100 per cent. For other schemes, the flow calculation needs to be worked out as objectively as possible with reference to records and further on possible outreach of benefits to women in consultation with the concerned Line Departments.

Column 5 is to record Actual Expenditure, scheme-wise, having Women component for the Annual Plan 2010-11. Such expenditure posting would call for detailed analysis. For dedicated women schemes there would exist no problem. Actual expenditure for such schemes for 2010-11 has earlier been captured at column 5 under Annexure-1. Now, out of them, actual expenditure of all women component-specific dedicated schemes have again to be captured at the first instance and then for other schemes having different nature of flow character of

Women component. Based on percentage of flow to WC, the actual expenditure has to be worked out.

Columns 6 and 7 refer to scheme-wise Approved Outlay and its flow to WC for the Annual Plan 2011-12. This column is to be filled in with reference to the approved letter of the Planning Commission for the Annual Plan 2011-12. However, women-scheme-specific approved outlay is not mentioned in the approved outlay of the Planning Commission. However, Scheme-specific Approved outlay for the Annual Plan 2011-12 has earlier been noted at column 6 of Annexure-1. From that column 6, only those schemes having Women component and its related outlay need to be posted here, i.e., at Columns 6 of Annexure VIII-A. Column 7 is the corresponding flow to WC.

Columns 8 and 9 are meant for Anticipated Expenditure for all schemes having WC and flow share of such expenditure to WC respectively for 2011-12. Here again scheme-specific anticipated expenditure have earlier been recorded at column 7 of Annexure I. From that column 7, only those schemes having Women component and its related Anticipated expenditure for 2011-12 need to be posted here, i.e., at Columns 8 of Annexure VIII-A. Column 9 is the corresponding flow to WC.

Column 10 is meant for the anticipated expenditure under WC for the Eleventh Plan period. These have to be computed with reference to expenditure figures on flow to WC of earlier three plan years, (i.e., 2007-8, 2008-9 and 2009-10) plus anticipated expenditure at column 10 (for 2010-11) and column 11(2011-12) of this Annexure.

Column 11 and column 12 are to indicate Tentative outlay for the Twelfth Plan for schemes having WC and of its flow to WC respectively. Here again, scheme-specific Tentative outlay for the Twelfth Plan have earlier been recorded at column 8 of Annexure I. From that column 8, only those schemes having Women component and its related outlay need to be posted at Columns 11 of Annexure VIII-A. Column 12 is the corresponding flow to WC.

Column 13 and column 14 are meant for proposals of the State Plan 2012-13 for schemes having Women component and its flow to WC respectively. Here again, scheme-specific proposed outlay for the Annual Plan, 2012-13 have earlier been noted at column 9 of Annexure I. From that column 9, only those schemes having Women component and its related outlay for 2012-13 need to be posted at Column 13 of Annexure VIII-A. Column 14 is the corresponding flow to WC.

12. Women Component (WC) in the State Plan Programmes: Physical Targets and Achievements—Annexure VIII-B

Annexure VIII-B is the Physical counterpart of Annexure VIII-A

ANNEXURE VIII-B

WOMEN COMPONENT (WC) IN THE STATE PLAN PROGRAMMES DRAFT ANNUAL STATE PLAN 2012-13 : PHYSICAL TARGETS AND ACHIEVEMENTS—PROPOSALS FOR WC

Sl. No.	*Major Head/ Sub-head/ Schemes*	*Unit*	*Eleventh Plan (2007-12)*	*Annual Plan (2010-11)*		*Annual Plan (2011-12)*		*Eleventh Plan (2007-12)*	*Twelfth Five Year Plan (tentative)*	*Annual Plan 2012-13 (proposed)*
			Target	*Target*	*Actual Achievement*	*Target*	*Anticipated Achievement*	*Anticipated Achievement*	*Target*	*Target*
0	1	2	3	4	5	6	7	8	10	11

FILE NAME: A-8B

At column 0, the consecutive serial numbers of the schemes are to be indicated.

Column 1 is to capture schemes having women component only under major and minor heads of development. As a matter of fact, both these segments have been captured separately in the previous Annexure VIII-A at columns 1 and 2. At this Annexure VIII-B, the corresponding figures have to be copied from VIII-A and schemes have to be posted under each minor head. Since minor heads are sub-components of major head, it will ensure major head-wise posting also.

Column 2 is the measurement index for column 1. Since there is no uniform measuring rod, the unit of measurement is bound to be different. Depending on the nature of items, units may be numbered thousand, lakh, million, crore, etc. It may be metre, square metre, acre, hectare, km, kg, tonnes, mt, etc. It is even possible to add description, e.g. number of beneficiaries and the like. It is, however, to be noted that the unit of measurement as adopted for Annexure II need also to be followed here.

Column 3 indicates the Eleventh Five Year Plan target for the items of column 1 expressed in terms of unit at column 2. Normally, these figures remain static throughout the Five Year Plan period as it were settled with the approval of the Five Year Plan of the State. However, in case any mid-term correction of plan targets takes place it may undergo that change only.

Column 4 indicates the Physical Target for WC for the Annual Plan 2010-11 and column 5 is to capture its Achievement. The physical targets set for Annual Plan 2010-11 for schemes having Women component need to be posted at Columns 4 of Annexure VIII-B.

The column 5 of Annexure VIII-B is the achievement counterpart of column 4 of Annexure VIII-B. In filling the figures for achievement care has to be taken to see the symbiotic relationship between expenditure and output. Though there is no system of verifying the actual physical figures by the office of the Accountant General, the figures as obtained from the implementing agencies need to be appropriately validated by field visits, wherever required.

Similarly, columns 6 and 7 are physical Targets and Anticipated Achievement for the Annual Plan 2011-12. Financial outlay were earlier settled with reference to column 7 of Annexure VIII-A. The physical targets set for therein for schemes having Women component need to be posted at Columns 6 of Annexure VIII-B.

Column 7 is the counterpart of column 6. In filling the figures for achievement care has to be taken to see the symbiotic relationship between expenditure and output. Though there is no system of verifying anticipated physical figures, the figures as obtained from the implementing agencies need to be appropriately validated by field visits and anticipated expenditure.

Column 8 is meant for the anticipated physical achievement under WC for the Eleventh Plan period. These have to be computed with reference to achievement figures on flow to WC of earlier three plan years (i.e., 2007-8, 2008-9 and 2009-10) plus physical achievement under WC at column 5 (for 2010-11) and column 7 (2011-12) of this Annexure.

Column 10 is to indicate Tentative Target for the Twelfth Plan for schemes having WC. Here again, scheme-specific Tentative outlay for WC for the Twelfth Plan have earlier been recorded at column 12 of Annexure VIII-A. With reference to that column 12 of Annexure VIII-A, scheme-wise physical targets for the Twelfth Plan have to be worked out and posted at column 10.

Column 11 is meant for Physical Target proposals of the State Annual Plan 2012-13 for schemes having WC. Here again, for schemes having WC proposed outlay for the Annual Plan 2012-13 have earlier been noted at column 14 of Annexure-VIII-A. With reference to that column 14 of Annexure–VIII-A, Physical Target proposals of the State Annual Plan 2012-13 for schemes having WC have to be worked out and posted at column 11.

13. Information Relating to Flagship Programmes—Annexure IX

Flagship Programmes are a set of important socio-economic programmes of the Central Government having enough far reaching potentialities to effect multi-sectoral base of the country. These Programmes are intended to contribute significantly to bring about envisaged economic and social sector transformation in the country. The essence of these programmes in the context of the State Planning is that dedicated schemes under them have inherent strength to address unmet development needs in the related sector and could normally be the lead or even supportive intervention initiative to meet the mighty challenges under the State Plan. Adequate and comprehensive coverage have to be made to obtain maximum advantage of the Flagship Programmes. Incidentally, the States have not much to contribute on these programmes as the funding for these programmes are made by the Central Government. Among the various programmes being implemented in the country, Planning Commission has sought to monitor the status of implementation of 15 Flagship Programmes for its crucial role in the economy as given below:

ANNEXURE-IX

DRAFT ANNUAL STATE PLAN 2012-13 : INFORMATION ON 15 FLAGSHIP PROGRAMMES

Sl. No.	Name of the Programmes	2007-08			2008-09			2009-10			2010-11			2011-12			Twelfth Five Year Plan Tentative Projected Outlay at 2011-12 Prices		Annual Plan (2012-13) Proposed	
		Centre Share Released	State Share Released	Actual Exp.	Centre Share Released	State Share Released	Actual Expenditure	Centre Share Released	State Share Released	Actual Expenditure	Centre Share Released	State Share Released	Actual Expenditure	Centre Share Released	State Share Released	Anticipated Expenditure	Centre Share	State Share	Centre Share	State Share
1	2	3	4	5	6	7	8	9	10	11	12	13	14	15	16	17	18	19	20	21
1.	Mahatma Gandhi National Rural Employment Guarantee Act																			

1	2	3	4	5	6	7	8	9	10	11	12	13	14	15	16	17	18	19	20	21
2.	Indira Awaas Yojana																			
3.	National Rural Health Mission																			
4.	Sarva Shiksha Abhiyan																			
5.	Mid-Day Meal Scheme																			
6.	Jawaharlal Nehru National Urban Renewal Mission																			
7.	Pradhan Mantri Gram Sadak Yojana																			
8.	National Social Assistance Programme																			
9.	Integrated Child Development Scheme																			
10.	National Rural Drinking Water Programme																			
11.	National Hortriculture Mission																			
12.	Accelerated Irrigation Benefit Programme																			
13.	Rajiv Gandhi Grameen Vidyutikaran Yojana																			
14.	Skill Development Mission																			
15.	Total Sanitation Campaign																			

Column 1 is the consecutive serial number and the column 2 indicates the name of the Flagship Programmes and is already given.

There are three columns each for indicating Central Share released, State Share released and actual expenditure for the years 2007-8 (columns 3, 4 and 5), 2008-9 (columns 6, 7 and 8), 2009-10 (columns 9, 10 and 11), 2010-11 (columns 12, 13 and 14), 2011-12 (columns 15, 16 and 17). These columns have to be filled in with reference to official records. For released figure of the Central Share, the records maintained by the nodal department for the related programme have to be cross-checked with those maintained by the State Finance Department. For the released State Share, again the records maintained by the nodal department for the related programme have to be cross-checked with those maintained by the State Finance Department and then post the figures. For Central Share and State Share for Twelfth Plan Tentative Projected Outlay (columns 18 and 19), the Central Share may be filled in with reference to the communication received from the related nodal Ministry and the corresponding counterpart outlay that the concerned State needs to provide as per present cost sharing arrangement. Similarly, for the Annual Plan 2012-13, Central Share and State Share for the Proposed Outlay (columns 20 and 21), the Central Share may be filled in with reference to the communication received from the related nodal Ministry and the corresponding counterpart outlay that the concerned State needs to provide as per present cost sharing arrangement.

Acronyms

ACA	Additional Central Assistance
AIBP	Accelerated Irrigation Benefit Programme
AID	Acquired Immuno Deficiency Syndrome
APEDA	Agricultural and Processed Food Products Export Development Authority
APL	Above the Poverty Line
ATR	Action Taken Report
AWP	Annual Works Programme
BP	Block Panchayat
BPL	Below the Poverty Line
BRGF	Backward Region Grant Fund
CAD&WM	Command Area Development and Water Management
CSS	Centrally Sponsored Scheme/Central Sector Scheme
DDP	Desert Development Programme
DHDR	District Human Development Report
DLBC	District Level Bankers Committee
DPC	District Planning Committee
DRDA	District Rural Development Agency
DPR	Detailed Project Report
EAP	Externally Aided Project
EWG	Economically Weaker Group
FAO	Food and Agricultural Organisation
FPI	Food Processing Industries
GOI	Government of India

GDP	Gross Domestic Product
GP	Gram Panchayat
GPS	Geographical Position System
GS	Gram Sabha
IAY	Indira Awaas Yojana
ICDS	Integrated Child Development Services
ICAR	Indian Council of Agricultural Research
ILO	International Labour Organisation
IMR	Infant Mortality Rate/Ratio
IRDP	Integrated Rural Development Programme
IWMP	Integrated Watershed Management Programme
JFMC	Joint Forest Management Committee
JNNURM	Jawaharlal Nehru National Urban Renewal Mission
JSY	Janani Suraksha Yojana
KVK	Krishi Vikas Kendra
KVS	Krishi Vikas Sevak
MDG	Millennium Development Goals
MGNRESS	Mahatma Gandhi National Rural Employment Service Scheme
MNP	Minimum Needs Programme
MoA	Ministry of Agriculture
MoRD	Ministry of Rural Development
MoWR	Ministry of Water Resources
MPC	Metropolitan Planning Committee
MPLAD	Member of Parliament's Local Area Development
NAP	National Afforestation Programme
NAREGA	National Rural Employment Guarantee Act
NDC	National Development Council
NeGP	National e-Governance Plan
NHB	National Horticulture Board
NGO	Non-Governmental Organisation
NRDMS	Natural Resources Data Base Management System
NREGA	National Rural Employment Guarantee Act
NREGS	National Rural Employment Guarantee Scheme

NRHM	National Rural Health Mission
NWDPRA	National Watershed Development Project in Rainfed Areas
PIA	Project Implementation Authority
PMGSY	Prime Minister's Gram Sadak Yojana
PSUs	Public Sector Undertakings
PWD	Public Works Department
RKVY	Rashtriya Krishi Vikas Yojana
RSVY	Rashtriya Sam Vikas Yojana
SC/ST	Scheduled Castes/Scheduled Tribes
SCSP	Scheduled Castes Sub Plan
SFC	State Finance Commission
SHG	Self Help Groups
SGRY	Sampoorna Grameen Rozgar Yojana
SGSY	Swarnajayanti Grameen Swarozgar Yojana
SSA	Sarva Shiksha Abhiyan
TFR	Total Fertility Rate
TSC	Total Sanitation Campaign
TSP	Tribal Sub Plan
UNAIDS	United Nations Programme on AIDS
UNDAF	United Nations Development Assistance Framework
UNICEF	United Nations International Children's Emergency Fund
UNEP	United Nations Environment Programme
UNFPA	United Nations Fund for Population Assistance
UNO	United Nations Organisation
WHO	World Health Organisation
WUA	Water Users Association
ZP	Zilla Panchayat

APPENDICES

Appendix 1

Extracts from the Constitution of India

PART IX
THE PANCHAYATS

243. In this Part, unless the context otherwise requires,—

(*a*) "district" means a district in a State;
(*b*) "Gram Sabha" means a body consisting of persons registered in the electoral rolls relating to a village comprised within the area of Panchayat at the village level;
(*c*) "intermediate level" means a level between the village and district levels specified by the Governor of a State by public notification to be the intermediate level for the purposes of this Part;
(*d*) "Panchayat" means an institution (by whatever name called) of self-government constituted under article 243B for the rural areas;
(*e*) "Panchayat area" means the territorial area of a Panchayat.

243B. (1) There shall be constituted in every State, Panchayats at the village, intermediate and district levels in accordance with the provisions of this Part.

(2) Notwithstanding anything in clause (1), Panchayats at the intermediate level may not be constituted in a State having a population not exceeding twenty lakhs.

[1][PART IX-A
THE MUNICIPALITIES

243P. In this Part, unless the context otherwise requires,—

(*a*) "Committee" means a Committee constituted under article 243S;
(*b*) "district" means a district in a State;
(*c*) "Metropolitan area" means an area having a population of ten lakhs or more, comprised in one or more districts and consisting

of two or more Municipalities or Panchayats or other contiguous areas, specified by the Governor by public notification to be a Metropolitan area for the purposes of this Part;

(*d*) "Municipal area" means the territorial area of a Municipality as notified by the Governor;

(*e*) "Municipality" means an institution of self government constituted under article 243Q;

243Q. (1) There shall be constituted in every State,—

(*a*) a Nagar Panchayat (by whatever name called) for a transitional area, that is to say, an area in transition from a rural area to an urban area;

(*b*) a Municipal Council for a smaller urban area; and

(*c*) a Municipal Corporation for a larger urban area,

in accordance with the provisions of this Part:

Provided that a Municipality under this clause may not be constituted in such urban area or part thereof as the Governor may, having regard to the size of the area and the municipal services being provided or proposed to be provided by an industrial establishment in that area and such other factors as he may deem fit, by public notification, specify to be an industrial township.

(2) In this article, "a transitional area", "a smaller urban area" or "a larger urban area" means such area as the Governor may, having regard to the population of the area, the density of the population therein, the revenue generated for local administration, the percentage of employment in non-agricultural activities, the economic importance or such other factors as he may deem fit, specify by public notification for the purposes of this Part.

POWERS, AUTHORITY AND RESPONSIBILITIES OF PANCHAYATS

243G. Subject to the provisions of this Constitution, the Legislature of a State may, by law, endow the Panchayats with such powers and authority as may be necessary to enable them to function as institutions of self-government and such law may contain provisions for the devolution of powers and responsibilities upon Panchayats at the appropriate level, subject to such conditions as may be specified therein, with respect to—

(*a*) the preparation of plans for economic development and social justice;
(*b*) the implementation of schemes for economic development and social justice as may be entrusted to them including those in relation to the matters listed in the Eleventh Schedule.

POWERS, AUTHORITY AND RESPONSIBILITIES OF MUNICIPALITIES, ETC.

243W. Subject to the provisions of this Constitution, the Legislature of a State may, by law, endow—

(*a*) the Municipalities with such powers and authority as may be necessary to enable them to function as institutions of self-government and such law may contain provisions for the devolution of powers and responsibilities upon Municipalities, subject to such conditions as may be specified therein with respect to—
  (*i*) the preparation of plans for economic development and social justice;
  (*ii*) the performance of functions and the implementation of schemes as may be entrusted to them including those in relation to the matters listed in the Twelfth Schedule;
(*b*) the Committees with such powers and authority as may be necessary to enable them to carry out the responsibilities conferred upon them including those in relation to the matters listed in the Twelfth Schedule.

COMMITTEE FOR DISTRICT PLANNING

243ZD. (1) There shall be constituted in every State at the district level a District Planning Committee to consolidate the plans prepared by the Panchayats and the Municipalities in the district and to prepare a draft development plan for the district as a whole.

(2) The Legislature of a State may, by law, make provision with respect to—

(*a*) the composition of the District Planning Committees;
(*b*) the manner in which the seats in such Committees shall be filled:

Provided that not less than four-fifths of the total number of members of such Committee shall be elected by, and from amongst, the elected members of the Panchayat at the district level and of the Municipalities in the district in proportion to the ratio between the population of the rural areas and of the urban areas in the district;

(*c*) the functions relating to district planning which may be assigned to such Committees;

(*d*) the manner in which the Chairpersons of such Committees shall be chosen.

(3) Every District Planning Committee shall, in preparing the draft development plan,—

(*a*) have regard to—

(*i*) matters of common interest between the Panchayats and the Municipalities including spatial planning, sharing of water and other physical and natural resources, the integrated development of infrastructure and environmental conservation;

(*ii*) the extent and type of available resources whether financial or otherwise;

(*b*) consult such institutions and organisations as the Governor may, by order, specify.

(4) The Chairperson of every District Planning Committee shall forward the development plan, as recommended by such Committee, to the Government of the State.

Appendix 1.1

Seventh Schedule (Article 246)

LIST I—UNION LIST

1. Defence of India and every part thereof including preparation for defence and all such acts as may be conducive in times of war to its prosecution and after its termination to effective demobilisation.
2. Naval, military and air forces; any other armed forces of the Union.1[2A. Deployment of any armed force of the Union or any other force subject to the control of the Union or any contingent or unit thereof in any State in aid of the civil power; powers, jurisdiction, privileges and liabilities of the members of such forces while on such deployment.]
3. Delimitation of cantonment areas, local self-government in such areas, the constitution and powers within such areas of cantonment authorities and the regulation of house accommodation (including the control of rents) in such areas.
4. Naval, military and air force works.
5. Arms, firearms, ammunition and explosives.
6. Atomic energy and mineral resources necessary for its production.
7. Industries declared by Parliament by law to be necessary for the purpose of defence or for the prosecution of war.
8. Central Bureau of Intelligence and Investigation.
9. Preventive detention for reasons connected with Defence, Foreign Affairs, or the security of India; persons subjected to such detention.
10. Foreign affairs; all matters which bring the Union into relation with any foreign country.
11. Diplomatic, consular and trade representation.
12. United Nations Organisation.
13. Participation in international conferences, associations and other bodies and implementing of decisions made thereat.

14. Entering into treaties and agreements with foreign countries and implementing of treaties, agreements and conventions with foreign countries.
15. War and peace.
16. Foreign jurisdiction.
17. Citizenship, naturalisation and aliens.
18. Extradition.
19. Admission into, and emigration and expulsion from, India; passports and visas.
20. Pilgrimages to places outside India.
21. Piracies and crimes committed on the high seas or in the air; offences against the law of nations committed on land or the high seas or in the air.
22. Railways.
23. Highways declared by or under law made by Parliament to be national highways.
24. Shipping and navigation on inland waterways, declared by Parliament by law to be national waterways, as regards mechanically propelled vessels; the rule of the road on such waterways.
25. Maritime shipping and navigation, including shipping and navigation on tidal waters; provision of education and training for the mercantile marine and regulation of such education and training provided by States and other agencies.
26. Lighthouses, including lightships, beacons and other provision for the safety of shipping and aircraft.
27. Ports declared by or under law made by Parliament or existing law to be major ports, including their delimitation, and the constitution and powers of port authorities therein.
28. Port quarantine, including hospitals connected therewith; seamen's and marine hospitals.
29. Airways; aircraft and air navigation; provision of aerodromes; regulation and organisation of air traffic and of aerodromes; provision for aeronautical education and training and regulation of such education and training provided by States and other agencies.
30. Carriage of passengers and goods by railway, sea or air, or by national waterways in mechanically propelled vessels.
31. Posts and telegraphs; telephones, wireless, broadcasting and other like forms of communication.

32. Property of the Union and the revenue therefrom, but as regards property situated in a State *** subject to legislation by the State, save in so far as Parliament by law otherwise provides.
33. [* * * * *]
34. Courts of wards for the estates of Rulers of Indian States.
35. Public debt of the Union.
36. Currency, coinage and legal tender; foreign exchange.
37. Foreign loans.
38. Reserve Bank of India.
39. Post Office Savings Bank.
40. Lotteries organised by the Government of India or the Government of a State.
41. Trade and commerce with foreign countries; import and export across customs frontiers; definition of customs frontiers.
42. Inter-State trade and commerce.
43. Incorporation, regulation and winding up of trading corporations, including banking, insurance and financial corporations, but not including co-operative societies.
44. Incorporation, regulation and winding up of corporations, whether trading or not, with objects not confined to one State, but not including universities.
45. Banking.
46. Bills of exchange, cheques, promissory notes and other like instruments.
47. Insurance.
48. Stock exchanges and futures markets.
49. Patents, inventions and designs; copyright; trade marks and merchandise marks.
50. Establishment of standards of weight and measure.
51. Establishment of standards of quality for goods to be exported out of India or transported from one State to another.
52. Industries, the control of which by the Union is declared by Parliament by law to be expedient in the public interest.
53. Regulation and development of oilfields and mineral oil resources; petroleum and petroleum products; other liquids and substances declared by Parliament by law to be dangerously inflammable.
54. Regulation of mines and mineral development to the extent to which such regulation and development under the control of

the Union is declared by Parliament by law to be expedient in the public interest.

55. Regulation of labour and safety in mines and oilfields.
56. Regulation and development of inter-State rivers and river valleys to the extent to which such regulation and development under the control of the Union is declared by Parliament by law to be expedient in the public interest.
57. Fishing and fisheries beyond territorial waters.
58. Manufacture, supply and distribution of salt by Union agencies; regulation and control of manufacture, supply and distribution of salt by other agencies.
59. Cultivation, manufacture, and sale for export, of opium.
60. Sanctioning of cinematograph films for exhibition.
61. Industrial disputes concerning Union employees.
62. The institutions known at the commencement of this Constitution as the National Library, the Indian Museum, the Imperial War Museum, the Victoria Memorial and the Indian War Memorial, and any other like institution financed by the Government of India wholly or in part and declared by Parliament by law to be an institution of national importance.
63. The institutions known at the commencement of this Constitution as the Benares Hindu University, the Aligarh Muslim University and the 1[Delhi University; the University established in pursuance of article 371E;] any other institution declared by Parliament by law to be an institution of national importance.
64. Institutions for scientific or technical education financed by the Government of India wholly or in part and declared by Parliament by law to be institutions of national importance.
65. Union agencies and institutions for—
    (a) professional, vocational or technical training, including the training of police officers; or
    (b) the promotion of special studies or research; or
    (c) scientific or technical assistance in the investigation or detection of crime.
66. Co-ordination and determination of standards in institutions for higher education or research and scientific and technical institutions.
67. Ancient and historical monuments and records, and archaeological sites and remains, 1[declared by or under law made by Parliament] to be of national importance.

68. The Survey of India, the Geological, Botanical, Zoological and Anthropological Surveys of India; Meteorological organisations.
69. Census.
70. Union Public Service; All-India Services; Union Public Service Commission.
71. Union pensions, that is to say, pensions payable by the Government of India or out of the Consolidated Fund of India.
72. Elections to Parliament, to the Legislatures of States and to the offices of President and Vice President; the Election Commission.
73. Salaries and allowances of members of Parliament, the Chairman and Deputy Chairman of the Council of States and the Speaker and Deputy Speaker of the House of the People.
74. Powers, privileges and immunities of each House of Parliament and of the members and the Committees of each House; enforcement of attendance of persons for giving evidence or producing documents before committees of Parliament or Commissions appointed by Parliament.
75. Emoluments, allowances, privileges, and rights in respect of leave of absence, of the President and Governors; salaries and allowances of the Ministers for the Union; the salaries, allowances, and rights in respect of leave of absence and other conditions of service of the Comptroller and Auditor-General.
76. Audit of the accounts of the Union and of the States.
77. Constitution, organisation, jurisdiction and powers of the Supreme Court (including contempt of such Court), and the fees taken therein; persons entitled to practise before the Supreme Court.
78. Constitution and organisation 1[(including vacations)] of the High Courts except provisions as to officers and servants of High Courts; persons entitled to practise before the High Courts.

2[79. Extension of the jurisdiction of a High Court to, and exclusion of the jurisdiction of a High Court from, any Union territory.]

80. Extension of the powers and jurisdiction of members of a police force belonging to any State to any area outside that State, but not so as to enable the police of one State to exercise powers and jurisdiction in any area outside that State without the consent of the Government of the State in which such area is situated; extension of the powers and jurisdiction of

members of a police force belonging to any State to railway areas outside that State.

81. Inter-State migration; inter-State quarantine.

82. Taxes on income other than agricultural income.

83. Duties of customs including export duties.

84. Duties of excise on tobacco and other goods manufactured or produced in India except—
   (a) alcoholic liquors for human consumption;
   (b) opium, Indian hemp and other narcotic drugs and narcotics, but including medicinal and toilet preparations containing alcohol or any substance included in sub-paragraph (b) of this entry.

85. Corporation tax.

86. Taxes on the capital value of the assets, exclusive of agricultural land, of individuals and companies; taxes on the capital of companies.

87. Estate duty in respect of property other than agricultural land.

88. Duties in respect of succession to property other than agricultural land.

89. Terminal taxes on goods or passengers, carried by railway, sea or air; taxes on railway fares and freights.

90. Taxes other than stamp duties on transactions in stock exchanges and futures markets.

91. Rates of stamp duty in respect of bills of exchange, cheques, promissory notes, bills of lading, letters of credit, policies of insurance, transfer of shares, debentures, proxies and receipts.

92. Taxes on the sale or purchase of newspapers and on advertisements published therein.

1[92A. Taxes on the sale or purchase of goods other than newspapers, where such sale or purchase takes place in the course of inter-State trade or commerce.]

2[92B. Taxes on the consignments of goods (whether the consignment is to the person making it or to any other person), where such consignment takes place in the course of inter-State trade or commerce.]

*[92C. Taxes on services.]

93. Offences against laws with respect to any of the matters in this List.

94. Inquiries, surveys and statistics for the purpose of any of the matters in this List.

95. Jurisdiction and powers of all courts, except the Supreme Court, with respect to any of the matters in this List; admiralty jurisdiction.
96. Fees in respect of any of the matters in this List, but not including fees taken in any court.
97. Any other matter not enumerated in List II or List III including any tax not mentioned in either of those Lists.

LIST II—STATE LIST

1. Public order (but not including 3[the use of any naval, military or air force or any other armed force of the Union or of any other force subject to the control of the Union or of any contingent or unit thereof] in aid of the civil power).

1[2. Police (including railway and village police) subject to the provisions of entry 2A of List I.]

3. 2***Officers and servants of the High Court; procedure in rent and revenue courts; fees taken in all courts except the Supreme Court.
4. Prisons, reformatories, Borstal institutions and other institutions of a like nature, and persons detained therein; arrangements with other States for the use of prisons and other institutions.
5. Local government, that is to say, the constitution and powers of municipal corporations, improvement trusts, districts boards, mining settlement authorities and other local authorities for the purpose of local self government or village administration.
6. Public health and sanitation; hospitals and dispensaries.
7. Pilgrimages, other than pilgrimages to places outside India.
8. Intoxicating liquors, that is to say, the production, manufacture, possession, transport, purchase and sale of intoxicating liquors.
9. Relief of the disabled and unemployable.
10. Burials and burial grounds; cremations and cremation grounds.

3* * * * *

12. Libraries, museums and other similar institutions controlled or financed by the State; ancient and historical monuments and records other than those 4[declared by or under law made by Parliament] to be of national importance.

13. Communications, that is to say, roads, bridges, ferries, and other means of communication not specified in List I; municipal tramways; ropeways; inland waterways and traffic thereon subject to the provisions of List I and List III with regard to such waterways; vehicles other than mechanically propelled vehicles.
14. Agriculture, including agricultural education and research, protection against pests and prevention of plant diseases.
15. Preservation, protection and improvement of stock and prevention of animal diseases; veterinary training and practice.
16. Pounds and the prevention of cattle trespass.
17. Water, that is to say, water supplies, irrigation and canals, drainage and embankments, water storage and water power subject to the provisions of entry 56 of List I.
18. Land, that is to say, rights in or over land, land tenures including the relation of landlord and tenant, and the collection of rents; transfer and alienation of agricultural land; land improvement and agricultural loans; colonization.

1* * * * *

21. Fisheries.
22. Courts of wards subject to the provisions of entry 34 of List I; encumbered and attached estates.
23. Regulation of mines and mineral development subject to the provisions of List I with respect to regulation and development under the control of the Union.
24. Industries subject to the provisions of 2[entries 7 and 52] of List I.
25. Gas and gas-works.
26. Trade and commerce within the State subject to the provisions of entry 33 of List III.
27. Production, supply and distribution of goods subject to the provisions of entry 33 of List III.
28. Markets and fairs.

1* * * * *

30. Money-lending and money-lenders; relief of agricultural indebtedness.
31. Inns and inn-keepers.
32. Incorporation, regulation and winding up of corporations, other than those specified in List I, and universities; unincorporated trading, literary, scientific, religious and other societies and associations; co-operative societies.

33. Theatres and dramatic performances; cinemas subject to the provisions of entry 60 of List I; sports, entertainments and amusements.
34. Betting and gambling.
35. Works, lands and buildings vested in or in the possession of the State.

    1* * * * *
37. Elections to the Legislature of the State subject to the provisions of any law made by Parliament.
38. Salaries and allowances of members of the Legislature of the State, of the Speaker and Deputy Speaker of the Legislative Assembly and, if there is a Legislative Council, of the Chairman and Deputy Chairman thereof.
39. Powers, privileges and immunities of the Legislative Assembly and of the members and the committees thereof, and, if there is a Legislative Council, of that Council and of the members and the committees thereof; enforcement of attendance of persons for giving evidence or producing documents before committees of the Legislature of the State.
40. Salaries and allowances of Ministers for the State.
41. State public services; State Public Service Commission.
42. State pensions, that is to say, pensions payable by the State or out of the Consolidated Fund of the State.
43. Public debt of the State.
44. Treasure trove.
45. Land revenue, including the assessment and collection of revenue, the maintenance of land records, survey for revenue purposes and records of rights, and alienation of revenues.
46. Taxes on agricultural income.
47. Duties in respect of succession to agricultural land.
48. Estate duty in respect of agricultural land.
49. Taxes on lands and buildings.
50. Taxes on mineral rights subject to any limitations imposed by Parliament by law relating to mineral development.
51. Duties of excise on the following goods manufactured or produced in the State and countervailing duties at the same or lower rates on similar goods manufactured or produced elsewhere in India:—
    (*a*) alcoholic liquors for human consumption;
    (*b*) opium, Indian hemp and other narcotic drugs and narcotics; but not including medicinal and toilet

preparations containing alcohol or any substance included in sub-paragraph (*b*) of this entry.

52. Taxes on the entry of goods into a local area for consumption, use or sale therein.
53. Taxes on the consumption or sale of electricity.
1[54. Taxes on the sale or purchase of goods other than newspapers, subject to the provisions of entry 92A of List I.]
55. Taxes on advertisements other than advertisements published in the newspapers 2[and advertisements broadcast by radio or television].
56. Taxes on goods and passengers carried by road or on inland waterways.
57. Taxes on vehicles, whether mechanically propelled or not, suitable for use on roads, including tram cars subject to the provisions of entry 35 of List III.
58. Taxes on animals and boats.
59. Tolls.
60. Taxes on professions, trades, callings and employments.
61. Capitation taxes.
62. Taxes on luxuries, including taxes on entertainments, amusements, betting and gambling.
63. Rates of stamp duty in respect of documents other than those specified in the provisions of List I with regard to rates of stamp duty.
64. Offences against laws with respect to any of the matters in this List.
65. Jurisdiction and powers of all courts, except the Supreme Court, with respect to any of the matters in this List.
66. Fees in respect of any of the matters in this List, but not including fees taken in any court.

LIST III—CONCURRENT LIST

1. Criminal law, including all matters included in the Indian Penal Code at the commencement of this Constitution but excluding offences against laws with respect to any of the matters specified in List I or List II and excluding the use of naval, military or air forces or any other armed forces of the Union in aid of the civil power.

2. Criminal procedure, including all matters included in the Code of Criminal Procedure at the commencement of this Constitution.
3. Preventive detention for reasons connected with the security of a State, the maintenance of public order, or the maintenance of supplies and services essential to the community; persons subjected to such detention.
4. Removal from one State to another State of prisoners, accused persons and persons subjected to preventive detention for reasons specified in entry 3 of this List.
5. Marriage and divorce; infants and minors; adoption; wills, intestacy and succession; joint family and partition; all matters in respect of which parties in judicial proceedings were immediately before the commencement of this Constitution subject to their personal law.
6. Transfer of property other than agricultural land; registration of deeds and documents.
7. Contracts, including partnership, agency, contracts of carriage, and other special forms of contracts, but not including contracts relating to agricultural land.
8. Actionable wrongs.
9. Bankruptcy and insolvency.
10. Trust and Trustees.
11. Administrators—general and official trustees.

1[11A. Administration of Justice; constitution and organisation of all courts, except the Supreme Court and the High Courts.]

12. Evidence and oaths; recognition of laws, public acts and records, and judicial proceedings.
13. Civil procedure, including all matters included in the Code of Civil Procedure at the commencement of this Constitution, limitation and arbitration.
14. Contempt of court, but not including contempt of the Supreme Court.
15. Vagrancy; nomadic and migratory tribes.
16. Lunacy and mental deficiency, including places for the reception or treatment of lunatics and mental deficients.
17. Prevention of cruelty to animals.

1[17A. Forests.

17B. Protection of wild animals and birds.]

18. Adulteration of foodstuffs and other goods.

19. Drugs and poisons, subject to the provisions of entry 59 of List I with respect to opium.
20. Economic and social planning.
1[20A. Population control and family planning.]
21. Commercial and industrial monopolies, combines and trusts.
22. Trade unions; industrial and labour disputes.
23. Social security and social insurance; employment and unemployment.
24. Welfare of labour including conditions of work, provident funds, employers' liability, workmen's compensation, invalidity and old age pensions and maternity benefits.
2[25. Education, including technical education, medical education and universities, subject to the provisions of entries 63, 64, 65 and 66 of List I; vocational and technical training of labour.]
26. Legal, medical and other professions.
27. Relief and rehabilitation of persons displaced from their original place of residence by reason of the setting up of the Dominions of India and Pakistan.
28. Charities and charitable institutions, charitable and religious endowments and religious institutions.
29. Prevention of the extension from one State to another of infectious or contagious diseases or pests affecting men, animals or plants.
30. Vital statistics including registration of births and deaths.
31. Ports other than those declared by or under law made by Parliament or existing law to be major ports.
32. Shipping and navigation on inland waterways as regards mechanically propelled vessels, and the rule of the road on such waterways, and the carriage of passengers and goods on inland waterways subject to the provisions of List I with respect to national waterways.
1[33. Trade and commerce in, and the production, supply and distribution of,—
(*a*) the products of any industry where the control of such industry by the Union is declared by Parliament by law to be expedient in the public interest, and imported goods of the same kind as such products;
(*b*) foodstuffs, including edible oilseeds and oils;
(*c*) cattle fodder, including oilcakes and other concentrates;
(*d*) raw cotton, whether ginned or unginned, and cotton seed; and

(*e*) raw jute.]

2[33A. Weights and measures except establishment of standards.]

34. Price control.
35. Mechanically propelled vehicles including the principles on which taxes on such vehicles are to be levied.
36. Factories.
37. Boilers.
38. Electricity.
39. Newspapers, books and printing presses.
40. Archaeological sites and remains other than those 1[declared by or under law made by Parliament] to be of national importance.
41. Custody, management and disposal of property (including agricultural land) declared by law to be evacuee property.

2[42. Acquisition and requisitioning of property.]

43. Recovery in a State of claims in respect of taxes and other public demands, including arrears of land-revenue and sums recoverable as such arrears, arising outside that State.
44. Stamp duties other than duties or fees collected by means of judicial stamps, but not including rates of stamp duty.
45. Inquiries and statistics for the purposes of any of the matters specified in List II or List III.
46. Jurisdiction and powers of all courts, except the Supreme Court, with respect to any of the matters in this List.
47. Fees in respect of any of the matters in this List, but not including fees taken in any court.

ELEVENTH SCHEDULE
(Article 243G)
(For the Panchayats)

1. Agriculture, including agricultural extension.
2. Land improvement, implementation of land reforms, land consolidation and soil conservation.
3. Minor irrigation, water management and watershed development.
4. Animal husbandry, dairying and poultry.
5. Fisheries.
6. Social forestry and farm forestry.
7. Minor forest produce.
8. Small scale industries, including food processing industries.

9. Khadi, village and cottage industries.
10. Rural housing.
11. Drinking water.
12. Fuel and fodder.
13. Roads, culverts, bridges, ferries, waterways and other means of communication.
14. Rural electrification, including distribution of electricity.
15. Non-conventional energy sources.
16. Poverty alleviation programme.
17. Education, including primary and secondary schools.
18. Technical training and vocational education.
19. Adult and non-formal education.
20. Libraries.
21. Cultural activities.
22. Markets and fairs.
23. Health and sanitation, including hospitals, primary health centres and dispensaries.
24. Family welfare.
25. Women and child development.
26. Social welfare, including welfare of the handicapped and mentally retarded.
27. Welfare of the weaker sections, and in particular, of the Scheduled Castes and the Scheduled Tribes.
28. Public distribution system.
29. Maintenance of community assets.

TWELFTH SCHEDULE
(Article 243W)
(For the Municipalities)

1. Urban planning including town planning.
2. Regulation of land-use and construction of buildings.
3. Planning for economic and social development.
4. Roads and bridges.
5. Water supply for domestic, industrial and commercial purposes.
6. Public health, sanitation conservancy and solid waste management.
7. Fire services.
8. Urban forestry, protection of the environment and promotion of ecological aspects.

9. Safeguarding the interests of weaker sections of society, including the handicapped and mentally retarded.
10. Slum improvement and upgradation.
11. Urban poverty alleviation.
12. Provision of urban amenities and facilities such as parks, gardens, playgrounds.
13. Promotion of cultural, educational and aesthetic aspects.
14. Burials and burial grounds; cremations, cremation grounds; and electric crematoriums.
15. Cattle pounds; prevention of cruelty to animals.
16. Vital statistics including registration of births and deaths.
17. Public amenities including street lighting, parking lots, bus stops and public conveniences.
18. Regulation of slaughter houses and tanneries.

Appendix 2

Conduct of Government of Business Under Article 166 of the Constitution of India

Art. 166. (1) All executive actions of the Government of a State shall be expressed to be taken in the name of the Governor.

(2) Orders and other instruments made and executed in the name of the Governor shall be authenticated in such manner as may be specified in rules to be made by the Governor, and the validity of an order or instrument which is so authenticated shall not be called in question on the ground that it is not an order or instrument made or executed by the Governor.

(3) The Governor shall make rules for the more convenient transaction of the business of the Government of the State, and for the allocation among Ministers of the said business insofar as it is not business with respect to which the Governor is by or under this Constitution to act in his discretion.

Appendix 2.1

Specimen of a Notification Under Article 166(3) By A State Government

EXTRACTS

Rules of Business published by Government of West Bengal under Article 166(3) of the Constitution of India vide Notification No. 1209 A.R. dated 5-6-1964

In exercise of the powers conferred by clause (3) of Article 166 of the Constitution of India, and in supersession of all previous rules made in this behalf, the Governor of West Bengal is pleased to make the following rules, namely:

1. These rules may be called the West Bengal Rules of Business.
2. In these rules, unless the context otherwise requires—
   (a) "Article" means an article of the Constitution of India;
   (b) "Council" means the Council of Ministers constituted under Article 163; and "Cabinet" means the Committee of the Council referred to in rule 11;
   (c) "Secretary" means a Secretary to the Government of the State; and includes—The Chief Secretary, the Additional Chief Secretary, a Special Secretary; an Additional Secretary, a Joint Secretary, a Deputy Secretary, an Under Secretary and an Assistant Secretary;
   (d) "Schedule" means the Schedule appended to these rules.
3. The General Clauses Act 1897, applies for the interpretation of these rules as it applies for the interpretation of a Central Act.

....

PART I
ALLOCATION AND DISPOSAL OF BUSINESS

4. The business of the Government shall be transacted in the departments specified in the First Schedule and shall be classified and distributed between those departments as laid down therein.
5. The Governor shall, on the advice of the Chief Minister, allot among the Ministers the business of the Government by assigning one or more departments to the charge of a Minister:

Provided that nothing in this rule shall prevent the assigning of one department to the charge of more than one Minister:

....

FIRST SCHEDULE
[See Rule 4]

....

Allocation of business among departments

Departments

I. Home Department
II. Finance Department
....
V. Agriculture
....
VIII. Department of Commerce and Industries
....
XI. Health & Family Welfare Department
....

1. "List I", "List II" and "List III" mean List I, List II and List III, respectively of the Seventh Schedule to the Constitution of India.
2. The business falling to each department is set forth in this schedule in three parts—

Part I defines the functions of the department.

Part II indicates, primarily by reference to List II and List III, the area within the sphere of the State's executive authority and power to make laws, within which the department exercise its functions. Items falling in List III are printed in italics.

Part III indicates, by reference to List I, the area within the sphere of the Union executive authority and power to make laws, within which the department transact such business as fails to the State Government (whether this be discharging agency functions or functions entrusted to it or merely furnishing advice or information by way of correspondence).

....

Department of Municipal Affairs

Part I

Promotion of local self government and financing, regulation and inspection of authorities established for local self government and for urban development other than the Board of Trustees for the improvement of Calcutta and the Board of Trustees for the improvement of Howrah.

Part II

2. Local government, that is to say, the constitution and powers of municipal corporations, district boards and other local authorities for the purpose of local self government referred to in entry 5 of List II, excluding village administration and improvement trusts.
5. Inquiries and statistics for the purposes of any of the matters specified in List II or List III with which the department is concerned (entry 45 of List III).
6. Tolls in respect of any matter with which the department is concerned (entry 59 of List II).
11. Communications, that is to say, roads, bridges, ferries and other means of communications (not specified in List I) with which local bodies are concerned, municipal tramways (entry 13 of List II).
13. Taxes on lands and buildings (entry 49 of List II).
14. Taxes on professions, trades, callings and employment (entry 60 of List II).
15. Taxes on animals and boats (entry 58 of List II).

16. Taxes on the entry of goods into a local area for consumption, use or sale therein (entry 52 of List II).
17. Taxes on vehicles, other than mechanically propelled vehicles, suitable for use on roads subject to the provisions of entry 35 of List III (entry 57 of List II).

....

Part III

2. Inquiries, surveys and statistics for the purpose of any of the matters in List I with which the department is concerned (entry 94 of List I).

Index